The Workplace Law Advisor

The Workplace Law Advisor

From Harassment and
Discrimination Policies to
Hiring and Firing Guidelines

What Every Manager and
Employee Needs to Know

ANNE COVEY

PERSEUS PUBLISHING
Cambridge, Massachusetts

Copyright © 2000 by Anne Covey

Cataloging-in-Publication Data is available from the Library of Congress
ISBN 0–7382-0374-2

Perseus Publishing is a member of the Perseus Books Group.

Find us on the World Wide Web at http://www.perseuspublishing.com

The author, Anne Covey, also has a Web page containing references on recent employment issues that readers may find helpful. Visit www.coveylawfirm.com

Perseus Publishing books are available at special discounts for bulk purchases in the U.S. by corporations, institutions, and other organizations. For more information, please contact the Special Markets Department at HarperCollins Publishers, 10 East 53rd Street, New York, NY 10022, or call 1–212–207–7528.

Text design by Tonya Hahn
Set in 10-point Daily News by Perseus Publishing Services

First printing, October 2000
1 2 3 4 5 6 7 8 9 10–03 02 01 00

The advice in this book should not be substituted for independent legal counsel. Each state has its own laws affecting the workplace and employment relationship. Consult your attorney regarding any particular matter.

Contents

Preface

I am a firm believer that the best teacher in life is experience, whether you learn from your own experiences or the experiences of others. Although the most powerful teachers are our personal victories and defeats, the most efficient and pain-free lessons are acquired from the knowledge of others. The purpose of this book is to make you the beneficiary of my professional knowledge and experiences as a practicing labor and employment attorney.

I love my profession and particular practice area of labor and employment law because of the diversity and challenges that lie within the human dynamics and interactions. I frequently thank my clients for calling because of the comic relief they provide through their inquiries. Although when they call their intention is not to be funny, life is truly stranger than fiction. I know they are telling the truth based upon the particular, and often unique, facts they relate to me. To all those clients and colleagues who have shared their life with me, I again thank you and dedicate this book to you. Without you this book would not have been possible and my life not nearly as fulfilling and interesting.

Most important, I acknowledge and give praise to God the Father, His Son Jesus Christ, and the Power of the Holy Spirit who placed the desire and words in my heart to write this book. They are the source of my being each day, through whom everything is possible. I am nothing without my faith and belief that everything is created for our good and that we each have the power and obligation to do good. The power of prayer and doing what is right at every minute of every day is true contentment. "The Lord is my rock and my fortress, and my deliverer; my God, my strength, in whom I will trust; my buckler, and the horn of my salvation, and my high tower." Psalms 18:2.

In addition to God's love and guidance, I have had the distinct privilege to experience personally the power a positive relationship can have on one's life. Michael S. Morris, Esquire—my best friend, law school classmate, colleague, partner, soul mate, husband, and father of our daughter—is that power source. I cannot begin to fully express my gratitude for his unfailing love, friendship, warmth, laughter, intelligence, acceptance, courage, and support. My life is complete through our mutual respect and admiration for each other—the greatest gift of life.

Mother and Dad, Marge and Bill Covey, I thank you for all those times you gave of yourselves to stand next to me, in front of me, and behind me to provide your support and encouragement to assist me to move forward when others told me my dreams and desires were not possible. From seeing your own perseverance and determination, I have incorporated these priceless qualities into my life. My sisters and brother, Marjorie, Bill, and Sharon, you have taught me the comfort of knowing that regardless of what happens, family is the most important life relationship. In our joyful experiences and those times we would rather forget, we will always be there for one another. I love you dearly and cherish you and our times together.

Mom-Mom, my maternal grandmother, taught me through her constant and consistent actions of unconditional love, tenderness, and faith that God does exist. Although she is no longer physically present, the impact of her life and spirit continues to live every day. Her presence made a huge difference in the lives of everyone she met. Aunt Helen and Aunt Elsie, you have demonstrated the power and grace of being a woman. I am forever grateful and will continue to pass these life qualities to others. Uncle Ed, a true leader, dedicated and humble man, we miss you, love you, and keep you forever in our hearts.

Through Mike's parents, Michael and Imogene Morris, and his sister, Pat Cameron, I have received additional love, strength, acceptance, and knowledge. Their actions have made me feel that I have always been a vital part of the family. They have created a powerful sense of belonging, which has blossomed into a wonderful and cherished relationship. I acknowledge you and thank you for your priceless gifts.

My friends, to whom I am totally dedicated and would be adrift without, I thank each of you with my whole heart for your presence in my life. You have seen me, heard me, accepted me, and shared with me all of you; I know no greater gift. Thank you, Kathy, Mary, Lucy, Meg, Patty, Susie, LuCinda, Chris, Lori, Joan, Donna, Tricia, Barbara, Roberta, Kara, Michelle, Pat, Roseanne—indeed, I am most fortunate in having been so blessed in friendship that the list is too long to name each friend individually. I know, however, that you will read this book with pride because your name is forever embossed herein.

My life has also been enriched with mentors who have taught me about people, life, work, professionalism, writing, communication, ethics, and the law. Thank you, Ira, Judge Craig, Peter, Craig, Gene, Jay, and Ted. Again, this list could go on, but each individual knows his or her contribution for which I am most appreciative and to whom I acknowledge my success. I praise your work and hope that I have accurately reflected all you have taught me.

Thank you, Diedra, for your talent, patience, and dedication in devoting so many hours of your life to assisting me in preparing this work and for always believing in the good to be produced by our labor of love.

Introduction

Good morning—or should I say good afternoon or evening? Well, it doesn't matter what hour of the day you picked up this book. At least once or probably more than twice during the day you thought about or talked about your job. Like most people, you probably spend the majority of your day thinking about, getting dressed for, commuting to, talking about, or planning for or around your job.

However, did you ever think about how little training or knowledge you were given to excel in your job or assist those you manage or supervise? Do you know your precise job responsibilities? Do you perform each workplace duty to the best of your ability every day? Whether you answer "yes" or "no" to any of these questions, this book will help you enhance your employment relationships and personal development.

Since we spend one of life's greatest commodities—time—focusing on or about work, how about giving yourself and your organization the gift of a successful employment relationship? The tools are simple and can be used at any time by everyone.

As a practicing labor and employment attorney, speaker, author, columnist, and university professor, I have personal experience with the inner workings of governmental agencies, the judiciary, and national law practice, in addition to the challenges of running my own law firm. In *The Workplace Law Advisor,* I offer to every reader the opportunity to step into my law office for consultation about the employment relationship without the obligation of paying my hourly fee. As my mentor, the Honorable David W. Craig, former president judge of the Appellate Pennsylvania Commonwealth Court, stated, "[a]ny lawyer can recite the law; only the exceptional lawyer can provide the practical application of the law." My eyes have forever remained focused on the practice of law as the exceptional lawyer.

The Workplace Law Advisor answers the most frequently asked questions posed by business owners, entrepreneurs, managers, and employees about the employment relationship and work environment. Each principle is illustrated through real-life examples drawn from actual letters I received and answered in my "Workplace Adviser" column published in *The Asbury Park Press* and *The*

Home News. The book is designed to help you navigate the legal issues associated with every stage of the employment relationship—from conception (even before the interviewing process and the hiring decision) through termination and life thereafter.

The book begins with an overview of the employment relationship and a discussion of its fundamental elements, such as trust and respect. It explores the elements that contribute to a healthy employment relationship and addresses how unions and litigation have been used by unhappy or dissatisfied employees in attempts to fill the void. In Chapter 2, I show how communication is the most powerful tool that can either build or destroy the employment relationship, depending on how it is used. I address the four key elements of communication—speaking, writing, acting, and listening—with examples, to teach you how to use your communication skills to a greater capacity in the context of the employment relationship.

Whether you are seeking a new employment opportunity or looking for a new employee, Chapter 3 will assist you in the interviewing and hiring process. Like the other chapters, this chapter gives you both the employer's and the employee's perspectives. It will walk you through the placement of the job advertisement to the employment application to the job interview to the job offer. It will also discuss some key areas that need to be given special consideration, such as the Americans with Disabilities Act and the importance of job descriptions.

If you have not followed the principles outlined in the first three chapters, or if you are facing a potential employment-related claim, Chapter 4 will have special interest: You will learn the top ten reasons employees sue their employers; the protections granted by the Civil Rights Act, the Age Discrimination in Employment Act, and the Americans with Disabilities Act; how lawsuits can be avoided; and what needs to be considered before a lawsuit is filed. The dual goals of this chapter are to help you determine whether you have the basis for bringing a discrimination lawsuit yet to recommend employment litigation only as a last resort.

Most employers and employees do not understand the origin or importance of employment-at-will, although this term is frequently used in describing the employment relationship. Chapter 5 will examine this term to provide you with an understanding of how and when it can be applied.

Chapter 6 provides new insights on sexual harassment, the most controversial workplace topic of the 1990s and beyond. The chapter offers a definition of sexual harassment, an overview of the rights and obligations of both employers and employees, and statistics on the number of sexual harassment claims that have been filed and the resulting damages that have been paid out. As with other areas of the employment relationship, employee education is key to eradicating this form of discrimination. However, unlike in other areas, training is mandated by the United States Supreme Court. I have furnished basic guidelines on how to protect your organization and yourself from the costly effects of sexual harassment.

The Americans with Disabilities Act (ADA) is the focus of Chapter 7, which includes discussion of the law's protections and obligations as well as definitions of its key terms, such as "disability," "reasonable accommodation," and "qualified individual with a disability." Many people do not fully understand the full impact of the ADA because they have no need for its protections. The chapter encourages an open mind toward differences and diversity.

Chapter 8 lays out the components of the Family and Medical Leave Act (FMLA), including which employers must comply with the law; which employees are eligible for FMLA leave and what their entitlements are; what constitutes a serious health condition; which employment benefits must continue while on leave; the employer's reinstatement requirements; special rules for key employees and instructors in educational institutions; what notices must be furnished by employers and employees; and how the law is enforced. Because of the breadth of this law, it interacts with a variety of other employment laws. I address how the FMLA impacts these other statutes and the differences among the laws to provide clear guidance on properly applying and understanding the various legal requirements.

Chapter 9 discusses an inevitable aspect of the employment relationship—employment separation. Employment relationships end for a variety of reasons and in a number of different ways, and the separation may have significant impact on the organization, the affected employee, other workers, and even the general public. When the employment relationship ends, regardless of who initiates its conclusion, there are several methods—some desirable, some not—to bring closure, and this chapter explores those options. Also addressed are specific issues, such as "Am I entitled to severance pay?" and "Does the organization have to pay the employee for unused sick time?"

The book's final chapter will help both the employer and employee see how each played a role in ending the relationship. This honest review is crucial to bringing proper closure and preventing similar situations from arising in the future. The evaluation will prevent employment litigation, generate employee morale, create confidence in moving forward in new relationships, and identify opportunities to avoid repeating unsuccessful and possibly costly mistakes. To emphasize the importance of the book's lessons, I conclude this chapter by walking you through the litigation process and its potentially disastrous effects upon all participants.

The pages that follow will assist you in creating a more fulfilling work environment and, consequently, a more peaceful atmosphere when you are away from work. Whether you are looking for employment, have been working for twenty-five years, or are managing a successful multibillion-dollar business, you will profit from your efforts to create a winning work environment—one built on mutual respect, communication, empathy, and growth.

—— ■ one ■ ——

The Employment Relationship

The essence of organizational life is the employment relationship—that is, a relationship at the workplace. *The Merriam-Webster Dictionary* defines "relationship" as "the state or character of being connected." (All subsequent definitions are also from this dictionary.)

Making the Connection

The employment relationship is like every relationship—it demands a tremendous amount of work and understanding, requires total commitment, and is based upon loyalty and trust. Without these essential components, there can be no connection. The success or failure of the employment relationship is the responsibility of both the employer and the employee. The relationship may fail for various reasons: The employer and employee have different perspectives or understandings of what is expected; they experience personality clashes or conflicting business objectives; conduct in the workplace is unacceptable or unlawful, such as sex discrimination or retaliation for asserting a legal right. Learning our employment responsibilities as well as our rights is critical for both employers and employees. This premise is as true for the new employee as it is for the longtime employee, supervisor, government official, or chief executive officer. Everyone is responsible for contributing to the success of the relationship.

To "employ," as defined by Webster's, means "to make use of something or someone advantageously." From the employer's perspective, that means ascertaining the employee's skills and abilities and evaluating how they fit into furthering the objectives and mission of the organization. Not surprisingly, the employee has the same goals—recognition and use of the employee's talents. When the employer and employee spend the necessary time to assess their assets fairly and accurately, they mutually benefit. Failure to make these critical assessments of yourself and the other party usually results in the inevitable—friction, conflict, and disharmony.

How often have you observed or experienced the fundamental problem that emerges when a person's natural abilities and interests do not match the essential functions of the job? How long did that employment relationship limp along? Who was happy in those circumstances—the employee, the coworkers, the supervisor, the manager, or no one? But why did the employment continue? In most cases people fear change and therefore take no action. From the employer's perspective, the excuses include lack of time to look for a replacement, difficulty finding qualified help, or fear of being sued for ending the employment opportunity. From the employee's perspective, usually he or she does not know what other opportunities exist, does not feel like exerting the energy required to find new employment, or is more afraid to be in a new environment than to maintain the uncomfortable status quo.

Unfortunately, we expend more time and energy rationalizing our circumstances than openly discussing them and looking for underlying connections or more productive alternatives. Thus, for both employers and employees, a key to establishing and sustaining successful employment relationships is to look at one's own qualities, philosophies, and objectives and evaluate how they complement or align with the other party's goals and interests. When compatibility exists, the employee and the organization are a powerful engine. But when it doesn't exist, the relationship is on an inevitable crash course. The following true workplace experience is such an example:

Worker Feels Squeezed Out by Her Managers

Q. I have a rather unique problem that has developed in my workplace. I hesitate to use any of the terms such as discrimination, bias, etc., but nevertheless it is a problem that I feel could lead to a serious situation. I have been an employee of the company for over 23 years. I am 55 years old. I have received nothing but above-average performance evaluations for this period. A few years ago my group was merged with another organization. This group is mainly technical, and I do not have a degree in that field.

I am being given fewer and fewer assignments that are on a par with my level. Now the majority of my work is clerical. I have taken classes with the hope of being involved in these computer systems. All of this has resulted in minimal responsibility or none at all.

Another person was hired from the outside to take over my work. Without my knowledge or an explanation, my job title was changed. I asked management if I could take on some other responsibilities and was told no. People are still being hired in the group, so it is not as if there is not enough work to go around.

I contacted the diversity group in my company and was advised to tell my supervisor again about my work situation. It took over three weeks and my contacting the diversity group again to get any action. All during this period I was almost idle every day.

In earlier years I almost preferred working to taking time off. This group does have a lot of interesting work to offer, but I am increasingly worried about my position within the group. I am looking for other positions inside and outside the company.

W. B.

A. You describe your situation as unique. I believe it is your commitment and dedication that are unique. You sound like the type of honest, conscientious employee so many of my clients long for. From what you have described, it is difficult to have a clear picture as to what is transpiring in your work group.

In addition to the steps you have already taken, consider asking your supervisor what action you need to take or if anything is lacking concerning your ability to assume additional responsibilities. I also suggest you speak with the company's personnel or human resources department concerning your current situation and future with the organization. Before this meeting, outline your qualifications and objectives. The better prepared you are, the more insight you can provide to someone who may be completely unfamiliar with the situation. You may also consider speaking with your supervisor's superior to find out what is happening within your group.

The objective is for you to obtain as much information as possible about the situation and at the same time educate those in decisionmaking positions about yourself and your desires and capabilities. Depending on how everything works out, it may be in your best interest to follow up your meetings and conversations with letters or other documentation to create a record. .

Although looking for a job elsewhere does not appear to be your objective, it may be a viable alternative worth exploring. Often this type of change leads to the opening of numerous exciting and rewarding experiences.

Maintain your perseverance and determination. In addition to being admirable qualities to have, they will help you feel more in control, less like a victim, and will lead you to an answer one way or another. It makes sense that you are not happy or comfortable with your current state of affairs. You are a dedicated worker, not a person who seeks to get paid for doing as little as possible. Never trade in who you are or the fine qualities you possess simply because life has thrown you an unexpected curveball.

Opportunity, Not Entitlement

How many résumés have you reviewed that reveal that the applicant has had numerous jobs within a short time? Perhaps this is your own résumé. What is the cause? In most cases job-hopping is not the fault of irresponsible, overly demanding, or negligent employers. Often, it's the individual who has refused to examine his or her personal value system and work ethics. Does this scenario sound familiar? *"Jack, I don't know why I can't find a good secretary. You know I've had eleven secretaries in the past six months. Not one of them knew what she was doing."* Could it be that the secretaries were fine, but that the complainer was failing to see something about himself or herself?

This was a real situation. The saddest aspect was that the people who worked with the complaining individual knew that the problem did not lie with the secretaries, but not one person was courageous enough to be honest. Who suffered here? Yes, the countless secretaries, the boss, the coworkers, the customers, and the organization. The recruiting, hiring, training and orienting process takes time and requires the expenditure of financial and emotional resources. Everyone pays here.

In contrast, have you ever met people who said they loved their job and found it personally rewarding even though it did not pay as much as they desired? Then the question becomes, what do you value in life? Money, prestige, good mental and physical health, or contentment? Only you can define your personal well-being and decide whether it is present in your relationships, including your employment relationship.

When the employer's and employee's goals do not intersect, a change may be needed. Change is an inevitable part of life. Most employees, however, mistakenly believe that employment is their right. Nothing could be further from the truth. No one is guaranteed life or good health. No one is guaranteed a job! We have all heard of "equal employment opportunity." But have you considered what that phrase means? "Opportunity" and "entitlement" are opposite ends of the spectrum. One is earned, and the other is given. Unless we recognize—as individuals and collectively—that an employment opportunity is *earned*, we will continue to pay costly errors of judgment in high employee turnover, skyrocketing insurance premiums, and employment litigation. Each person either contributes to the explosive employment-related costs or counters that trend by seeking to prevent those costs. Where do you stand on the issue—spending the money or living the words printed on the money, "In God We Trust"?

On Character

Good interpersonal relationship skills, talents, experiences, abilities, ethics, and morals are the true source of good business and job security. Recall how hard you worked your first day on the job. Do you continue to bring that same dedicated vitality and commitment to the job each day? Think about how you would like to be remembered and respected if today was your last day of life. Take a few minutes to see yourself. Then write your own epithet. Does it create a mental picture of what you desire others to know about you? The picture is your barometer of how each day is to be lived and your acceptance of individual responsibility on the job. Do your actions and words reflect your mental picture?

Webster's defines "character" as "the complex of mental and ethical traits marking a person." "Characteristic" means "a distinguishing trait, quality or property." In order to understand more about our characteristics and the impact they have on our lives and the lives of the people we touch, write down 15 characteristics that you respect in your coworkers or other workers where you shop. Take your time. This is your life. If you are finding this task difficult, you are not alone. Most individuals struggle to list five positive qualities.

Now list 10 characteristics that you disrespect in other employees. Like many people, you may find this exercise easier. Unfortunately, this revelation tells us where we spend most of our mental energy. The insight gained from clearly examining this aspect of your life is valuable. If you make the investment to evaluate and change any part of your life that is hindering your happiness, well-being, or growth, you will be rewarded many times over.

After you have completed the preceding two exercises, write down 10 characteristics that you display on a daily basis in the workplace or with coworkers. Be honest. Don't sugarcoat the truth. No one is reading this list except you. Remember, other people are fully aware of what characteristics you put on view everyday. If you have any doubt or need assistance, ask colleagues or coworkers; you may be shocked at what they report. Of the three lists you have created, which fits a person you most desire to work with?

Next, write down 15 characteristics you *choose* or *will choose* to display on a daily basis to all persons you encounter, paying particular attention to how you treat your coworkers and customers or clients. Put this list in your wallet or pocket and carry it with you wherever you go. Have it become your permanent cheat sheet. When you are having a difficult day or you just cannot seem to get peaceful, read your list as a reminder of what skills and abilities you possess and put them into practice. You will be surprised by the results. People who have taken this exercise seriously have reported feeling better about themselves and life, and their coworkers have related how much they enjoy working with these individuals and the positive influences that have been created in their own lives.

We all have rough times, but that momentary lapse of sanity does not give anyone the right to disrespect, lie, cheat, hurt, scream at, or lash out at another human being. No excuse is acceptable. Here are a few popular characteristics:

1. Courteous.
2. Kind.
3. Patient.
4. Jovial.
5. Gentle.
6. Sensitive to others' needs or concerns.
7. Consistent between actions and words.
8. Responsive to inquiries.
9. Observant.
10. Attentive.
11. Supportive.
12. Encouraging.
13. Honest.
14. Flexible.
15. Respectful.

Do the characteristics that you respect and admire in others match the characteristics you have chosen to exhibit on a regular basis? Following are examples of how to make these traits work for you in your employment relationship:

1. Praise good work.
2. Counsel and redirect poor work.
3. Furnish the necessary informational tools so that others can properly perform their jobs.
4. Listen without interruption.
5. Maintain respect for all persons even in the face of disrespect.

6. Serve those who serve you.
7. Offer assistance.
8. Get involved.
9. Answer inquiries honestly.
10. Be enthusiastic.
11. Welcome suggestions.
12. Lead by example.
13. Present the solution.
14. Create cooperation.
15. Find common objectives.

These examples apply to all employees—coworker to coworker, supervisor to subordinate, subordinate to supervisor—and employee to customer.

On Responsibility and Influence

In my seventeen years of practicing labor and employment law, people still continue to amaze me. An example is the employee who filed a lawsuit because he was angry when the employer fired him after he had failed to report to work on time for the fifteenth time in several weeks. Maybe the employee chose to end his employment relationship; after all, he chose to report to work late consistently. If you had acquaintances who were constantly late for events you planned to attend together and you explained how you felt about their lateness but the chronic disrespect continued, would it surprise anyone when the outings came to an end? What, then, makes employees believe that being terminated from their job gives them the right to file a lawsuit? There is a clear distinction between equal employment opportunity and equal employment entitlement—and the law provides for only the former.

Janitor, pianist, teacher, doctor, construction worker, postal worker—it does not matter your personal calling. Each service is necessary, and each person who provides a service or manufactures a product has an impact on others. How you conduct your affairs is important to your local community and the global universe. One person is enough to get the process started. Each one of us has not only the ability but the *responsibility* to stand up and out in being a positive influence.

Where do you begin to make changes? The answer is simple. Select your most respected role model or other people in your life whose behaviors you admire. Then practice those positive traits and incorporate them into your daily living on a minute-by-minute basis. This process is not a temporary fix but rather a life-long educational commitment for your well-being and the betterment of the environment in which you work and live. Remember, you spend most of your time, physically and mentally, in the workplace. Therefore, isn't it worth your while to make it a comfortable and positive environment? As children we mimicked behavior we liked. We learned how to place the square peg in the square hole. This exercise is no different. If we could succeed at this art in our youth, we can unquestionably carry this ability forward with us as adults who now possess years of wisdom and experience.

The choice is yours. No one can force you, nor can you require someone else, to take the necessary steps. How many of us know people who constantly place the blame for their circumstances on another or find an excuse for the situation in which they find themselves? Do you admire or respect those people? Have you reached the point that you can repeat, verbatim, another person's woes? Even if you are intolerant of such behavior, do you find yourself engaging in such conduct in some form? If you answer yes to any of these questions, your most important inquiry is, what can I do differently? Here is an example:

Worker Not Given Right Tools to Do Job

Q. I am writing with regard to a problem that I believe relates to workplace standards. I have been employed with the same employer for eight years working in a secretarial position. During this period of time, I have had many supervisors resulting in a steady decline of assistance, direction, etc. I recently returned from being out on disability leave, and while I was out, my desk, etc., were moved to another facility. I was advised by certified mail that upon my return from disability, I would report to this new location. When I arrived at my new work location, I found the following:

1. Insufficient work space.
2. My obsolete computer is not functioning for what I believe to be a variety of reasons.
3. No typewriter.
4. No stationery supplies.
5. No clear indication of work assignment.

I have spoken with both my immediate supervisor as well as the regional supervisor; however, as in the past, no clear answers or direction are offered. No reason has been given for my transfer.

The regional supervisor asked me what I am doing since I do not have equipment or supplies. I expressed my concerns, and she suggested I put them in writing. She also stated that she does not believe she will be able to get me a typewriter or computer, since any new ones have been distributed and there will not be any new purchases until July.

My question is this: What are the responsibilities of an employer with regard to providing sufficient work space, reasonable equipment, supplies, and direction such as job responsibilities in the workplace? Any advice you can give me would be greatly appreciated, since I am quite frustrated.

B. F.

A. Your situation and how you were treated do sound frustrating. As for an employer's obligation to provide sufficient work space, the federal Occupational Safety and Health Act (OSHA) imposes a general mandate that employers furnish their employees a safe and healthy work environment. In addition, OSHA lists numerous specific workplace requirements, such as providing a fire extinguisher, having employees wear certain protective equipment, and abiding by other mandates that support an employee's safety and health. If the size of your work space is not unsafe but merely insufficient to allow you to perform your work assignments properly, OSHA most likely is not applicable.

No mandate exists for an employer to provide employees reasonable equipment, supplies, and direction, as long as the employer is not failing or refusing to provide these items on account of an employee's race, sex, religion, disability, age, veteran status, marital status, sexual preference, or some other protected classification. Nevertheless, it is generally understood that an employer provides equipment, supplies, and direction based upon sound business practice. You are an employee, not an independent contractor, as indicated by some of the factors you list; these are necessary elements for employees to perform the services for which they were hired.

It is unrealistic for your employer to expect you to perform your secretarial responsibilities without the necessary means. Consider speaking with someone superior to your regional supervisor who has the ability to assist you. I encourage you to continue your search for someone with the answer. Also consider documenting all such communications to protect yourself and your job and to demonstrate your attempts to be loyal in fulfilling your responsibilities. In addition, be creative in finding ways to complete your assignments with the tools you do possess. There is often more than one way to accomplish a task. Finally, seek out coworkers who have tools or equipment they could share; teamwork of this sort benefits the organization as a whole.

Try to get past your frustration and have fun with the challenge you are facing. Be a leader in creating solutions, new ideas, and possibly a whole new work environment.

Think about how you like to be treated. Do you like to be screamed at or heard? Included or made fun of? Respected or mistreated? Praised or criticized? Remembered or ignored? Most of us would agree that being heard, included, respected, praised, and remembered is the greatest wealth, better than a pay raise. As with any new behavior, such as learning how to walk, ride a bicycle, play the guitar, or operate the computer, it takes time, practice, and diligence to change your environment. Yes, it also requires standing up and maybe falling down and then standing up again and again. But what option do you have—to continue in the same routine with no direction and no positive influence? One path is debilitating; the other is invigorating.

Manager Not Dealing with Worker Issues

Q. I am writing on behalf of the staff. We are having problems with our manager and are at a loss as to how to handle it. Due to downsizing, our manager has the formidable task of running two units. Both units come under the same general category but are entirely different in their composition, routine, and staffing. Management refers to us as "sister floors" and says we are "administratively combined," but we consider ourselves the unwanted "stepchildren."

The problem lies with management. Our manager clearly cannot handle two floors. She is inconsistent, indecisive, and outright lies to cover up her mistakes. On one day, she will overstaff so that she can "pull" us to cover her other floor, and on the next day, she will understaff our floor so that we are forced to run around like crazy to get our work done. She will tell us how she wants things done on one day, and the next day, we are told we should be doing things another way. Then she denies that she told us something different the day before.

This month she actually put out three separate work schedules. She posts one schedule, then replaces it with another. She expects us to keep checking it to see if there are any changes. We cannot work this way. We recently were told we must inform the person in charge where we will be for lunch, so that we can be contacted if needed. We do not get paid for lunch, so this is our own time. Also, some of us work 12-hour shifts, and we consistently do not get the breaks we are entitled to under the law.

These are just a few quick examples of the situations that have arisen, but the list is never-ending. Overall, it seems this manager has a power struggle and needs to control everything we do. She has assistant managers, but they are not permitted to make decisions, even in her absence. We made an attempt to set up a meeting with her direct supervisor, but were stonewalled. He would not even talk to us, even if only to find out what the request for a meeting was about. We were told through his secretary that we must go to our manager. Well, we tried that many times. To top it off, her boss informed her we were trying to set up a meeting with him.

Needless to say, the staff morale is at an all-time low, with much fighting among us. We feel oppressed and helpless. Please help us.

M. C.

A.   You have described a truly unpleasant situation. As you stated, "the problem lies with management," with management being not only your manager and her supervisor. You are correct in stepping out and clearly communicating your concerns and struggles in order to create a better working environment.

Your letter also conveys a high level of stress in an intense work environment. I recommend in this type of situation that employers schedule group meetings with their employees to air concerns. Unfortunately, from what you have described, you are being stonewalled in your efforts for such a meeting. Although most organizations have a chain of command an employee must adhere to in asserting employee matters, you might consider taking your concerns outside of the conventional framework of communication. Often, writing a letter outlining the specific topics for discussion, with your coworkers' signatures attached, sent to either the board of directors or owners of the organization will generate some type of response to your inquiry.

You have described an employment relationship that is in decay. In companies experiencing both financial and morale problems, the hardship is borne by all in the organization. A company that eventually is able to stabilize rewards those employees who chose to weather the storm rather than desert the organization at its hour of need.

As for your question concerning your lunch period and your manager's direction to inform the person in charge as to your whereabouts during your lunch period, the federal Fair Labor Standards Act (FLSA) requires employers to pay their employees only for actual time worked. Therefore, if you are required only to notify your supervisor as to your whereabouts during lunch but in fact do not work during that time, no compensation is due. It may be frustrating to inform the person in charge of where you will be during lunch, but because of the staff shortage you described, such request is not surprising. With respect to breaks, the FLSA does not require employers to provide employees who are over age 18 a break regardless of the number of hours worked, except in certain businesses such as the airlines and trucking industries.

I hope the contention between the staff and management improves over the next few months. At some future time, you will have to examine your employment position in light of the totality of the circumstances to make an informed decision on whether to stay or to move on to new opportunities.

Good luck in bringing this matter to a workable and win-win solution for all parties.

If you are content in your job, you are probably also productive at work. However, if you are unhappy at work, lack direction, or feel unappreciated, you are probably not effective or focused and are more likely to be absent or to sustain a workplace injury—whether the injury be physical, mental, or emotional. The following example illustrates the destructive results of disrespect and reinforces why supervisory training is so essential.

Worker Was Harassed by Her Manager

Q.   I recently resigned my job after a series of incidents that were hostile and harassing. The first verbal attack came approximately two weeks after my starting date. It involved books that are kept on top of a filing cabinet. My administrator actually scolded me for not having them in a perfectly straight row.

More problems occurred. All letters, invoices, and statements that had been returned to our service center marked "undeliverable" were kept on my desk. The number had grown considerably, and I was unable to use the top of my desk efficiently. I put them in my bottom desk drawer. The administrator shouted at me, "Put them back where they were, now!"

Within approximately one week's time, she asked me a question from across the office. I could not hear her. After I replied, "Excuse me, I cannot hear you," she asked, "What, are you deaf?" I felt this was inappropriate behavior under any circumstances, but particularly so in an office/corporate environment.

In my enthusiasm to make this situation workable, my behavior was seen as a mandate to continue her verbal abuse. It did not cease. It took several more insults and humiliations that then culminated in my resignation. I would like to return to the job if this situation can be resolved amicably.

In a recent letter to employees, my former employer wrote, "Last, but probably most important, treat every employee, regardless of position, with dignity and respect. We are a team, and we cannot succeed without working together."

I was refused unemployment benefits and therefore have no income presently. I am 59 years old, and as I was recently widowed, this is very stressful to me. If need be, I would consider a lawsuit.

S. S.

A. From what you describe, it appears that in addition to your work environment being unpleasant, the message conveyed to employees was contrary to how at least one person in a managerial position treated you.

It is understandable that you did not desire to be disrespected, nor should you have been. Resolving an employer-employee problem or concern internally often produces more favorable results when there are two parties willing to discuss the situation openly and fairly. Addressing these concerns face-to-face is preferable. Your letter does not indicate whether you communicated to the employer's human resources director or other managerial representative the problems you were experiencing before you resigned. However, it is extremely difficult to resolve your type of situation after you have taken the strong step of resigning.

In order to prove employment discrimination, such a case must be based upon your membership in a protected classification, such as your age, race, sex, religion, disability, or similar personal characteristic. From what you describe, it is unclear whether the administrator was disrespectful to everyone, treated you differently simply because she did not care for you, or treated you differently because of your age or some other protected classification.

In the first two scenarios, there is no basis for a lawsuit. But if the last scenario is the case, you may have a cause of action against your former employer for its supervisor's behavior.

I frequently advise employers about the importance of supervisory training for the reasons you have set forth in your letter. In most cases, top company officials are unaware of the acts of their managers and supervisors, and without the proper training, these individuals can generate litigation against the company.

As you go forward, list your skills and abilities, focus on the positions for which you are qualified, and make prospective employers aware of how you can be an asset to their organization. You are 59 years old and therefore possess enormous wealth in wisdom and experience. Good luck and congratulations on not tolerating disrespectful behavior.

The Role of Unions

The history of labor relations in the United States reveals a scarred past. At the turn of the twentieth century, labor unrest continued to influence every facet of economic, social, and political life. Labor strikes, boycotts, and picketing were viewed as destroying the nation's economy, creating social unrest, and fostering a communist movement to destroy the democratic society. Thus, it became necessary to balance the employer-employee relationship through means other than criminal statutes, tort actions, and antitrust laws.

The first congressional statute to provide the foundation for the development of a federal labor policy was the Norris–La Guardia Anti-Injunction Act passed in 1932. The legislation gave labor the legal right to organize, free from restraint. Further, it limited the power of the federal courts in issuing injunctions against labor organizations, a power they had previously used to abrogate such groups. The law was a congressional reaction to the need for equalizing the employment relationship, creating industrial democracy, and restricting federal courts in order to uphold employees' rights.

Labor organizations did not arise as a matter of chance but rather as a direct result of employers' lack of concern for and interest in their employees. This disrespect poisoned every aspect of the employment relationship. Consequently, union representatives became the employees' mouthpieces until such time that labor organizations lost sight of their primary objective—the employees. Like employers, unions also became blinded by the silver and gold rewards of big business that they have now become.

Concerns Unanswered by Union

Q. I am writing regarding my daughter, who for the past seven years has worked as a relief counselor. She was given her first raise a few months ago. She was told that because she works only one day a week, they could not give her a raise every year, and they cannot give her any benefits.

Now my daughter has to join the union. The initiation fee is $100, plus she must pay union dues. The fees are the same for her as for someone working full-time. There are still no benefits for her.

She has made many calls to the union representative, but he will not respond. I would appreciate your advice on this matter. Thank you.

M. M.

A. As you have pointed out, unions have many requirements that in most cases are unfortunately not communicated to employees before a union becomes their exclusive representative. Many employees do not realize the cost of unions, for themselves personally and the organization that employs them.

In addition, as you note, unions are expensive in many ways. When employees elect to be represented by unions, they must pay the union financially as well as personally by giving up their right to speak for themselves. Unions are big businesses and charge for their services of being the employees' spokesperson with management regarding wages, hours, and other terms and conditions of employment.

There are two typical types of union environments, a "closed shop" and an "open shop." A closed shop, which appears to be the type of environment where your daughter works, is where the union has mandated as part of the collective bargaining agreement between itself and management that all bargaining-unit employees must be union members in good standing to have continued employment with the employer.

Generally, a union member in good standing is defined as an employee who has paid the union's initiation fee, regularly pays the union's monthly dues, and complies with the union's constitution and by-laws. The union's constitution and by-laws regulate union members' conduct and obligations. For example, a union member may be required to pay additional fees to the union, commonly referred to as a special assessment. The assessment may be used to help fund a strike occurring at another company with whom the union member has no affiliation, or an individual union member must pay a fine for failing to follow union rules, such as crossing a picket line. Union membership is expensive in that it not only may literally cost employees their job but also entail financial expenditures.

An open shop is where all individuals in the bargaining unit are given the option to join the union. Union membership is not a condition of continued employment. Of course, most unions require that the work environment be a closed shop for financial reasons: The initiation fee and monthly dues finance the union's expenses, such as salaries for the officers, organizers, and other employees; costs associated with attempting to organize other workplaces; and other expenses associated with running a business as well as political campaigns.

The union representative is being disrespectful of your daughter in failing to respond to her inquiries. Your daughter might consider writing a letter to a higher union official and make that individual aware of how she has been mistreated and ask the reason for the enormous initiation fee and monthly dues in relationship to her compensation and no benefits. As another option, your daughter might also speak with the union shop steward at her workplace. However, it is important for her to make a top union official aware of her concerns.

As part of my practice in counseling companies regarding unionization efforts and decertifications of union representation, I strongly suggest that the employer furnish employees with information that unions seldom provide their members. This education of the employees is appreciated by all concerned so that the employees may make an informed choice of whether to accept or keep a union. Your daughter, although not the beneficiary of such information, is certainly the recipient of the consequences of it.

Here's another example of employee frustration over union policies:

Work Days Are Stipulated in Contract

Q.   I am a licensed nursing professional. The employer's standard hours of operation are 8:30 a.m. to 4:30 p.m. Monday through Friday. However, the nurses also work rotating weekends. The union contract stipulates management can make a nurse work up to three weekends per quarter or one weekend per month, in addition to working the five full days during the week. A nurse who pulls a weekend stint winds up working 12 days in a row. A hospital also requires nurses to work weekends, but the nurse gets the day before the weekend and the day after the weekend off. My employer says it is not allowed by law to do that. Is there such a law? The nurse does get paid time-and-a-half for anything over 40 hours; that's not the point. After putting in 37.5 hours, the nurse then faces a weekend of work plus another 37.5-hour workweek before getting a day off. The nurses call this forced overtime. Please clarify this situation for me and my coworkers.
　　　J. S.

A.   There is no statute that prohibits your employer from granting you and your coworkers the day before the weekend and the day after the weekend off when an employee works the weekend. However, from your description, it appears your employer has a contractual obligation that would prohibit the type of work schedule you and your coworkers desire. The employer's obligation arises from its contract with the union. Your employer's failure to honor the terms of that contract may constitute an unlawful breach of the contract, a violation of the federal National Labor Relations Act, and possibly a violation of the federal Civil Rights Act and state law.

　　　A union contract is a legal document. Once a majority of the employees have decided that they desire to have their interests represented by a labor organization, the employer has a legal obligation to bargain in good faith with the union concerning wages, hours, and other terms and conditions of employment. The employer's and union's bargaining obligations and relationship are governed by the National Labor Relations Act. Thus, failure to bargain in good faith or actions contrary to the terms of a collective bargaining agreement may constitute a violation of the law as well as a breach of contract. In addition, it is extremely important for employers to apply their employment policies and procedures uniformly and consistently. Failure to adhere to this practice may result in intentional or unintentional employment discrimination in violation of the federal Civil Rights Act and state law.

As you can see, your employer is correct with respect to the work schedule and the possible consequences should it alter the schedule as you propose. One of the major debilitating components in the employment relationship, as in any other relationship, is the meddling of a third party. As you and your coworkers are experiencing, the involvement of the union, which a majority of the employees invited into the relationship, has restricted flexibility in the employment relationship. When I talk to management and employees about the ramifications of a labor organization, I make everyone clearly aware of all the possible consequences of their decision. Unions don't discuss these items with employees before they sign union authorization cards or vote in the representation election. However, management as a whole is becoming more proactive in its relationships with employees because of the escalating number of employment-related lawsuits. I continue to conduct an increasing number of legal awareness seminars nationally and locally for organizations of all sizes with varied backgrounds in all types of industries and public works. Consequently, management has the necessary tools to understand its legal obligations to prevent such claims from being filed.

Depending upon when the union contract expires, you and your coworkers might consider changing the work schedule provisions during union negotiations or decertifying the union. But for now, all parties must live with the express language of the union contract regardless of the dissatisfaction with the current method of operation.

As the twentieth century progressed, unions spent more time on furthering their own business objectives and less on responding to employees' needs. Thus, employees were again left on their own in seeking protection in the workplace. This time they began soliciting and receiving the support of their legislatures. There is a strong correlation between the enactment of fair employment practice laws and the decline in union membership. Employment laws, like the creation of labor organizations, were enacted in direct response to the cries of employees to have their interests protected and their needs addressed.

Union Member Is Frustrated by Givebacks

Q. I am a member of a union. For two years now my company has been claiming it is losing business. First, the company brought in nonunion workers off the street to unload trailers. The union allowed this to happen. Then, the company laid off 38 percent of the workforce. So, for two years now we have been understaffed, and we are made to work whenever needed.

Next, the company asked for a wage reduction and took away our lunch break, therefore paying us only for 37.5 hours a week, and took away two sick days, one personal day, five holidays, and a lot more. The proposal was put up for a vote, and people were told the company would close the doors if we did not vote it in. Workers who were laid off were allowed to vote, and the company offered them $1,000 to vote yes. I understand they should not have been allowed to vote if their dues had not been paid up.

Right after that, upper management gave themselves a 3 percent raise. I am still trying to get my pension squared away, for they have shorted me for almost a year. Now we find out that after all we gave back, the president and his henchmen stole a lot of money—millions, in fact—but the company is hiding this information from us.

R. M.

A.   You apparently believe that both the union and your employer have cheated you and have been less than forthright. When a majority of employees have chosen a union to be their exclusive bargaining representative, the employment relationship is governed by the terms of the collective bargaining agreement, which is negotiated by the employer and the labor organization.

The National Labor Relations Act mandates that the employer discuss the employees' wages, hours, and other terms and conditions of employment with the union and not the individual employees. The employees who at one time could speak for themselves must now talk through their union representative. The union has the obligation to represent the employees' interests fairly. It must also act in accordance with the collective bargaining agreement as well as its own constitution and by-laws or other internal rules and regulations.

If you believe that the union has not represented the employees fairly or has violated its constitution or by-laws, you may file a claim for relief against the union in federal court. You, or the other employees who file the complaint as the moving party, will have the burden of proving that the union acted unlawfully. Similarly, if you believe that the employer defrauded the union or made known misrepresentations about the company's financial status, then the union may seek to have the agreement with the company rescinded because it was made on false pretenses.

With respect to your pension, the law is extremely strict in protecting employees' interests. Ascertain whether the union or the employer has the responsibility for your pension money, and document your request for information concerning your pension through written correspondence with the appropriate party.

Cooperation, Not Litigation

Has regulation of the employment relationship gone too far by creating too many employee rights and not focusing sufficiently on employee accountability? Although employment legislation educates and informs employers how to treat employees, it has in many regards altered the nature of the relationship. Multiple employment-related laws, which often are conflicting, have made it extremely difficult to run a business without consulting legal counsel who concentrates solely in labor and employment law. Complaints concerning overregulation are similar to those raised about the interjection of unions into the employment relationship. The statutory law of the workplace has become so highly specialized that attorneys who do not practice in this field will not handle such cases. How, then, is a "relationship—the state or character of being connected," to exist in an atmosphere of mercurial regulation and the intrusion of a third party, be that party a union or the government?

The many employee lawsuits that continue to be filed with federal and state courts and administrative agencies reveal that employers and employees are still not working together. This result is contrary to the very purpose of the employment relationship—the connection of working together advantageously. It is time to recognize and learn the missing ingredients—*communication, education, accountability, respect,* and *empathy.*

Failure to use these simple tools will lead to increased litigation. Litigation is a last-resort, lose-lose situation. Employment-related claims are often filed out of anger, lack of knowledge, or fear of the unknown in something or somebody being different. Litigation costs money, productivity, quality, resources, and morale.

Worker Fights Frustration in His Lawsuit

Q. For three years I have pursued a civil case against my former employer for an illegal dismissal. As I have limited financial means, I have done this pro se (on my own). My former employer, fearing a jury trial by my peers, has thrown obstacle after obstacle in my path to a trial. First my former employer asked for an extension of time to answer my complaint, then sent me a notice to be more specific in my complaint. They filed a motion to dismiss, which was denied. They sent me an 18-page questionnaire that I answered, and then they claimed they wanted more specific answers and requested some additional documents. At considerable time and expense, I complied with all these requests.

Finally, after a standard-track court date had been set, they asked for a change of venue. This request was a ploy to find a sympathetic judge in their home county. They found such a judge, who granted their motion for summary judgment without oral argument. My former employer has used its unlimited expenses and power to stifle my right to a trial.

What are my options? Can I request an "impartial" judge to review the judge's decision, or have I been effectively excluded from the judicial process? Any advice you may offer would be deeply appreciated. Thank you.

J. L.

A.   You have accurately described the difficulties of litigation—time and expense. Although you may feel that your former employer manipulated the system, the nature of the court proceeding is set forth in the rules of court. From what you describe, it appears that your former employer was merely exercising its rights. For example, the court rules concerning the discovery of all pertinent facts are broadly construed in the search for the truth.

The judge who granted your former employer's motion for summary judgment is also subject to the court rules and judicial precedent. Because of the backlog of cases and their desire to move cases through the judicial process so that justice is not denied, most judges will not grant oral argument when the matter before them is clear on the law and on the facts. Generally, oral argument is granted in more complex matters.

If you believe that the judge's decision is not supported by the law, that there was a misapplication of the facts to the law, that the judge was biased, or that some similar unfair event occurred, you have a right to file an appeal from a final order. This appeal right must be exercised in accordance with the court rules and gives you merely a review of the original judge's decision. The matter itself cannot be retried on appeal.

Unfortunately, litigation is not an easy mechanism but rather requires a tremendous amount of effort, energy, resources, and knowledge of the process. If you have no grounds for appeal, there is little you can do, except look to creating your future. You cannot control the effects of your employer's or the judge's decision, but you can control how you will go forward for your own well-being.

When a relationship is not working, avoid continuing to play the same notes; try singing a new song. Change direction, flip the situation around by doing something, *anything,* different so long as it is at all times respectful and sets you on a productive path. Provide a positive influence, even if implementation of the change is difficult. In most circumstances, forward motion presents a challenge and requires internal strength and endurance. But you have much to lose if you don't take steps to initiate a different result.

Employers have an obligation not only to individual employees but also to the organization as a whole. Employees typically are focused singly on their individual needs. However, we must never lose sight of the complete picture—the organization must remain healthy in order to provide employment opportunities.

We often forget or ignore the fact that people who apply for a job with an organization make a personal, *voluntary* choice as to whether they desire to work for that employer. This decision is not thrown upon applicants. When they sign the employment application or express the desire to work for the organization, they are making a personal commitment to perform to the best of their ability in carrying out their job responsibilities and adhering to the organization's policies and procedures. An employee's failure to honor this personal commitment creates turmoil and results in breach of the basic covenant of the relationship.

Similarly, employers must honor their commitments. They must fulfill promises or representations they made. The courts have long held that the basis of the employment relationship is trust and loyalty. Absent these qualities, there can be no relationship. Again, personal commitment and personal responsibility must prevail. These are the keys to keeping the doors of success wide open.

Each failed relationship, regardless of whether one likes the true picture, must be considered in light of everyone's role. More frequently than not, employers and employees choose the consequences of their relationship through their words and conduct. When the relationship comes to an end, unfortunately they blame each other or another person without considering that their actions might have contributed to the result. Employers do not fire good employees, and happy employees do not quit. It is costly to an organization to recruit, hire, and train good employees. Therefore, employers have become more responsible to the organization by conducting exit interviews when employees leave. The primary purpose of these interviews is to learn why the relationship did not work and where the organization can improve.

When employers and employees create fulfilling employment relationships in an environment built on mutual respect, communication, and empathy, the result is contentment, productivity, and success. The objective is to create a win-win atmosphere in which everyone wins. The alternative is described by a reader of my column:

Wage Law May Have Been Violated

Q. After a long and stormy relationship with my now-former employer, I resigned effective March 1. I gave notice by certified mail, return receipt requested, more than two weeks before then. In an apparent fit of anger at me, company officials have withheld sending my final check to me, claiming they "were not going to go out of their way for me" by sending the check to my place of employment where I had received it since the start of my employment. Instead, they are saying that "if" I want this check, which is supposed to include my final two weeks' pay along with accrued vacation, I will have to go to some office in a different state where I have never been. They say this is their policy. I have a copy of their policy manual. There is no such policy delineated. Other former employees have not been subjected to such abusive treatment. It appears this "policy" is directed at me as a punitive measure.

Can they make me travel interstate to collect this final check when it was never a condition of my employment? I worked exclusively at this one facility during the five years of my employment with this company. Do I have recourse against them?

Also, I am fairly confident that they have been gouging me on my insurance contributions over the years. When I asked them how much employees were required to contribute, they gave me three different answers (75 percent, 50 percent, and the balance above $1,000 paid by the company). When, and if, I get the COBRA statement showing how much the actual premium is, will I have any recourse if I find they have gouged me? In addition, they withheld more than $2,000 for my single-person coverage. Thank you.

J. S.

A. The law in most states, and your state in particular, requires employers to communicate to their employees at the time they are hired the amount of their wages or salary, when they will be paid, and the method of payment. Further, employers must pay employees on regular paydays at least twice during each calendar month. However, employers may establish less frequent but regular paydays for bona fide executive, supervisory, and other special classes of employees provided they are paid in full at least once each calendar month on a regularly established schedule.

The law also requires employers to pay employees upon employment separation or suspension all wages due. This payment is to be made no later than the regular payday for the pay period during which the employee's termination, suspension, or cessation of employment took place. If compensation is by an incentive system, the employer must pay a reasonable approximation of all wages due until the exact amount can be determined. Payment is to be made either through the regular pay channels or by mail if the employee so requests. Thus, your former employer's directive that you must travel to a different state to pick up your final paycheck appears to be contrary to its established pay practice and to state law.

As for your medical insurance premium, you may request from the company, or possibly your medical insurance carrier, documentation evidencing the amount of medical insurance coverage. An employer must inform an employee of the cost of the medical benefit when the employee is paying for the coverage. Any overpayment you made should be reimbursed to you. The law regulates employee health and welfare plans administered by employers in order to protect employees and other plan beneficiaries. In addition, the law states that before a medical contribution may be deducted from the employee's paycheck, such deduction must be authorized in writing by the employee.

When people apply for a job, they are applying for an employment *opportunity*. This opportunity depends first on how they conduct themselves in the employment interview and later in the performance of their job duties. All employees, including the chairperson of the board, the manager, and the line worker, must occasionally recommit to the employment relationship by ensuring that they are bringing their best to the workplace everyday. In your work-related activities, always be mindful of the nature of the employment relationship and what your obligations and role are in that relationship, regardless of how others are acting.

In the next chapter, I discuss the single most important relationship requirement—communication. This critical skill has four essential elements—speaking, writing, acting, and listening—that will provide you direction on how to have a more fruitful employment relationship.

━━■ two ■━━

Communication

Communication is the single most powerful tool in creating and maintaining good relationships, whether they involve employment, customers, family, or the public. Unfortunately, most people have not received formal training on how to use and develop their communication skills. Inability to exercise communication skills to the fullest is at the root of employer-employee nonproductivity, lack of direction, noncommitment, frustration, poor morale, and litigation.

Everyone wants to be heard and feel respected. But when these qualities are missing or there is no clear direction on where the relationship is headed, employees resort to sources outside of the employment relationship, such as unions and litigation. If you have any doubt that poor or no communication is a powerful negative force within the workplace, a common example might influence your opinion. In reading the example, ask yourself this question: If open, direct communication between the employee and his manager were in place, would the disrespect and uncooperative spirit be present?

Communication Is Key

Q. I have worked for the same employer for the past 10 years on the same work schedule, and when requested, I have worked additional hours. My performance reviews have been above average or outstanding. Recently, a manager was hired who I believe directed the personnel department to change my work hours to accommodate her personal schedule.

I was hurt that she did not confront me first because I would have obliged. I am now required to work on Sundays. At one time, my employer had provided additional pay. Because I did not typically work on Sundays, I am ineligible for any additional compensation. I feel it is unfair that I am now required to work Sundays but do not have the opportunity to receive extra pay.

In addition, my new manager frequently changes my work schedule and requires me to perform new job responsibilities, which include strenuous physical labor. Other than my pay, I receive no extra consideration for the additional hours I work above 7.5 hours per day. For the first time in my 10 years of employment, I have received a borderline performance review. I am uncertain about what to do, and any direction you can provide would be greatly appreciated. A coworker has also experienced difficulty with this new manager.
    K.D.S.

A. The ideal path, of course, would be for you and your manager to meet to discuss the needs of the department and your desire for a consistent work schedule and an outline of your job responsibilities. However, because your manager seems unwilling or incapable of such an amicable resolution, I recommend that you schedule a meeting with the personnel department to apprise someone there of the difficulties you are experiencing and your dissatisfaction with how the manager has treated you. Also, inform personnel of your outstanding performance evaluations and of your coworker's similar experience.

I suggest that you prepare for the meeting by outlining what you seek to achieve. Have a solution in mind to create a win-win situation—be a part of the solution, not the problem.

To assist you in preparing for the meeting, I can tell you an employer has the right to schedule an employee's work hours, including additional hours, in order to meet business or customer demands. Although the hours may change as the demands change, it is in the employer's and employee's best interest to have a common understanding as to what the hours are or, at the very minimum, if the schedule periodically changes, have a specified day when the weekly schedule will be created.

Similarly, an employer is free to establish what compensation it will pay employees, so long as it meets the minimum wage and pays nonexempt employees overtime of one and one-half their regular hourly rate for all time worked in excess of 40 hours in any workweek.

If the federal and state minimum wage rates are different, the law more beneficial to the employee governs. Whether an employee is exempt from the wage and hour overtime provisions depends on several factors, such as the employee's position, workplace responsibilities, and salary, and must be evaluated on an individual basis.

During your meeting with personnel, you might consider requesting reevaluation of your performance review. Keep a positive frame of reference and inform your employer of your employment-related assets. If your items of concern cannot be resolved to your satisfaction, perhaps look for other employment opportunities that meet your desires and goals.

Although changing jobs after 10 years with the same employer may be difficult, you need to consider what is best for you. You sound as if you are a reasonable employee who works hard and is a team player. Thus, you are a valuable employee and will be an asset to numerous other organizations.

This story is not the exception but the rule, common in many organizations. Are you aware of what is occurring within your work environment, or have you received complaints from employees and decided, consciously or unconsciously, to take no action to address the concerns raised? Such behavior costs an organization hundreds of thousands of dollars in lost productivity; generates poor employee morale and bad publicity; and if it leads to litigation, entails court costs and fees for expert witnesses, consultants, and attorneys.

Organizations that have a proactive employee relations program make all of their employees accountable, starting at the top of the organization, and provide training to all employees. These organizations experience higher productivity, lower absenteeism, fewer work-related accidents, lower insurance premiums, and less employment-related litigation. Such success is generated by encouraging candid communication among all employees.

We all communicate on a regular basis through our actions as well as our words. How we present ourselves is largely by choice, and in most situations, our attitude and what we have to bring to the relationship, good or bad, are obvious. Notwithstanding that we know the power of communication, how is it that we can ignite frequent explosions by speaking, writing, acting, or listening inappropriately, or by not speaking, writing, acting, or listening at all? We often elect our life's consequences by our words and deeds. Here is a common example:

> The employer has a well-established and publicized attendance policy. Employee Sam is frequently late and leaves early. Although Sam can give good reasons for his absences, he fails to follow the organization's policies and procedures. Consequently, the organization decided to fire Sam because of his poor attendance and lack of respect for his position. In fact, on the very day the employer plans to give Sam the news, Sam fails to report to work and does not call. When he finally shows up and is informed of the organization's decision, he starts screaming that the action is unfair and that he has been mistreated.

This real-life situation could have had a different result if Sam's "excuses" were not used and made part of the equation. Sam chose his own path.

Communication requires an affirmative step or movement. "Communication," as defined by Webster's, is an "act of transmitting, to make known, an exchange of information or opinions." The four basic components of communicating are *speaking, writing, acting,* and *listening.* This basic four-part framework enables us to understand where to focus so that we can apply and improve our communication skills.

Speaking

For most of us, this first communication skill appears to be easy enough. However, not everyone can speak. In addition, many of us come from different countries and speak a different language. Even people from the same country speak different tongues based upon their diverse backgrounds, understandings, and experiences. What seemed to be a simple concept suddenly appears to involve much more thought and energy.

Since no two people are alike, not even husband and wife, brother and sister, or best friends, the constant question is, how can I speak so you can understand me? Or stated another way, how can I speak in a manner that is familiar to you? I must place *you* first in the equation of understanding before we can move forward together. Speaking is no different from singing—when we read from the same music sheet, we sing a beautiful melody, but when we sing different notes, we create disharmony. How I select my spoken words, although they cannot be seen, can wound another person emotionally and mentally.

Accusations Cause Woman to Quit Job

Q. I was forced to quit my job as manager, which I enjoyed, after $7\frac{1}{2}$ years. My job duties consisted of preparing the payroll, scheduling employee hours, ordering supplies, firing employees the male co-owner had hired and could not fire, easing problems between employees and customers, writing checks, handling the bookkeeping and banking, and filling in wherever needed. When I wrote payroll checks for all the other employees, it was not unusual to pay myself. I was also left alone to manage the business while the owners were on vacation.

Now, I will tell you why I left this job. The male half of this partnership accused me of stealing. He said this to other employees and customers. I was not confronted with this accusation. The unemployment office was unable to obtain an exact date or amount of money taken. Since he could not furnish a date or amount of money taken, he gave them a date after I quit. Because of this, I was able to collect unemployment compensation. When the male owner would want to get rid of an employee he would lie, lie, lie about the person to others so the employee would quit.

My work history of the past 25 years was unblemished, and others would seek me out for employment. Now he has tarnished my name by telling prospective employers that we had a "business problem." He has ruined my reputation as well. How do I get him to stop spreading lies? What do I tell prospective employers? By the way, his wife is co-owner, and she knew I was paying myself and only what was rightfully mine. I am desperate and determined to have my name and my reputation back. Any advice you can offer me would be greatly appreciated.

C. M.

A. The saying that "actions speak louder than words" is true. You have a 25-year unblemished work history. Employers must have had a reason to seek you out for employment. Your reputation is a known. Proven experience cannot simply be ignored and overturned by another's words.

Your previous employer's use of the phrase "business problem" does not necessarily reflect negatively upon you. It will probably be interpreted literally to mean that there was a business dispute. The phrase carries no judgment of good or bad or right or wrong. You, of course, will infer a negative meaning because of your experience, but you also know his accusation to be untrue.

The law of several states, and in particular your state law, prohibits an employer from maliciously or recklessly disregarding the truth in communicating with others regarding the reason for an employee's employment separation. However, an employer does have a qualified privilege to answer inquiries regarding the reasons for such a separation when they are based on what the employer reasonably believes to be true. If you believe your former employer is making untrue statements about your employment relationship and you desire to file a claim, you will have the burden of proving these allegations. Obtaining the evidence to prove these assertions is generally difficult, at best.

As for other actions you can take, first and foremost, remember that you chose to end the employment relationship because you did not desire to work with someone who was treating you with disrespect by saying untrue statements about you. If asked why you left the job, simply respond that you chose to work elsewhere because you and the co-owner had different business practices and philosophies. Most important, continue to be a success and keep your unblemished work history with employers seeking you out for the next 25 years. Also keep in mind that just as they know you are a good employee, others also know that your former employer is not the easiest person to get along with and has behaved in ways or made statements to cause his employees to quit.

Unfortunately, lack of or breakdown in communication has destroyed numerous employment relationships. In the example, the employer never informed the employee that he had a problem with her work performance or sought to learn the circumstances surrounding what he perceived to be a problem. Rather he leaped to a conclusion of theft. The employer's approach left many unanswered questions, wounded individuals, and possibly persistent problems to this day. Failure or refusal to address a problem head-on only heightens the initial concern. Only full discussion will uncover sufficient information to find either an amicable resolution or closure.

Writing

The written word is easily marked by its symbols. Although writing might seem the easiest of the four communication tools because it is readily seen, do not let this illusion lure you into a false sense of security.

Man Questions Vacation Policy

Q. My wife works for a very small company. The owner is very cheap, pays minimum wage, and his conduct, in some instances, is very questionable.

   My wife will be working there one year as of August and had expected her one-week vacation. Although the employee handbook states vacation is calculated according to your anniversary date, he maintains that you must work a year of working days, 365, which would be much longer. His attitude is "If you don't like it, quit."

   He asked that all employees work the Sunday after July 4. He said anyone who did not work that Sunday would not get paid for the holiday. The employee handbook says nothing about an employee having to work the day before or the day after a holiday to be paid for it. These are a couple of examples of his harassment of the employees. He claims he is the owner and he will run his business as he wants.

The handbook states that this company abides by employment-at-will, which permits employer or employee to terminate employment at any time for any reason.

My question is, do these employees have any rights at all? Thank you for any advice you can give us.

J. S.

A. The general rule of law is that the employer may establish the policies and procedures that govern the employment relationship, so long as they are consistent with federal and state law. Over the years, the courts have created numerous exceptions to this general rule. For example, when an employer has communicated its employment policies and procedures to employees in an employee handbook and has widely distributed that handbook to employees, a court may find that the handbook is a binding contract between the employer and employees.

In such circumstances, the employer must adhere to its written statements, or it may be liable for breach of contract. If there is any ambiguity in the wording, the doubt will be resolved in the employee's favor. This rule of construction is based on the premise that the employer wrote the policy and therefore had the opportunity to clarify the message it desired to communicate to employees.

However, a handbook may be found not a contract if it contains a proper disclaimer. For a disclaimer to be effective, it must clearly communicate to employees that the employment relationship is "at will" and that either the employee may quit or the employer may fire the employee at any time for any reason, with or without notice, and that the employer may change the handbook at any time without advance notice. The disclaimer must be placed in a conspicuous location, such as the first page of the handbook, and be clearly visible, such as through use of bold print, capitalization, and underlining. Generally, where this type of disclaimer exists, employees have no recourse based upon the handbook. I recommend that your wife review the handbook to ascertain whether it has a disclaimer, and if so, what the disclaimer says and where it is located.

Not all employment policies are put in writing. It is difficult and not always possible to reduce every aspect of the employment relationship to writing. Therefore, employment practices may be created by an employer's conduct in particular circumstances.

When an employer has created a past practice, employees may reasonably expect to be treated in the same or similar manner. If the employer's actions do not match the established practice, the employer may be liable for not acting in accordance with that practice. For example, if the employer has a history of paying its employees holiday pay even though they do not work the day after the holiday, the employees may reasonably expect that, absent any communication to the contrary, the practice will continue. Therefore, prior practice becomes a supplement to a written policy, and failure to follow it may leave an employer liable for a breach of contract action. An employee's relief from any such breach lies in filing a complaint with the state court.

Employers are advised to treat similarly situated employees in the same manner to avoid discrimination lawsuits. For example, if your wife or others were being treated differently because of their membership in a protected classification, such as sex, age, or race, then she or they may file a discrimination action against the company with the state's Division on Civil Rights or the federal Equal Employment Opportunity Commission.

In addition, the law of many states, including your state, and the federal Fair Labor Standards Act broadly define wages to include, among other items, holiday, vacation, and sick pay. Therefore, if an employer has a policy that it refuses to follow in regard to the payment of its employees' wage benefits, an employee may file a claim with the state or federal Office of Wage and Hour Compliance.

Your wife and her coworkers do have certain rights regarding their employment terms. However, they first need to ascertain what the employer has communicated, either in writing or orally, concerning their wages, hours, and other terms and conditions of employment. Then they can decide how best to proceed.

Because relationships require work, we must expend the necessary time and thought before writing down information or opinions. The written word can confuse, intentionally or unintentionally, if not properly used. The objective is to convey information or opinions that others can receive readily with clarity. A writing serves little purpose if I understand what I have communicated, but others fail to comprehend and take in the message.

You probably have heard the comment "It's your problem that there is no communication or you failed to understand what I said or wrote." No matter how powerful that self-serving, self-defeating message may be, it often carries the day with no end product. The underlying frustration persists—"I wasn't heard and consequently I've failed to achieve my objective." Here is an example of this principle in action:

Employer Unclear on Vacation Policy

Q. I am looking for information as to proper business practices when hiring and the follow-up as to adhering to them. My daughter was advised when hired that she would have three weeks' vacation after one year. She assumed that meant effective on her hire date. Not so. This year, she was recently advised that vacation time started after the three months' probation time. Not so. Again, she was advised that she must have one full month of work in before she can start to accumulate time.

I had never heard of this practice, but some friends said they had. Since she was given no employee handbook or anything to read on these policies, I would like to know if this company is acting properly. I can not believe that an employer is allowed to take this approach with its employees and the employee has no recourse.

H. C.

A. For the numerous reasons you point out, employee handbooks are extremely valuable tools in that they clearly communicate to employees their employment benefits and dates of eligibility as well as the employees' obligations to the organization. When this important information is not documented, the potential is great for inconsistent application of the policies as well as lost employee productivity in using work time to ascertain the various policies and procedures.

Many employers are concerned about reducing their employment policies and procedures to writing based upon several court decisions that have ruled that absent a proper disclaimer, an employee handbook may be considered an employment contract. However, with the correct counseling, employers can meet the legal requirements and prevent the type of situation you describe. Again, good communication is imperative to have a successful relationship. The investment an employer makes in creating a properly prepared employee handbook is small compared with the benefits gained.

Even more important is a fact of which most employers are not aware: An employment policy and procedure need not necessarily be reduced to writing to make it enforceable and the organization responsible and possibly liable. The courts have held that when an employer has an established practice upon which employees have relied or may reasonably rely, that practice will be enforceable against the employer. The primary considerations are what the employer has communicated, by actions or words, to employees and what the employee's reasonable expectation is based upon that communication. Similarly, if an employer makes an oral representation to an employee upon which the employee has relied to his detriment, the employer may be expected to honor its commitment.

The courts will require employers to keep their commitment to employees. A claim may be filed with the court for breach of contract, whether the contract is written or oral. The difficulty with an oral contract is having the evidence to prove its existence. Your daughter's situation exemplifies the importance of clearly communicating with employees regarding the terms of the employment relationship. Handbooks have proved to be valuable employment tools and a good business practice. We have assisted hundreds of clients with our model employee handbook to educate management and nonmanagement employees properly about their employment benefits and responsibilities.

Acting

Like the written word, body language can be seen by most people. How you act tells others how you desire to be treated. For example, when you act with disrespect, you will receive no respect; when you cut someone off in the middle of a sentence, you will not be heard; when you give no assistance, none will be provided to you.

Most managers and supervisors are unaware of or would prefer to ignore the fact that their actions set the tone for the work atmosphere. For example, a manager complains to the director of human resources that many of the employees he supervises are reporting to work late, leaving early, not paying attention to how they are performing their job duties, and not completing assigned tasks. After investigating these problems, the director of human resources learns that the complaining manager also has been reporting to work late and leaving early, has not been responding to employees' questions or providing direction, and has been unavailable to give assistance. The employees were merely taking their lead from the person responsible for setting the stage. Is there any doubt that actions speak louder than words? What kind of example are you setting? Does your conduct serve as inspiration for others to admire, or does it create disdain?

Solution Sought for Sick-Time Abuses

Q. I have been working for the federal government for nine years. Approximately two years ago, I was promoted to a first-line supervisor's position.

This gave me access to the time and attendance records of employees in the section I supervised. At that time, I came to realize I was the only individual not abusing my sick leave.

In the federal government, there is no restriction on the amount of sick leave that may be accumulated. Full-time employees earn sick leave at the rate of four hours for each full biweekly pay period or 13 days per year. Sick leave is a qualified right in that the employee is entitled to use it only when warranted. My concern is employees are using their sick leave as soon as they accrue it. Furthermore, no employee has a significant accumulated sick-leave balance, since nothing is saved for the future. This is a problem because it represents lost productivity, and sometimes when people really get sick, they run out of leave.

I would like to take action to curb the excessive use of sick leave, but I have been advised by other managers and supervisors to turn a blind eye to the matter. Since everyone is abusing the sick-leave policy, it is hard to crack down on the abuse. The situation is mass disobedience similar to when the speed limit is 55 mph and everyone's going 65 or 70.

What is your advice? Should I turn a blind eye to the matter? If I take action to curb the excessive use of sick leave, I am told other offices will continue their liberal leave policies, and my employees will resent being subjected to a stricter policy. So, I will have accomplished nothing by enforcing the rules, since a morale problem will occur. Is it better simply to consider the sick leave as 13 days additional paid vacation per year?

D. C.

A.   I respect your conscientiousness in desiring to fulfill the reason employers provide their employees paid sick time: to assist employees financially when they are unable to work as a result of a non-job-related illness or injury. The frustration you communicate is understandable because abuse of paid sick time negatively impacts upon the organization, the coworkers who must perform the absent employee's responsibilities, the public or customer, and employees themselves, who may not have any paid time available when it is truly needed.

Unfortunately, regulating employees' proper use of paid sick leave is a monumental task at best. However, there are certain steps that employers do take in defining under what circumstances an employee will be eligible for paid sick time. For example, many employers require employees to call in at least one and one-half hours prior to the start of their workday if they are going to be absent. When an employee is absent because of illness for more than three days, some companies require the worker to submit a doctor's note on the first day back to substantiate an absence.

I agree with the other managers and supervisors that if you implement a stricter enforcement policy than what other offices are applying, you will have a lot of unhappy and nonproductive employees. Perhaps you might consider initiating a government-wide program whereby employees receive an award for perfect attendance. Consider offering the Cal Ripken Jr. award for perfect attendance, the Lou Gehrig award for one absence per year, and another prize for persons with two absences per year. You could also look into whether a program could be instituted to buy back unused sick time.

Like Cal Ripken Jr. and Lou Gehrig, those employees who have perfect attendance are heroes and entitled to be recognized for their dedication and achievement. These programs create a win-win situation for everyone, including us taxpayers. I hope you also will be recognized for your dedication, commitment, and strong work ethic beyond the compliment and commendation I give you. You too are a hero!

Because your actions are readily seen, ask a trusted friend whom you respect to reflect back to you, like a mirror, your actions so that you can see clearly how they are being communicated to others. Although the thought of having someone tell us of our imperfections is worse than public speaking, it is far worse to be humiliated or humbled in public out of our own ignorance. Inability to see our self-portrait creates a problem that continually arises in sexual harassment complaints:

Workplace Social Butterfly

Q. Call me old-fashioned, but I am in love with women, which these days can often be construed as "politically incorrect." I can be considered a "tease" to women at work. I very often subtly and sometimes overtly flirt with those above and below me on the corporate ladder. Is the act of flirting with a coworker while on the job construed as sexual harassment? Your response is important. My social nightlife depends on it.

B. D.

A. The U.S. Supreme Court and the New Jersey Supreme Court have stated that a hostile work environment based on sexual harassment exists if

1. The unwelcome conduct would not have occurred but for the employee's gender.
2. The conduct was sufficiently severe or pervasive.
3. A reasonable employee would believe that the conditions of

employment have been altered (the reasonableness of the belief is viewed from the perspective of the gender of the individual who alleges sexual harassment).

4. The conditions of employment are altered in that the working environment is hostile or abusive.

Although in most cases the harassing conduct takes the form of unwelcome touchings or comments with sexual overtones, the conduct need not be sexual in nature in order to be considered "sexual harassment." Your act of flirting with coworkers while on the job may very well be construed as constituting sexual harassment. You may consider your conduct as "flirting and therefore harmless," but another individual may find your behavior offensive and thus harassment.

A person is hired to perform a service for the employer, in return for which the employee is paid; the job is not intended as a scoping ground for one's social life. Should other people be offended by what you refer to as "flirtation," and a claim of unlawful sexual harassment is filed with a governmental agency or court, you and your employer each may be found liable, with the obligation to pay monetary damages. You may lose your job as well. Thus, you should consider scouting out spots other than your place of employment for your nightlife and focus your mind and energies on your job responsibilities. Who knows, this newly directed attention may result in a raise, a bonus, or a promotion.

Listening

The most important—and most overlooked—component of the four communication skills is listening. It is also the easiest tool to use but the most difficult to practice. In most conversations we have our own agenda to complete, and because of our preoccupation with our list or defenses against what is being said, we often do not hear what the other person is saying.

Right or wrong, each person has a perception. The individual who takes the time to listen and understand the perception of another demonstrates a great communication ability and is better equipped by possessing pertinent knowledge. In the following example, the manager's failure or refusal to hear that the employee injured himself in furtherance of the organization's interests may cost the employer a lot of money as well as employee morale through the filing of a discrimination lawsuit, increased insurance premiums, other workplace accidents, payment of additional medical expenses, lost time from work, and disgruntled, nonproductive employees who are concerned about their safety and upset about the treatment of their coworker. Had the manager taken in the information provided to him, the entire matter could have been avoided.

Employee May Be Entitled to Workers' Compensation

Q. I am an employee of an organization where I have been for employed 32 years. I was hurt at work after lifting 93 catalogues. I pulled my left shoulder out due to an impinged nerve. Instead of my manager being concerned that I hurt myself, he gave me a letter of warning, which was later rescinded.

After that, I was denied medical attention unless I took care of it on my own. I am still in constant pain.

J. K.

A. I am very sorry to hear about your injury and pain. The purpose of workers' compensation insurance is to provide employees and their families quick and certain payment for injuries or illnesses that occur in connection with their employment. To fulfill this statutory objective, the legislatures of most states have mandated that employers provide adequate insurance coverage for the payment of workers' compensation benefits.

Employees who suffer an on-the-job injury or illness are entitled to workers' compensation benefits regardless of any negligence, including their own. In exchange for receiving benefits, injured workers gives up many of the claims of damages to which they would otherwise be entitled. Thus, workers' compensation statutes represent a compromise by providing workers essential benefits at a cost that allows employers to remain in business.

In addition to providing statutory benefits, the workers' compensation statutes protect employees in the filing of a workers' compensation claim. The laws specifically prohibit employers from retaliating in any manner against an employee for filing a claim or testifying in a proceeding.

From what you have described, it appears that your injury occurred while you were performing your job responsibilities. If so, your injury would be compensable under the workers' compensation statute. Your manager's letter of warning may constitute retaliatory action unless you had failed to follow safety procedures in the performance of your job or he had some other legitimate business reason for his actions unrelated to your potential claim.

Although one of the purposes of workers' compensation insurance is to keep the costs of providing benefits at a manageable level, the insurance is still expensive and paid for in full by the employer. The premium charged is based upon the number of workers' compensation claims filed against the employer. This experience rating remains with the employer from three to five years. Thus, as a cost of doing business, employers need to educate their managers and supervisors concerning their responsibilities to provide a safe and healthy work environment and how to respond to workplace injuries.

During my management educational programs, I emphasize the importance of good communication skills and documentation involving work-related accidents. The employer must accurately understand how and where the accident occurred to prevent further injury to the employee and injury to other employees and to verify that the accident occurred in the workplace. An employer's failure to properly educate its employees may result in additional injuries or lawsuits alleging an unsafe workplace or retaliation.

In regard to your situation, definitely obtain medical assistance to protect against further injury and potential time lost from work due to this injury. Many organizations have specific doctors to whom they refer all employees who sustain a work-related injury. Possibly speak with upper management concerning your accident and your immediate manager's response. It is in your organization's best interest to possess all relevant information about the health of its workers and to ensure proper documentation of injuries. Often, knowingly or unknowingly, managers and supervisors do not act in the employer's best interests. Your situation clearly demonstrates the importance of management training programs on the employment laws and their practical implications.

Most important, tend to your medical needs immediately. Your health is of utmost importance so that you can continue to live a happy, productive, and fulfilled life.

The most practical way to better your listening skills is to keep your mouth closed and your ears open. While the other person is speaking, forget your agenda that is playing in your head. We often completely miss what has just been said because we were focused on what we wanted to say next. To ensure you have heard what has been told to you, repeat back your understanding as to what has been relayed. Continual practice of these devices will improve your listening ability.

Applying All Four Communication Skills

How many times have you seen relationships—marital, customer, friendship, employment—dissolve as a result of lack of or poor communication? Unfortunately, probably more than you care to recall. A frequent inquiry I have received over the years involves an employer not knowing what to do concerning the status of an employee who has been on a workers' compensation leave of absence for the past sixteen weeks and with whom the employer has had no communication during the entire leave period. The employer desires to end the employment relationship because the organization needs to fill the position, but the employer is concerned it will be sued. On the other hand are the employees on leave who during the first several weeks of their absence feel uncomfortable and disconnected as a result of not being in their regular routine. By then, however, they have come to enjoy the newly found television shows and other activities as a result of not having any work obligations. The parties who are suppose to be working together are traveling on two separate paths.

To prevent this type of stressful situation, for both the employer and the employee, I strongly urge my clients to put into place a written policy that clearly outlines employees' responsibilities should they take a leave of absence, whether the leave be on account of a workers' compensation injury, non-work-related disability, serious health condition of a family member, or other personal reason. Regardless of the nature of the leave, employees are required to call in at least every week or every other week, depending upon the circumstances, and speak personally with their supervisor to provide a status report. Speaking with the receptionist or leaving a message on voice mail is unacceptable. Personal connection is necessary to keep the relationship vital.

In addition, if an employee fails to adhere to the policy, the employer should telephone and ascertain the employee's status and ability to return to work *before* ending the relationship. This one telephone call by no means transfers the contact responsibility to the employer. I have frequently had clients who in fact did undertake the obligation of calling the employee for status reports. When the employer stopped calling and thereafter fired the employee as a no-call/no-show, and the employee sued, the court ruled in favor of the employee. The court's reasoning was that by its actions, the employer communicated that it would call, thereby relieving the employee of any such requirement. Consequently, the employer, not the employee, had failed to do its part. If this scenario seems archaic and lopsided, it is. This situation is an accurate description of an employer, usually with good intentions, doing too much for the employee. Unfortunately, an employer's good intentions often get the organization into trouble. Documentation describing what transpired is also essential in protecting the organization's interests.

This example again clearly demonstrates that communication—speaking, writing, acting, and listening—is key. On the other hand, failure of on-leave employees to adhere to a well-publicized policy of regularly checking in with their supervisor communicates their disrespect for the organization and disinterest in serving it and its people.

The following lists contain some simple communication skills that will produce success in applying the four different communication methods. The contrast in not using the representative set for each category is demonstrated through an actual workplace situation.

Speaking

1. Questioning applicants about their prior work experience.
2. Praising good work.
3. Telling employees about their poor work performance.
4. Discussing inappropriate workplace behavior.
5. Asking where you can improve.
6. Verbalizing the need for assistance.
7. Clarifying your job responsibilities.
8. Inquiring about a pay raise.
9. Talking about a promotional opportunity.
10. Expressing concern about low productivity.

By contrast:

Vacation Time Used for Leave

Q. I have been working for a small firm for the last 10 years. I work on salary plus sales commission. This past March I had major surgery—total knee replacement. I was out of work three weeks, and management decided to take my three weeks' vacation as a substitute for the time off. I was told it would not be legal to just let me take the time off that was needed for this operation.

Should I have filed for workers' compensation? I feel I was not treated fairly by this new office manager, and I would like to know if I can do anything about this situation.

T. D.

A. When an employee needs a leave of absence, it is important for the employee and employer to discuss in advance, absent an emergency, the reason for the leave, the approximate duration of the leave, the employee's obligations during the leave, and whether the leave will be with or without pay. This communication will enable everyone affected by the leave, including the employee's coworkers, to plan and be prepared for the employee's absence.

As to whether you should have filed for workers' compensation, it depends on why you needed knee replacement surgery. If it was the result of a work-related injury, either occurring at work or while you were providing a service for the employer's business, the surgery would likely be covered by workers' compensation. However, you have an obligation to make your employer aware of a work-related accident or injury when it happens. If you do not, you may not be able to claim later that the injury or disease was work-related and thus may be precluded from receiving workers' compensation benefits.

On the other hand, if your injury was not work-related, it may be covered by the state temporary disability law. To receive temporary disability benefits, you must complete the necessary paperwork and request your physician and employer to complete their sections of a form that is submitted to the state. In addition, some employers offer coverage under an individual temporary disability plan.

Whether your employer can use your vacation time to cover your disability leave depends on your employer's policies. You need to discuss this matter with your employer. Perhaps you would have preferred to save your vacation time, or perhaps your employer has no reallocation policy in place. Often employees prefer such reallocation, because it provides them with pay for part of their leave that would otherwise be an unpaid leave of absence. Most disability leaves are unpaid.

An employer is free to establish under what circumstances employees may use sick, personal, and vacation time, as there is no law requiring employers to provide these benefits.

Writing

1. Keeping records of work-related accidents for workers' compensation insurance coverage.
2. Documenting a voluntary resignation to evidence unemployment compensation ineligibility.
3. Memorializing an act of insubordination.
4. Preparing a job description.
5. Creating an employee handbook.
6. Completing an employee performance evaluation.
7. Detailing a work status report.

8. Applying for a job posting.
9. Filling in time and expense reports.
10. Nominating an employee of the year.

By contrast:

Employers Who "Bug" Should Have Policy

Q. Is it legal to "bug" a record room or office and conversations and monitor the telephones in a workplace without informing the employees of such activities? And if employees are informed, what are the implications or liabilities toward visitors and vendors who use our telephones on-site?
    N. E.

A. Advanced technology and electronic devices in the workplace have generated many questions such as yours. Privacy issues are of primary concern to employers and employees alike. Whether an employer may "bug" a record room or office generally depends on what the employer has communicated to employees and on employees' reasonable expectation of privacy. For example, an employee would have a reasonable expectation that the employer is not recording any sound or conversations if

- The employer has not informed employees that it has recording devices in its offices or conference rooms,
- The employer has provided these rooms for the employees' use without restrictions, and
- These areas are not generally opened to the public or are used for private meetings.

Similarly, an employer generally does not have the right to monitor all telephone calls an employee makes unless it has provided employees with advance notice of such monitoring and the employer has a legitimate business interest for the practice or has obtained the employee's written consent.

An employer's failure to adhere to these rules may be a violation of federal and state wiretapping laws, which provide for compensatory and punitive damages.

In addition, an employee may have an invasion-of-privacy claim against the employer that may make the employer liable for compensatory and punitive damages. The general rules discussed previously also apply to voice mail and electronic mail.

To prevent a lawsuit from being filed or to place the organization in a good defense posture should a claim be filed, an employer is advised to have a written employment policy that sets forth its practice and procedure regarding whether it has recording devices in the workplace or monitors telephone calls. This policy should also address the employer's position regarding searches of employees' desks and lockers. An employer's unauthorized eavesdropping and recording not only may result in monetary liability but also, and even more important, may cause damage to employee morale by destroying any sense of trust and loyalty.

The same rules and recommendations also generally apply in the case of visitors and vendors who use an employer's telephones. In addition, an employer's monitoring or recording of their conversations could have incalculable damages as a result of lost business. Again, the employer should have a written policy outlining its practice and procedure as well as a recording on the telephone informing all telephone users that their conversations may be monitored or recorded, or both.

Furthermore, the employer is urged to have a legitimate business purpose for implementing a telephone monitoring or recording policy. In addition, simply having such a policy does not give the employer the right to publish or disclose the telephone conversations to third parties. Such action may also result in liability.

The various employment laws and regulations affecting the workplace are based upon and encourage employers to have open communications with their employees regarding what is present in the employment environment and relationship. Therefore, it is important to keep these basic principles in mind in developing and maintaining the employment relationship.

Acting

1. Being respectful to superiors and coworkers.
2. Serving as a liaison for others.
3. Associating with coworkers.
4. Reporting to work on time.
5. Assisting others in completing work product.
6. Following workplace rules.
7. Getting along with others.
8. Extending greetings to new employees.
9. Participating in organization-sponsored events.
10. Furnishing work project materials.

By contrast:

Worker Puzzled by Her Firing

Q.   A company employed me on a 90-day probationary period. During this
     time I was written up for reasons that I did not agree with, and I wrote a re-
     buttal to the human resources manager. My next scheduled workday after
     management received my rebuttal, I was fired for no specific reason. I was
     told I would be better off working somewhere else.

     I feel my firing was more on a personal level than on a professional one.
     Management had no criticism about my work since I was employed with the
     company.

     Management's written warning to me and my rebuttals are as follows:

     • Thirty minutes late. First scheduled day to work, not aware of traf-
       fic flow.
     • Left two hours and 30 minutes early due to snowstorm. I have an
       hour-and-a-half commute.
     • Left one hour early to pick up car. I had to return a rental from a
       previous accident before the store closed.
     • Left 15 minutes early. It was not busy this day.
     • Fifteen minutes late. Traffic was heavy.
     • Fifteen minutes late. Traffic was heavy.
     • Fifteen minutes late. Traffic was heavy.
     • One hour and 45 minutes late. I had a flat tire and was waiting until
       the shop opened to get the tire repaired.
     • One hour late. My alarm did not go off because the power went off
       overnight.

     My coworkers were and still continue to come in late and some leave
     early, including other employees who are also on a 90-day probationary pe-
     riod. None of them was given a written warning.

     I do not feel the company had a real reason to fire me. I believe if I had
     signed the written warning without a rebuttal, I would still have a job, and it
     would have blown over in a couple of weeks. I feel this may be a case of dis-
     crimination.

     J. G.

A.   In your letter you state that management had no criticism with your work.
     However, you also state that management gave you a written warning dur-

ing your first 90 days of employment, and when you were fired, you were told you would be better off working somewhere else. Doesn't this information, in addition to your cited unreliable work record, indicate that management was not pleased with your work performance?

Regardless of what other employees were or were not doing regarding their job duties, the focus needs to be on the commitment you made to your former employer to report to work on time and provide the stated service for the duration of the scheduled work hours.

Every employer has the right to expect its employees to respect the terms and conditions of employment, especially in the beginning of the relationship, when most workers are on their best behavior. However, on the first day of your employment, you arrived for work 30 minutes late because you did not take the time to learn the traffic flow in advance. Your behavior sent a strong message to the company that you simply did not value the relationship.

You reinforced this message when on your fourth day you left work two hours and 30 minutes early because you have an hour-and-a-half commute. During your second week you again left early to return your rental car and because the company was "not busy" that day.

Your initial actions, which continued in a similar vein, clearly communicated your lack of loyalty to the organization, its employees, and its customers and were contrary to the reasons you were hired.

The purpose of the probationary period is for both the employer and employee to get to know each other, learn whether they have common interests and goals, and decide whether they can work together. The probationary period highlights the employment-at-will relationship, in that either the employee may quit or the employer may fire the employee at any time, with or without notice, for any reason or no reason, so long as the action is not contrary to law.

Although you state that your former coworkers arrived for work late and some left early, the more important question is what the individual circumstances are for each person's conduct. Perhaps an employee has a prearranged flexible work schedule, or another had a death in the family, or perhaps others were also fired. You may not know the exact details of their situation.

The reason you believe your employment was ended also appears to be conflicting. On the one hand, you state that if you had not written the rebuttal to the written warning, you would still be employed. On the other hand, you state that your firing was discriminatory.

If the first reason is true, then you have no legal protection. If the second reason is true, then you have the burden of proving that you were treated differently from similarly situated employees on account of your sex, sexual preference, race, religion, creed, color, age, martial status, veteran status, or disability.

Before deciding how best to proceed, you need to possess full and accurate information. With the ending of every employment relationship, it is critical to see what your role was in producing that result. Refusing to take inventory may invite a similar unwelcome ending in the future.

Listening

1. Possessing detailed knowledge of conversation topic.
2. Receiving oral direction at the conclusion of a meeting.
3. Gaining insight from employee meetings concerning job duties.
4. Understanding others' needs or desires.
5. Empathizing with another person's situation.
6. Heeding advice.
7. Paying attention to what is being said about an old method.
8. Being receptive to ideas on expanding operations.
9. Hearing the problem.
10. Knowing how to solving employees' vocalized concerns.

By contrast:

Worker Learns a Lesson on the Expense of Tardiness

Q. I love my sales job but hate the daily call reports and weekly expense reports expected of me. In an effort to "teach me a lesson," my boss demanded back reports that were overdue. He then refused to compensate me for legitimate out-of-pocket expenses from Jan. 1 to May 31, amounting to $1,500 for gas, tolls, telephone, etc.

Although I have clearly brought this on by my tardiness in submitting reports, can my boss deny me just compensation as a disciplinary action? Ironically, my sales showed the largest increase in our company during this period.

C. B.

A. Employers need to establish organizational policies in order to maintain smooth business operations. Violation of those policies causes deterioration of the organization's stability and negatively impacts each employee. Employers have obligations to their employees, but employees also owe responsibilities to their employer and coworkers.

Most employers have a written policy requiring workers who seek reimbursement to submit business-related expense reports with original receipts. The failure to comply with the requirement results in no reimbursement.

In addition, these policies usually require the employee to submit the report within a specified time in order to be reimbursed. An employee has an obligation to adhere to the employer's policies, and the failure to do so may result in disciplinary action or employment termination.

As you state in your letter, "I have clearly brought this on by my tardiness." If your employer has a policy requiring its employees to submit expense reports in a certain manner and you failed to adhere to that policy, then it seems only fair that you be treated in a similar fashion as every other employee who violates the policy.

The employer's policies and practices are established for good reason. Just as you have bills to pay, so does your employer. When bills are not paid on time, there is usually a penalty attached.

There is no law specifically addressing the issue of whether your employer has the right to refuse to reimburse you for late-reported expenses. Although you refer to the out-of-pocket expenses as "just compensation," the federal Fair Labor Standards Act and state Wage Payment Law require employers to pay employees for all hours worked. Payment of out-of-pocket business expenses is not included in the definition of "wages." Neither is it expressly illegal for an employer to refuse to cover an employee's out-of-pocket business expenses if the employee failed to comply with the employer's policies.

However, each employee must receive at least minimum wages for all time worked. Should the nonreimbursement of business-related expenses take an employee below minimum wage, there may exist a violation of the minimum-wage requirements.

It is unfortunate that you had to experience the consequences of your actions. However, the lesson of listening and respecting another person's words in the face of disliking a job responsibility is worth more than $1,500.

Take a minute to review the four lists. In doing so ask yourself these questions: (1) How often do my coworkers and I use these or other similar communication skills? (2) How well do I perform these skills? (3) What is common among the items listed? (4) Who wins when I use these communication skills? I hope you can answer that you are currently practicing these or other similar communication methods and that you perform them well or are seeking to improve upon them. As for the third question, each communication task requires *action*. With respect to the last inquiry, each item creates a win-win environment. Now create your own action lists.

What are the consequences if you choose not to practice the basic communication skills? Consider the following situations:

1. You did not ask enough questions or listen to the applicant's objectives or work values to learn that his method and skill level were incompatible with that of the organization. Now you are responsible for firing the individual from his job.

Consequence—Every employment termination exposes the organization to a potential lawsuit, and every incompatible employee creates frustration for everyone.

2. You did not create the necessary documentation to substantiate the employee's habitual tardiness and poor performance to take the next step of feeling legally comfortable in ending the relationship.

Consequence—A nonproductive employee is adversely affecting employee morale and the organization's profit margin.

3. You did not speak with Jack about his inappropriate workplace behavior. Now you have five employees who spend more time focusing their attention on Jack and the upcoming sexual harassment lawsuit than carrying out their job duties.

Consequence—You are named as a defendant in the lawsuit.

4. You did not listen to your supervisor's instructions and now you have lost the big account and your job.

Consequence—You are humbled by your need to collect unemployment compensation benefits.

5. You failed to read the employee handbook and now you have lost the opportunity to use your personal days.

Consequence—You have lost the opportunity to have the much overdue and needed eye examination.

Notice that the key is not how good we are in using these tools, but rather the brass ring is won each time we practice these skills. Equally as important is that not one of the above disasters was caused by using one of the communications tools but rather was the direct result of not using a key communication component.

When I counsel people on how to take a different approach to the employment relationship or on how to defend against employment-related claims, I
frequently hear the following responses:

1. I don't feel very skilled at speaking, writing, acting, or listening when
   people raise sensitive matters.
2. I don't have the desire or energy to deal with difficult people or
   tough situations.
3. Maybe someone else will address the problem, or better yet, maybe
   no one will notice.
4. I've never done this before.
5. No one else is doing anything about it, so why should I stick my
   neck on the chopping block?
6. It isn't my job.
7. I'm hoping things will get better.
8. I have too many other items that need my attention.
9. If the relationship doesn't work, we will simply get a replacement.
10. I'm overwhelmed.

If any of these answers sound familiar, you know how the story ends, "and
the list of excuses just goes on and on and on." The one item we are never
short on is excuses. The Army's motto is that at all times you have only two
choices—the right decision or the wrong decision—because the third choice—
inaction—will get you shot every time.

Good communication skills practiced on a minute-by-minute basis are invaluable to a successful employment relationship. Using them shows respect
for yourself and everyone else. As the examples in this chapter demonstrate,
the ability to communicate must be seen fully and clearly for the value it can
add or the destruction it can create in a relationship. The importance of this
powerful tool will be highlighted in the next chapter, as the interviewing and
hiring process sets the stage for whether an employment relationship will
come into existence, and if so, how it will proceed based upon the parties' initial interactions.

three

The Interviewing and Hiring Process

Most applicants and employer representatives dislike the interviewing and hiring process and fail to see it as a valuable educational tool for learning more about themselves and others. In addition to its being a vehicle for growth in supplying new information and/or affirming current beliefs, the process can produce great benefit if perceived correctly and approached with the right attitude. However, if the purpose of the process is not understood and the parties don't invest time in preparing themselves, the consequences could be, and often are, devastating and costly. In this chapter I discuss the purpose of the interviewing and hiring process, walk the applicant and employer through the process, and outline for both parties how to prepare for what could be the best or worst meeting of their career. Thus, the prospective employee and the employer will be able to see the process from the perspective of both parties.

The interviewing and hiring process for most people is the beginning of the employment relationship, although many never proceed beyond the initial contact. The old adage "the first impression creates a lasting impression" is a common theme for most first contacts, written or in person.

In addition, the process is an information-gathering opportunity for both the employer and employee. The employee can ascertain as much as possible about the available position, the organization, and its people; the employer can learn whether the candidate is qualified, well-suited for the position, and a good investment. The purpose of this process is to decide whether the parties desire to create a work relationship. Regardless of the urgency of finding a job or an employee, the interviewing and hiring process takes time. Like any other employment-related decisions, hiring decisions made without preparation usually lead to disappointment.

The hiring process consists primarily of the job advertisement and other recruiting devices, the employment application/résumé and interview(s), and new employee orientation. Each part of the process serves a distinct purpose. Recognizing and using the objective of each independent hiring function will allow you to be more effective.

Job Advertisement

The job advertisement is a valuable tool for the employer and employee when it clearly delineates the employer's objective. This goal is achieved when the ad contains sufficient specific information to apprise applicants of whether they would desire the job and are qualified for the position. They need this information to determine whether the details fit their objectives and abilities. Preparation of the job advertisement helps the employer focus on its employment needs and clarify the position's purpose within the organization *before* the creation of an employment relationship. Neither party desires to spend time on an incompatible match. Have you heard the story about the blind date who arrived an hour late, never apologized, had bad breath, chewed his food with his mouth open, had no cash, check, or credit card to pay for dinner, and asked for a good-night kiss? Like the failed blind date, if the parties do not have the same or similar interests, the relationship will not work. The initial investment in evaluating what is important can prevent future disappointment, frustration, and litigation.

The employment advertisement should contain the following information to attract those prospective employees most suited for the position: (1) title; (2) requisite skills; (3) additional desired skills; (4) minimum education and/or experience; and (5) summary of essential job functions.

Before the job advertisement is placed, it must first be reviewed by someone familiar with the state and federal pre-employment guidelines to ensure that it is void of any information extraneous to the job description and qualifications. Federal and state laws strictly prohibit any reference to sex, race, color, religion, creed, national origin, age, sexual preference, marital status, veteran status, and non-job-related physical, mental, and emotional disability, unless one of these characteristics is a "bona fide" job requirement. A "bona fide" qualification is one that is reasonably necessary to the employer's normal business operations. The existence of the business necessity is strictly construed against the employer, who has the burden of proving the job requirement. For example, an ad for a food server is not to state "waitress" but rather "waitress/waiter" or "server." Similarly, an ad for a "salesman" needs to read "salesperson" or "salesman/woman."

As demonstrated in the next example, employers also need to consider the timing of the announcement of employment openings.

Disabled Man Thinks Town Discriminated

Q. Please help. Sorry for the poor penmanship; a few years ago I had a stroke and this is the best I can write.

Here is the situation. I work for a town, and the officials hire who they please and give out job titles for political cronies. The town hired three people; however, the town also had a layoff, and some people are still laid off. How can they hire these new people when there are people on layoff?

I feel I have been discriminated against due to the fact I am a handicapped person. The town is discriminating against me by not offering me a lateral promotion. The union I belong to says the town can hire whom they please. I say hogwash, because I have seven years' seniority. I say this is discrimination and misrepresentation on the part of the town and the union.

Your advice will determine what recourse I can take. Please help. Thank you.

T. P.

A. An employer has the right to hire whomever it desires, so long as the employer does not make an employment decision, whether it be to hire or not to hire, based upon an applicant's race, creed, color, national origin, ancestry, age, marital status, sex, sexual preference, veteran status, disability, or other protected classification. There is no prohibition against offering employment to friends.

In the public employment setting, however, the employer needs to be prudent in how it spends the taxpayers' money, which would include hiring persons who are qualified for the position. Unlike a private employer, a public employer also has specific civil service rules to follow, which govern the terms of the employment relationship.

Although seemingly unfair for the town to hire new employees at a time when laid-off employees have not been returned to work, perhaps there are extenuating reasons for this situation, such as the laid-off employees are not qualified for the positions that needed to be filled. Depending upon the terms of the employment relationship, such as the provisions of a collective bargaining agreement and what representations the town made to employees at the time of the layoff, an employer may hire employees while other employees are laid off. Again, this action may be taken as long as the hiring is not contrary to an agreement or representation or for an unlawful discriminatory reason.

For the reasons you point out, when possible, it is in the employer's best interest to return laid-off employees to work before hiring new employees. To maintain good employee relations and morale, employers may consider telling its employees the legitimate business reasons for its actions.

The Americans with Disabilities Act and most state laws prohibit employers from discriminating against an applicant or employee in hiring, compensation, promotion, or other terms or conditions of employment on account of a person's disabilities. To make a claim against an employer for unlawful disability discrimination, the applicant or employee must show that he was disabled, qualified for the position he applied for or desired, a nondisabled person was placed in the job, and the disabled person sustained damages as a result of the employer's decision, such as lost compensation.

An applicant or employee who believes he has been discriminated against because of his disability may follow any available internal grievance procedure, file a claim with the federal Equal Employment Opportunity Commission or the state Division on Civil Rights, or file a lawsuit in state court.

If you are a union member, the union has a similar obligation as that imposed upon employers not to discriminate on account of a person's disabilities. A union also has the obligation to represent fairly the interests of its members. The union's failure or refusal to carry out this responsibility may result in liability by an aggrieved member's filing of a lawsuit in federal court.

Although you have several available legal arenas if your claim is filed in timely fashion, perhaps you may first consider where your energy and effort would be best spent. For example, because you are concerned with your particular employment relationship, I would suggest that the focus be on yourself and not on what the town is doing with respect to other employees. Then consider scheduling a meeting with the appropriate decisionmakers to ascertain why you did not receive the lateral promotion. It is important to ask specific questions and request specific answers to your questions so that if there are valid reasons for your not receiving the promotion, you may improve in those designated areas. On the other hand, if there are not specific reasons for your not receiving the promotion, you then may make an informed decision as to whether you will pursue filing a legal claim.

Keep the focus on yourself, where it is that you desire to be with your career and life, and what steps you can take to receive the necessary data to make an informed decision, and then proceed with confidence and grace in taking care of yourself. These preliminary steps will enable you to cause change and achieve your goals. Good luck.

Employment Application

The employment application is an introduction or screening. The employer informs applicants that it offers equal employment opportunities regardless of the various characteristics previously outlined (sex, age, religion, etc.), that applicants need not provide any information pertaining to those personal characteristics, and that the application is an informal information-gathering process. All the questions on the employment application are to be job-related. In turn, applicants tell the employer their name, address, qualifications, skills, experiences, and other pertinent information related to the job for which they are applying. Because the employment application is the cornerstone upon which the relationship will be built, prospective employees have an obligation to represent themselves honestly. The courts have consistently held that falsification of an employment application supports an employer's decision not to hire the applicant and may be grounds for terminating the relationship if discovered later.

Past Illnesses Are Taboo Topic for Employer

Q. This year I was diagnosed with breast cancer. I began a series of tests and had surgery. So far there's been no spread to the lymph nodes, and I completed radiation a few weeks ago.

I am now actively looking for a job. In two separate cases I have come across the following question right on the initial application: "What diseases have you had in the past 6 months? What medication are you taking now?"

These are huge companies. The assumption would be that they can only ask legal questions on their applications, but this does not seem fair to me.

If I am honest, I know that I will never be called back. In both cases I left the questions blank and I have been called back for second interviews with these companies. What should I do if I am asked directly at my second interviews or if I confront these questions on an application again? Also, if I am hired, how do I handle the obligatory insurance forms?

If I am not honest, they can fire me for being dishonest. My medical coverage is very important. If I am hired, what prevents the insurance company from giving my medical information to my new employer?

I am 50 years old. I need a secure position that I can count on.

K. H.

A. The Americans with Disabilities Act and most state laws prohibit an employer, including large companies, from soliciting from applicants any information that may reveal certain protected information, such as the applicant's disability. This prohibition applies to job advertisements, employment applications, and the interview process. A limited exception exists that allows an employer to solicit certain information from an applicant if that particular characteristic has an impact upon a job for which the applicant is applying.

For example, an employer may not ask an applicant about the existence of any physical or mental handicap or distinguishing physical characteristics, scars, or markings. However, an employer may ask whether the applicant is able to perform satisfactorily the job duties in question. In addition, an employer may inquire or invite individuals with handicaps to identify themselves as handicapped to satisfy affirmative action requirements or a court order or to implement a special program for the benefit of disabled persons.

The two questions you quote from the employment applications you were asked to complete do not fit within the limited exceptions to the general prohibition against soliciting protected information. Multinational corporations as well as small companies make mistakes.

You made the most prudent decision in not answering the medical-related pre-employment questions. Should these questions be raised during an interview, you might consider answering the question with a question, such as "How does this information relate to the essential job functions of the job for which I am applying?" The fact that you had breast cancer will rarely, if ever, preclude you from satisfactorily performing the essential job duties.

With respect to completing obligatory insurance forms, at that point in time a job offer will have been made, and in most cases you will have been working for several months and your medical condition rarely becomes an issue.

You are absolutely correct to always tell the truth. Should the worst-case scenario occur and you are fired on account of your disability, you may file a claim with the federal Equal Employment Opportunity Commission, state court, or state Division on Civil Rights.

Job Interview

After the initial screening and the determination has been made that the two parties have a mutual interest, the formal meeting or interview is the time to discuss the position's essential job functions, the organization's history and objectives, and the benefits of being an employee. It is also the time for applicants to discuss thoroughly, by way of examples, their ability to perform the required duties, prior experience, and personal goals. The purpose of the interview is to determine whether the applicant and employer have complementary needs

and compatible objectives. To achieve a mutually successful employment relationship, three basic questions must be asked and answered: First, what are the
organization's needs and what are my needs? Second, what is required to have
the organization's needs met and my needs met? Third, after a review of all the
data, are the organization's needs and my needs compatible?

The interview is a sales meeting where the employer and employee seek to
determine whether there is the basis for a mutually beneficial work relationship. Both the employer and employee, like all good salespeople, must be fully
prepared in knowing what they are selling and that the representations made
are accurate to the best of their knowledge. Therefore, preparation is essential.
Incorrect or misleading information, whether provided by the applicant or the
employer, can ruin the relationship.

Assistant Needs to Decide Whether It's Worth Staying with Employer

Q. I am in desperate need of advice in two separate areas, but they are some-
what related. Two years ago, I was hired by a company with the verbal
promise that I would be given my own office to manage in no more than
three months. Within two months of my hire, several changes took place.

First, the office I was pegged to take over was handed over to a new vice
president. I was handed over to her, too. This put me in the awkward position of working for someone who not only did not hire me but also knew
nothing about me or the type of manager I am.

Second, the supposedly incompetent manager I was to replace had a
change of heart about stepping down. Although this decision basically left me
high and dry, I graciously accepted the decision. The new vice president asked
me to wait for an opening in an office where she herself had just hired a new
manager, and I gladly agreed to do so. From there, it became a nightmare.

The new manager apparently had a huge ego and was deeply insecure, despite the fact that she had a lot of great qualities, too. She proceeded to wreak
havoc upon the office and, completely unbeknown to me, my career as well.

Although I was never given any indication in writing or otherwise that my
work was less than excellent, the new manager made several off-handed
comments to me concerning the fact that managers in general with my particular background tended to be more like mothers than managers, and that
my natural enthusiasm and openness on the job were going to be a detriment in my career. (It certainly never had been before!)

Apparently, because of her own insecurity and lack of knowledge of the
business itself, the vice president took the new manager's word as gospel and

determined to see me remain where I was in an assistant capacity. To make a long story short, the vice president and incompetent manager have both left the company, and the new manager has taken a totally different position with the company. My professional reputation is very much in question among the new supervisors who have replaced them due to what was said about me by the new manager.

I would like advice from you as to what steps, if any, I should take to get my career back on track. I have been casually exploring other job opportunities, which leads me to my second problem.

A headhunter called me at work to tell me of a position that sounded perfect for me in my own town. After an interview, the headhunter told me that the human resource person, upon hearing my name, said "Know her, not interested." I had worked for the company briefly 13 years ago in a lower-level capacity and had left on good terms for a good career advancement. I do not think I am being paranoid when I say that I believe I am being blackballed by the company.

I am not in any minority group, so I cannot pursue the matter in terms of discrimination. Is there any recourse? Believe me when I tell you I am holding back nothing in terms of my past job performance, which has always been very good, particularly in the area of people and communication skills. I have never done anything unethical or offensive to others, and yet I seem to be spiraling downward for no apparent reason. Any advice you could give would be so greatly appreciated.

E. H.

A. Your situation sounds very difficult, but you are taking good steps to protect yourself and keeping your eyes open.

In response to your first inquiry, when an employer (or one of its representatives who has the authority or apparent authority to act on the employer's behalf) makes a promise that an applicant or employee relies upon to his detriment, the employer has the responsibility to make good on the promise.

For example, suppose you took your current job based upon the representation that you would receive the next manager position. To accept the position, you had to relocate and give up another job that paid substantially more. Under those circumstances, you might be able to show how you detrimentally relied upon the employer's promise.

However, the applicant or employee has the burden of proving the oral representation and the specific terms and conditions of the promise. Without knowing more, I cannot determine whether you have a breach-of-contract claim against your current employer, but from what you describe, I suspect you do not.

It doesn't appear that actions are being taken against you because of your membership in a protected classification (race, religion, etc.). If that is true, there is little you can do legally. The law does not provide a remedy for every unfair treatment.

What might be helpful is for you to evaluate, by listing on paper, where you would like to be with your career and your strengths that support those career objectives. If you want to stay with your current employer, determine whom you need to educate within the organization about your skills and why you are an asset to the company.

No one presently is standing in your way, since the other individuals who may have blocked any movement have either left the company or your section. Keep in mind that you now have two years of experience with the organization and have observed different management styles. Therefore, you have the ability to assess what action will support the company's mission. In addition, you know your own strengths and limitations and have the ability to evaluate others. Use all of this information and your skills to carry you forward in your career goals. If you encounter a barrier, pursue another direction until you reach your destination. No one can hold you back unless you permit it.

If you don't want to remain with your current employer, consider your career options based upon what you have written in your career assessment evaluation. Although it is unlawful for an employer intentionally to damage someone's reputation and business opportunities, this does not appear to have occurred in your situation, and as you correctly point out, such a claim is difficult to prove.

It is distressing to be rejected, especially based upon false information. However, I encourage you to focus on areas you can control. Any further energy expended on this situation will be lost time. In addition, why would you want to work at a company where you were not readily received?

Keep doing the footwork. None of this time has been wasted but rather will give you clarity about and the ability to make your next career advancement.

In addition to furnishing information, both the employer and prospective employee need to use the interview time to solicit facts. Both parties must expend time preparing questions for the interview, so that by the end of the meeting they have a colorful descriptive picture of how the employment relationship will look. If you have any unanswered questions or do not see the full picture, you do not have enough information. Remember, this decision you are making is very important. Therefore, you need to invest the time and ascertain all of the pertinent details. Failure to be proactive and to exert the energy now has demonstrated consistently the expenditure of at least double the time, resources, finances, and other costs later to correct or cure the mistake. Most people take the interviewing and hiring process lightly—"Well, if it doesn't work, we'll hire someone else," or "I'll find a different job." You know the results either through personal experience or general news reports—anger, frustration, and disappointment, which often translates into pain, suffering, monetary expenditures, and litigation. Isn't it worthwhile for everyone to take the correct steps initially to avoid negative consequences?

Most jobs are not for life, and the courts have recognized this general principle. However, you possess the ability to safeguard yourself and others by making the best decision possible.

Looking for a Job? Ask Tough Questions

Q.   I had recently been employed part-time, leading to full-time. During my job interview, it was explained that I would be relieving the secretary who was having surgery in the near future. I specifically asked whether the position would terminate after the secretary's recovery, and I was assured that not only would I be needed, but because the company would be taking on new accounts, they would probably be hiring additional help.

Once hired, I was given a general noncompete agreement and a nondisclosure-of-trade-secrets form to sign, since the work I was doing was of a confidential nature. During the summer, I trained extensively and took my work seriously. I began to notice that visitors to the business did not show much interest in getting to know me. It seemed as though, and the secretary hinted, that there had been many temporary workers in this position. However, at one point, I heard the secretary assure one of the clients that the company was pleased with my work performance and that I should be considered permanent.

After three months on the job, I felt secure enough to purchase an additional car for my newly licensed daughter, counting on my income to cover the car payments. Then suddenly, the secretary informed me that business was slowing down. My boss, who had assured me that new business was coming in and I would soon be working full-time, cut my already part-time hours even shorter without an explanation. A short time later, I received a phone call from the secretary informing me that I was being laid off due to a lack of work. According to her, she too was being laid off. Officially, she stated the reason was lack of work. But privately, she hinted the boss did not want to pay her workers' compensation insurance after the surgery and had hired me so that when he fired us both, he would not get into trouble. The boss's wife would be replacing her.

Unfortunately, I had been terminated just short of the time necessary to qualify for unemployment benefits. I was wondering if there was any way to investigate past employees of this company to see if he had a habit of hiring people and firing them just short of their qualifying for unemployment benefits. I contacted the state Department of Labor, and they said there was no record of this, he was within his legal rights, and there was nothing that I could do.

Since I had no contract with the employer, I realize there is no recourse I can take against his promise of future work that was broken. But perhaps you could print an article urging future employees to look out for themselves by scrutinizing a prospective employer in the same manner as that employer may investigate you, and if at all possible, have a written contract with specifics regarding job description, specific duties to be performed, length of expected employment, benefits, company rules and regulations, sick days, lunch/break times, and so on.

B. H.

A.   Your situation is unfortunate, especially in light of your full commitment to your job. Many employees do not take personal pride in how they perform their job responsibilities, and everyone would profit by having more dedicated employees like you. Although the end result is not what you desired, you can be proud that you were true to yourself and your work ethic. In addition, it is probably best that your employment relationship was short, because your investment in a relationship where your skills were not appreciated was not protracted.

The law in general provides that absent an employment contract, collective bargaining agreement, or oral representation, the employment relationship is "at-will." The definition of an at-will employment relationship is one in which the employee may quit or the employer may fire the employee at any time for any or no reason, with or without notice.

It is a good idea for employees to investigate and interview prospective employers just as employers investigate and interview prospective employees. The employment relationship is like any other relationship in that it requires the commitment and dedication of both parties to work toward common goals and support each other in the process.

With respect to obtaining a written contract that outlines the terms of the employment relationship, much of that information often is contained in an employee handbook rather than a contract. Regardless of how the organization communicates its policies, procedures, and other terms and conditions of employment, it is important for employers to inform employees what they can expect from working with the organization as well as what the organization expects from them. Again, this type of dialogue supports a good, open working environment where everyone benefits from working together in carrying out the organization's mission.

An employer is not required to enter into written contracts with its employees and may terminate the relationship at any time, unless to do so would violate state or federal law or be against public policy. What constitutes public policy can be found in the state legislature's rules and regulations, judicial decisions, and other similar pronouncements. For example, most state workers' compensation laws specifically state that an employer may not fire an employee because he or she has filed a claim for benefits. There is no similar provision in most state unemployment compensation laws.

I can't determine why your employment was terminated, but it does appear that you were told you would have full-time employment. What is not clear is for how long that employment would last, which again relates to your being an at-will employee. The courts have consistently held that they will not recognize lifetime employment contracts absent a specific provision to that effect. If the company is having financial difficulty, it may be best that you take your skills and strong work ethic to a work environment that supports the organization's growth and development as well as your own.

As in the employment application, no information is to be solicited during the interview that directly or indirectly reveals an applicant's race, color, religion, creed, sex, sexual preference, national origin, age, marital status, veteran status, disability, or other protected characteristic. Because this information is protected, it cannot be used as hiring criteria. Any protected information that is solicited before an employment offer has been made is presumed to have been used in the hiring decision and, consequently, unlawful.

In today's legal climate, it is essential that individuals who conduct job interviews as the employer's representative have a solid understanding of what actions are and are not appropriate and legal. Interviews are not to be held in a hurried fashion without sufficient preparation time having been expended by the interviewer. For example, the interviewer should be familiar with the applications or résumés of candidates about to be interviewed in order to make them feel comfortable, create a good first impression of the organization, and give the interviewer an opportunity to see what relevant experience applicants may have had in order to discuss thoroughly and predict accurately the compatibility of the parties' objectives.

In addition, it is imperative that the interviewer know the position for which the candidate is applying prior to the interview. Because the range of permissible questions is to some degree limited to a candidate's ability to perform the essential job functions of the given position, an interviewer who is unaware of these essential functions is likely to ask a question that may not be relevant and may, under certain circumstances, be construed as discriminatory. It is also advisable to ask all interviewees the same or similar questions in order to provide a better foundation upon which to base the hiring decision as well as to avoid any claim of unequal discriminatory treatment. A consistent interview will enable the organization to rate more objectively the abilities of one candidate against another. In addition, a consistent interview practice will save the organization significant money in at least three areas: (1) best use of interviewer's time; (2) smaller percentage of unqualified candidates being hired; and (3) less likelihood for the company to be a target of litigation.

Worker Misled About Status as Independent Contractor

Q. Recently, I started a new position. During the interview process, meetings were held over three dates with nine individuals. In the last appointment, an offer was made that I accepted immediately and a start date was agreed upon for 10 days later. Between the acceptance and start, three planning phone conversations were held.

When I reported to the new job, I was shocked to find that papers were drawn requiring my signature to acknowledge that I understood I was an independent contractor, not an employee, and that my monthly compensation was a draw, not a salary, that I would have to repay if not covered by future commissions. I asked why these provisions were never told to me during the interview process. Needless to say, no answers have been provided.

Under pressure from the person who hired me, I signed the paper about the draw being repaid because when he saw how upset I was over this issue, he assured me that the level of business in the office would cover the amount concerned.

Papers referring to my status as an independent contractor also outline specific duties to be performed by me at the specific office I am assigned to that has established set work hours for me. Furthermore, I am not allowed to perform these duties for anyone else. I am certain that the Internal Revenue Service would consider me an employee, based upon the tests they use to determine such.

Should I formally submit the proper form to the IRS requesting they make this determination? I am certain the company will be unhappy over that, as there are perhaps 15 others who they handle in this same manner. Could they fire me for simply filing the form?

In that event, I might not be able to collect unemployment because I would be viewed as self-employed, despite my previous work history as an employee. Is this a correct assumption? Can I sue the company for not disclosing all the facts prior to my resignation that resulted in my giving up a secure position as an employee?

Please advise how I could best handle these problems, because the stress I feel now is affecting my attitude and work performance.

S. B.

A.   Your situation sounds most distressing, since you were not provided all the pertinent information prior to resigning from your former job and commencing your new position.

Whether you should file a claim with the IRS concerning the company's classification of you as an independent contractor and not an employee is a personal decision that should be based upon what you ultimately desire to achieve. If you want to be paid as an employee, you may achieve your objective if the IRS finds in your favor. Such a finding, however, may have adverse economic consequences for you and the company should the company decide to reduce or restructure its workforce because its independent contractors are considered employees.

Several states, including the state where you work, and several federal laws have "whistleblower" protection provisions that prohibit an employer or business entity from terminating an individual's employment or contract because that individual reported what he or she reasonably believed to be a violation of the law. Therefore, the company cannot legally fire you for your filing a claim with the IRS. However, if such a firing did occur, you would have the burden of proving that the company terminated the work relationship because you filed the claim.

Most state laws, and yours in particular, and the federal Fair Labor Standards Act require employers to communicate before an employee begins work the amount, method, and day the employee will be paid. Although the company did not provide this important information in accordance with those laws, it would most likely respond that it considered you an independent contractor, not an employee, and therefore was not obligated by these requirements. Unless you can show that the company made a misrepresentation to you or in some other manner discriminated against you, there does not appear to be a strong basis for you to sue the company. Keep in mind that you agreed to work for the company and be paid as an independent contractor, notwithstanding that you disagreed with the company's position.

In evaluating how to proceed, determine what you desire to achieve. For example, if you want to work with this organization, perhaps you should talk with the decisionmakers about your method of compensation or possibly an increase in the amount of your compensation to cover your costs.

If the real issue is that you are angry because you feel the company was not forthright in its communications with you, then maybe you should resign or file a claim with the IRS. It may be that you have no desire to continue to work with the company based upon its actions, and that may be the true source of your stress and discontentment at work. Additionally, you may explore the possibilities of returning to your prior job.

You have much to consider in determining how to proceed. I encourage you to spend the time, to work through the various issues and opportunities, and then to make an informed decision. At that point, take steps to move forward with confidence in your actions of achieving your goal.

As for your eligibility for unemployment compensation benefits, such claims are made on a case-by-case basis depending upon the facts of the particular situation. Should you file a claim, you may assert that you were an employee, and because of the improper classification, the employer terminated your services. You also may be eligible to receive benefits if it is found that you are still within the base year of your previous employer.

Whatever action you decide to take, consider where you ultimately want to be so you are enjoying the fruits of your labor within the right work environment. Good luck.

In general, the only appropriate questions during interviews are those inquiries that are job related and aimed at determining candidates' skills and qualifications for the job applied for. To assist employers in conducting job interviews, many states publish a list or guidebook on permissible pre-employment inquiries. These publications are a good reference tool and should be reviewed before commencing the interviewing and hiring process.

Because each prospective employee's characteristics impact and help form the work environment, it is permissible and important to ascertain this information. Similarly, the applicant will want to know about the work atmosphere and therefore will need to make similar inquiries. In addition to discussing job-related requirements and skills, an employer and prospective employee may desire to inquire about the other party's (1) personality; (2) interest in joining the organization; (3) interpersonal skills; (4) maturity; and (5) accountability. The interview is for the employer as well as the employee. Both parties need to deliver and receive pertinent details about what is expected and how the relationship will work in order to make an informed decision.

Similarly, prospective employees need to prepare for an interview by delineating, in writing, their objectives in the prospective employment relationship. For example, how can I assist the organization? What are my goals, abilities, experience level, compensation requirements, and benefit needs? What are the work hours, work environment, opportunity for advancement, and travel requirements? In addition, applicants should learn as much as possible about the organization and the available position. This knowledge communicates to the employer the applicant's interest in the organization and provides the applicant valuable insight to assist in making a decision. Taking the time and forethought to prepare turns what is often described as an uncomfortable and laborious process into an exciting and educational adventure.

The interview process is formal and should be treated accordingly. During the interview, listen to what words are being used and the tone in which they are spoken. Observe body language, facial expressions, mannerisms, attire, and surroundings. Note whether the person with whom you are meeting arrived on time and how the individual greeted you. Think about the examples or experiences cited or not cited and the depth or shallowness of information provided. Use all of your senses during this meeting.

Employer and employee alike, regardless of the applicant's qualifications and the employment opportunity, need to ask and honestly answer, "Can I comfortably spend a large percentage of my day and energies with this person, and will my objectives be advanced by consummating this relationship?" Successful and rewarding relationships do not exist in an environment filled with resentment. For example, if the applicant continually interrupted you during the interview, how do you think the person will respond when you are giving direction at the job site? Personal characteristics such as rudeness, poor judgment, refusal to follow direction, lateness, and dishonesty are not protected by law. These characteristics need to be considered in making the best possible hiring decision and are equally as important for the prospective employee. Failure or refusal to seriously evaluate these subjective qualities have proved costly for both parties in many cases.

The next area of concentration involves acknowledging your human selfishness and asking, "What do I gain from this relationship?" "Will I earn a good salary?" "Is this applicant a hard worker?" "Will I have a short commute?" "Will the candidate's background take us to the next step in our development?" And so on. Everyone wants to win. Acknowledge this fact up front so that a determination can be made as to whether the essential elements of a win-win relationship are present. If these qualities are not present, never proceed on the false premise that somehow they will magically appear. This wishful thinking has proven consequences of disaster. As a healthy reminder, consider the relationships, employment and others, that have failed and the scars that have festered. Each job and each person have various parts, and like everything else in life, with the good comes the not so good. No one part of either the person or the job is the total package. Both parties need to be open to learning as much as possible about the other.

Employers are advised to have more than one interview with a candidate, preferably with three or four interviewers on different days. This procedure serves a variety of important purposes. First, it communicates to applicants that the organization respects itself and its employees and customers and therefore it is important to find the most qualified individual for the position. Second, several individuals get to see the candidate and use their collective experience to place the organization in a position to make a well-informed decision. Third, the organization can see how applicants interact with different personalities, in different scenarios, on a number of occasions. Fourth, successful candidates will feel proud that they jumped numerous hurdles in receiving a job offer.

Although this process takes time and commitment from both the prospective employer and prospective employee, each gains invaluable insight and clarity from the experience. The more we observe individuals, the more they reveal themselves to us. Again, the decision whether to spend the majority of your day in a close environment with a certain person is a big investment, and you must act accordingly. This process also allows candidates to make an informed decision as to whether they still desire to join an organization after meeting all the players.

By contrast, the short-term strategy of having only one or two interviews can produce long-term failure. For example, imagine preparing a job advertisement, contacting the newspaper for placement of the ad, spending money for publication of it, reviewing employment applications or résumés, interviewing applicants, making an offer, training the new employee—and then the employment relationship collapsed. How costly was that chain of events simply to learn that the new employee was not as he or she represented himself or herself or lacked the ability to perform the job? On the other hand, perhaps the employer misrepresented the work opportunity, the topic of the preceding question and answer. A few simple reference checks in both situations could have saved thousands of hours and dollars and emotional energy.

"Time is money," so spend it wisely. Although nothing is forever, the time and costs associated with interviewing are less expensive than employee turnover, poor employee morale, and employment litigation.

An interview is preferably held in a comfortable setting to help the candidate feel relaxed and to create an atmosphere of openness. Physical barriers such as desks and tables should be removed between an interviewer and a candidate. The interviewer is advised to schedule the interview at a time that is strategically important to the employer. For example, if a particular position requires a candidate to be particularly alert early in the morning, schedule an interview for that time to get an idea of how the candidate reacts under those conditions. Document the interview by listing the necessary skills, qualifications, and experiences, and the applicant's ability to meet the hiring criteria. This documentation will address the organization's legitimate business reasons for hiring or not hiring a particular candidate.

The hiring process has a beginning, and similarly it needs an ending. When a job offer is extended, it may be conditioned upon the successful completion of a specified event, such as a drug or alcohol examination. However, whatever the condition, it must be job-related, applied uniformly and consistently, and not solicit protected information. (More information about preoffer and postoffer testing is discussed in Chapter 7.) Upon successful completion of the specified condition and the applicant accepts the job offer, the hiring process is ended. If no employment offer is extended or the applicant fails to satisfy the specific condition, the employer should inform the applicant of the *true* reason(s) for not being offered the job. Failure to close this circle or provide an honest explanation for not hiring the person may leave the employer exposed to a claim of unlawful employment discrimination, tarnished reputation, or unfounded rumors, none of which enhances the employer's reputation or is inviting for future candidates.

Single Mom Getting Unfair Shake

Q. I was hired in November. There was a 45-day probationary period after which I would be entitled to health insurance, beginning January. My health insurance did not go into effect until February, and I have, upon many occasions, asked that I be personally reimbursed as they have done for another employee for the personal coverage I paid. I am still being told that they are "looking into this matter." I have a written New Hire Package, which was signed by the administrator indicating insurance would begin as mentioned above.

In addition, I have been told that I could not take lunch until payroll is finished, which one day was 6:30 p.m. I normally work 9 a.m. to 5 p.m. There are times payroll is not finished until late afternoon, maybe 3 p.m. or so. When I was hired, I was given materials that indicated I would get a 30-minute lunch break and two 20-minute breaks. Now I am being told that I am not entitled to any break; however, they will try to give me a 15-minute relief during the day. I am dependent upon others to relieve me at the phones and many times have been told that my coworkers were too busy. I have stopped asking.

Please help me rectify this situation. I am a single mother who cannot easily leave this job and take time off to search for another. However, I know what they are doing is wrong. I would appreciate any help you could offer. I have thought about going to small claims court, but fear that I would lose my job.

Thank you for your attention to this very troubling situation.

R. B.

A.   Yes, your situation does sound troubling. As a general rule, an employer has the right to establish an employee's wages, hours, and other terms and conditions of employment, so long as the employment policies and procedures are not contrary to law. Similarly, an employer has the right to change or modify the workplace rules.

However, when an employer makes a written or oral representation to an employee and the employee has reasonably relied upon the employer's statement, the employee may seek to hold the employer responsible for any damages he or she incurred as a result of the representation and reliance. Similarly, when an employer has an established past practice upon which an employee reasonably relied to his or her detriment, the employer may be liable.

The employment discrimination laws also prohibit employers from treating employees differently with regard to their wages, hours, and other terms and conditions of employment on account of their age, sex, marital status, or similar classifications.

Your employer may be required to reimburse you for your out-of-pocket medical insurance payment based upon its representation and past practice. However, this answer depends, in large part, on whether you had any obligations, such as completing forms or notifying the employer of your desire to have medical insurance benefits, and your intention to pay for coverage if it was not provided as promised. As a practical matter, it is difficult, if not impossible, to force others to take a desired action if they choose not to so act. Therefore, you have few alternatives if your repeated requests for reimbursement fall upon deaf ears.

In deciding how to proceed, make sure you are speaking with the correct person regarding reimbursement, and also consider whether there is anyone else within the organization with whom you may speak. Should you decide to pursue a court action, it may provide you some reassurance to know that employers are prohibited from retaliating against employees by terminating the employment relationship or by taking any other adverse employment action because employees took steps to protect their employment rights.

The hours of work and break situations are similar to the insurance payment question in that it appears the employer is not honoring its original commitment to you. Yes, it makes sense that payroll is a priority to be completed by a specified time because of the consequences if it is not. However, if the rush deadlines continue on a regular basis, you might consider communicating to management what you need to finish payroll in a timely manner. Although an employer, under most circumstances, has no obligation to provide breaks or meal periods, these rest periods serve the interests of the employer, employee, and customers.

You do not seem to be an employee exempted from overtime premium pay—such as an executive, administrator, professional, or outside salesperson as those terms are defined by the law. If you are not exempted and are working more than 40 hours a week, you are entitled to 1 1/2 times your regular hourly rate for all time worked in excess of 40 hours in any workweek.

From what you have described, I believe you need to decide what is important to you and set your boundaries accordingly. For example, take your lunch break each day, including payroll days. You and your boss may be surprised to learn that payroll gets done faster after you have had time to refuel. It appears that you are allowing people to walk on you. It is okay to take care of yourself and make others responsible for their actions and words also.

Generally, looking for a job is a full-time job. However, you can also simply make people aware of your skills, experience, and desire for other employment opportunities. Some of the best employment positions occur by way of referrals and recommendations. Start talking and taking care of yourself. You deserve good treatment and have options available to you.

The question is often raised, "How do I know whether the person I am hiring or the organization that has offered me a position can be trusted and will respect the relationship and stated goals?" Trust, like other pure and time-honored qualities, is earned. Unfortunately, these precious qualities often cannot be readily seen, and only time will reveal their existence or nonexistence. However, gaining knowledge about the prospective employer or prospective employee by conducting reference checks often can prevent costly mistakes.

A good basis from which the employer may work in conducting a successful interview is a written job description. A job description should set forth a short, general description of the job; the duties and responsibilities incident to the job; designation of which duties are essential; any physical and/or mental requirements of the job; and the knowledge, skills, and ability requirements of the position. The Americans with Disabilities Act (ADA) assists in this area by defining what constitutes "an essential job function":

1. Whether a position exists for the purpose of performing a particular function. For instance, the position of "secretary" exists for the purpose of preparing typed communications, either for internal or external use. The position of "chemist" exists for the purpose of developing and preparing formulations of products.

2. Whether sufficient numbers of employees having similar jobs are available to permit a distribution of tasks. For instance, a secretary in an isolated situation may be required to answer the telephone, take messages, act as a receptionist, take dictation, and type correspondence and reports. A secretary in a group may well be able to share those responsibilities with others.

3. Whether particular tasks require expertise or particular skills. For instance, sales functions in Mexico may require the ability to speak Spanish. Boiler operation may require a license. The work of a chemist may require a degree in chemistry.

4. Whether experienced employees are available to assist new employees. For instance, the position of chemist may require an advanced degree or extensive experience if other chemists are not available to consult, but may require a lesser degree or lesser experience when experienced employees are available.

5. Whether there are particular physical requirements associated with a position, such as heavy lifting, manual dexterity, or visual acuity.

6. Whether a substantial amount of time is spent in performing a particular function. For instance, a data processing operator who spends the majority of each day inputting data may require greater typing skills than an inventory clerical person who types only occasionally.

7. Whether it is necessary for an employee to perform particular por-

tions of a job. For example, forklift operators may traditionally install the battery in their assigned forklift truck. A particular forklift operator may be unable to lift the battery into position. It should be determined whether alternate arrangements can be made for the installation of the battery.

Whether a particular function is essential is determined on a case-by-case basis. Marginal job functions, such as a filing clerk being able to stand on a step stool to reach high shelves, do not qualify as an essential function. Another method for determining whether a function is essential is to determine whether removal of the function in question would fundamentally alter the position. Although a job may require an individual to possess certain skills and abilities to perform the job, a person may have different skills and abilities to achieve the same result. Thus, in determining whether an individual is qualified for a position, the employer must communicate with the person regarding his or her *ability*, with or without a reasonable accommodation, to perform the essential functions. So long as business decisions are made consistent with the job description, this procedure will serve as an asset in hiring, promotion, and termination decisions.

A written job description should have the following information stated clearly and concisely for each employee job classification:

1. Title;
2. Requisite skills;
3. Additional desired skills;
4. Minimum education and/or experience;
5. Essential job functions;
6. Physical and mental ability, if any, required as essential job function;
7. To whom position reports;
8. What employees, if any, the position supervises;
9. Exempt or nonexempt from the overtime wage law and basis for exemption.

This information will serve as the foundation in ascertaining an individual's abilities to perform a particular job and will provide the organization a snapshot picture of each position and how that position fits into the organization's overall structure. In addition to addressing the ADA issues, the job description will provide the basis for the organization's wage and hour overtime exemption decisions.

The written job description is the basis for the interview conversation—what the employer expects from the prospective employee and the applicant's abilities and interests in performing the essential job functions. In addition, the job description is the framework upon which the relationship is built. Both a carpenter who is eager to build a house and a sailor who desires to cross the ocean need to have well thought out written descriptions as to where they are headed and how they are going to get there. One has a set of prints and the other a chart. Neither would commence the journey without the proper navigational tools. Similarly, the job description is the foundation of the employment relationship to provide for smooth sailing.

The benefit of the written job description is that it can be used throughout the employment relationship. It is a compass to evaluate performance, promotion opportunities, and termination decisions. Therefore, the job description must be well written and accurate; otherwise, it will create confusion and can be used as a weapon against the employer. On the other hand, a properly prepared written job description can serve as a vital piece of evidence in thwarting or defending against an employment claim. The individuals most qualified to write the job description are the person who is currently performing those essential functions and that employee's supervisor.

Because the job description reflects the daily relations between the employer and employee, it must be treated as a living, breathing component of the relationship. Written job descriptions must accurately reflect work that is actually performed. They must reflect physical demands, mental requirements, psychological factors, and environmental conditions to which individuals will be exposed. If the tasks within a particular job or position should change, the job description needs to be updated.

Employers are not required to develop or maintain written job descriptions. However, the current policy of the federal Equal Employment Opportunity Commission (EEOC) and state civil rights agencies is to consider job descriptions as evidence when those descriptions are prepared in advance of advertising or interviewing applicants for a particular job. For example, if individuals claim that they have been disqualified for a position on the basis of a disability, an objective job description setting forth the essential factors associated with a particular job may furnish a defense.

The ADA raises some particular concerns pertinent to the interviewing and hiring process. First, the interviewing process must be made accessible to people with disabilities. For example, a blind candidate may require assistance in completing the employment application, or a wheelchair user access to the interviewing location. Second, the interviewer is never to assume that a person with a disability needs assistance. Third, interviewers may not ask a candidate with a disability any of the following: (1) the nature of the candidate's disability; (2) the severity of the candidate's disability; (3) how the disability was caused; (4) any questions regarding when or if the disability will be cured; and (5) if the candidate requires specific periods of leave for treatment of the disability. Although these questions are off-limits, the interviewer should ask questions of the candidate such as (1) the candidate's ability to perform the essential job functions and (2) whether the candidate will be able to accomplish such functions with or without reasonable accommodation. The ADA is discussed in further detail in Chapter 7.

Orientation

After a successful candidate has been selected and accepted the position, the orientation begins. The orientation process is as critical as the interviewing phase because of the immediate and long-term impact it has on the relationship if it is not conducted properly. An employer's failure to spend the necessary time with new employees to orient them can create a disastrous time ahead. In addition, employers have certain legal obligations that must be fulfilled, such as the completion of the Employment Eligibility Verification Form and clear communication of the employee's hours of work, rate of pay, day of pay, and employment benefits.

As with the start of any new relationship, the various pebbles when molded together can create the foundation for a strong, mutually beneficial relationship or a slippery slope. Just as the beginning of a play foreshadows the remaining acts of the show, so too the players in the employment relationship, through their initial interactions, lay the foundation for the future of their relationship. The orientation process is the concrete upon which the employment relationship may be solidly built.

When you and your colleagues participate in the interviewing and hiring and orientation process, each of you are making a personal covenant to serve yourself, your superiors and co-workers, and the organization and its customers to the best of your ability, to be fair and honest in all things large and small, and to be respectful and courteous at all times. Are you living up to these promises?

■ four ■

Why Are Discrimination
Lawsuits Filed?

Failure to master the necessary communication techniques or to have a solid interviewing and hiring procedure can generate animosity and employment litigation. The explosion of employment-related claims has created a new hue and cry among employees and employers: "When in doubt, sue my employer" and "Beware of the discontented employee." The most common question employees and employers ask remains, "Why are employment discrimination lawsuits filed?" There are some general categories: Some lawsuits are filed because applicants believe their employment opportunity was denied because of their race or their request for a reasonable accommodation, such as to not work on the Sabbath. Others are filed as a result of employees being transferred to other positions after they lodged complaints of sexual harassment against major rainmakers at their respective firms. Still others are filed because the employer objects to employees' desires to speak their native language in the workplace. On the other hand, applicants or employees may file complaints out of anger, to get revenge, or to be heard.

However, generalities do not fully explain such an epidemic as employment litigation. The tremendous increase in broken employment relationships, which carry a costly repair bill or total loss factor, dictates the need for more specific information. The federal Equal Employment Opportunity Commission's statistics provide insight into the major reasons discrimination lawsuits are filed. These statistics and employer/employer feedback have generated the following list of the top ten reasons employees sue their employers:

1. Race discrimination
2. Sexual discrimination
3. Disability discrimination

4. Sexual harassment
5. Age discrimination
6. National-origin discrimination
7. Religious discrimination
8. Anger/frustration
9. Retaliation
10. Unfair or inequitable treatment

Discrimination

Webster's defines "discrimination" as "to make a distinction in favor of or against one person or thing as compared to others." Implicit in this term is different treatment. Most persons equate it with unequal treatment or unfairness. Although life is filled with unequal, unfair treatment, each wrong does not necessarily have a legal remedy. Rather, only those acts that the federal and state legislatures and courts have declared unlawful are compensable in the eyes of the law. Therefore, it is important to be familiar with and understand the employer's and employee's rights and obligations with respect to the administration of the employment relationship.

An Unfair Firing Is Not Necessarily an Illegal One

Q. In one of your columns, you wrote that "an employer has the right to fire a worker for any legitimate business reason." As someone who was fired from a job without a seemingly legitimate reason, I wonder if in a future column you would elaborate on the legal definition of what is a "legitimate business reason."

My particular situation involved being fired, with no prior written or verbal warnings, and told that the reason I was being let go was "because you were not doing your job." Not only did the company advertise several weeks prior to my termination for an assistant to replace me, they subsequently hired two people to assume my responsibilities. Do these sound like legitimate business reasons? I still am left wondering if I may have some legal recourse and am at a loss to explain why I was fired.

Most workers are totally ignorant of their legal rights when faced with firing. Although I am certainly not suggesting that every worker who loses his job run to a lawyer, most people just have no idea whether they have been treated fairly and legally.

E. M.

A. What constitutes a "legitimate business reason" is not specifically defined
    by statute or case law. Rather, the existence of a legitimate business reason
    is dependent on whether the reason provided is supported by the facts,
    such as a reduction in the employer's business, an employee's failure or re-
    fusal to properly perform the job, a poor performance evaluation of an
    employee, customer complaints about an employee, or a company reorga-
    nization. Each situation must be evaluated in light of all the circumstances
    to determine whether the business reason stated by the employer is the
    true reason.

    If an employee disputes the reason provided by the employer and chal-
    lenges the firing before an administrative agency or court, the employee has
    the burden of proving that the business reason provided by the employer is
    not the true reason but rather is a pretext for discriminatory conduct. For ex-
    ample, if a company tells a female employee she no longer has a job be-
    cause of a lack of work and the next day the employer hires a man to per-
    form her duties, it is more probable than not that the lack of work was not
    the real reason for her discharge. Employers are advised to document the
    business reason prior to and at the time they take any disciplinary or adverse
    action against an employee.

    An employer is not required, without some contrary agreement or repre-
    sentation, to provide written or verbal warnings regarding poor performance
    by workers before firing them. However, prior counseling is preferable for
    many reasons. First, it allows employees to correct their performance and
    promotes communication. Also, it keeps operating costs down because the
    employer doesn't have to spend time and money to recruit and train new
    employees. Last, prior counseling improves an employer's defense should a
    discrimination claim be filed.

    Because you received no warning about not "doing your job" before be-
    ing fired, you understandably are questioning why the action was taken.
    However, merely because your former employer did not discuss your job
    performance does not mean that your employer did not have a legitimate
    business reason for firing you.

    Whether an employer treats an employee fairly is a separate question
    from whether an employer acted legally. An employer's unfair treatment of
    an employee is not tantamount to illegal conduct. Rather, both the em-
    ployer's and the employee's conduct must be examined in light of the law to
    determine whether the employer has acted unlawfully.

The first and most effective step for complying with the employment laws is
employee education. Therefore, the following sections outline the most fre-

quently used antidiscrimination laws that also encompass the top ten reasons discrimination lawsuits are filed.

The Civil Rights Act

The United States Congress and state legislatures have enacted various equal employment opportunity laws to protect applicants and employees from being discriminated against based upon personal characteristics unrelated to the position they are seeking or holding, in receiving the benefits of the job they are performing, or from being denied the opportunity for further advancement in the organization. The most controversial civil rights statute enacted by Congress was the Civil Rights Act of 1964, which prescribed how people were to treat one another in the workplace. In short, Congress told each and every one of us that we cannot treat someone differently by denying opportunities or placing barriers to earning a living simply because that person is female, male, Caucasian, Afro-American, Hispanic, Asian, Catholic, Jewish, Buddhist, or a member or nonmember of some other ethnic group or religious denomination.

Woman May Have Strong Case

Q. My employer announced that it was closing. We were told that every effort would be made to find jobs for people. We were also told that we would have support until the end.

In my particular position, because I chose not to relocate, I left the plant that day feeling I would be out of a job in 18 months. The next morning, my supervisor called me into his office and proceeded to tell me that each manager had been allowed to pick one employee and guarantee the person a job. He told me that I was his pick. He asked for my help in keeping things running smoothly, and said I would be taken care of.

The next day, I met with the manufacturing director and human resource manager, and told them I would like to stay with the company even if it meant taking an hourly position. During that meeting, I was asked if my husband still worked with the same company, and I said that he did.

A few months later, I was called into my supervisor's office to discuss how I would feel about taking on additional responsibilities, since people were leaving and not being replaced. Being an exempt employee, I did not get paid for overtime. My supervisor and I discussed the possibility of changing my status to nonexempt. My supervisor thought it best I remain an exempt employee because it would, in his words, "provide better protection." I asked him if exempt employees were protected more than nonexempt, and he said "absolutely."

Thereafter, I had countless discussions about my working at another company location. I was told that I would be a perfect fit, and there were constant meetings with the other location to convey this information. The people I spoke with always seemed very confident that there would be a job there for me. One time, I was told it was "99 percent a done deal."

Some time later, I again met with the human resource manager, and he again asked if my husband was still with his same employer. At this meeting he told me that there did not appear to be any jobs open. I asked many fellow male employees if they were ever asked where their wives worked, and I could find no instances where they were. I voiced my concern about other people getting their feet in the door at the other company location and I was not getting the opportunity to do so because I had to fill in for everyone.

My supervisor told me not to worry—that the other location knew my reputation and they wanted me. Later at a plant meeting, we were told that the other location was "a dead issue" and that we should look for jobs elsewhere in the company through the job information system. I find it very suspicious that most of the jobs people found were not on the system. It appeared that jobs were created for certain people, and I find it questionable as to why males were found jobs at an overwhelmingly higher ratio than females.

Thereafter, I went on an interview for an internal job at a different location. During the interview, I was asked if I had children and what were their ages. The interviewer commented on the fact that my children were still young, and he seemed very intent on discouraging me. The next day the plant supervisor of where I worked told me that he had the dubious honor of handing me my last paycheck. He proceeded to tell me I should stay home and that my husband was the main breadwinner and my income was "supplemental." He again told me I should stay home and "enjoy my kids while they were still young."

My supervisor took the same path. I had to endure lecture after lecture about how I would miss my children growing up and how sorry I would be later. I sincerely doubt that I would have had to put up with the intrusions if I were a male. In the big picture, I am one of only two salaried employees out of 35 who did not either secure a job or was old enough to go on preretirement leave or retire.

My reviews have always been exemplary, and on my last review, I was rated "exceptional." I feel I got a double dose of discrimination. I feel that the attitude prevailed that since I was a female, they did not have to knock themselves out looking for a job for me. I also think that because I am white and my husband is black, which is something that bothered the human resource manager and many of the employees, racism was present. I do not think I was treated fairly. After almost 23 years with the company, I think at the very least I deserved that.

T. M.

A.   The federal Civil Rights Act and the state antidiscrimination law prohibit employers from discriminating against applicants and employees in hiring, compensation, promotion, training, discharge, and terms and conditions of employment based upon an individual's sex, race, color, marital status, age, creed, religion, veteran status, national origin, or disability.

When an individual can show that he is a member of a protected class, that a person not in the protected class was selected for the position or treated differently, that he was qualified for the job, and that he has sustained damages, then the employer must prove that it had a legitimate business reason for the action it took.

A plant closing or workforce reduction is a generally accepted business reason for certain employment-related decisions. However, this conduct must still be nondiscriminatory. The aggrieved individual then has the burden of showing that the employer's reason is merely a pretext for the alleged action. Based upon your description of receiving different treatment from that of your male coworkers, the interview inquiries, and representations, it appears that you may have a claim of unlawful sex and marital-status employment discrimination.

Just as an employer may not provide preferential treatment to male employees over female employees, an employer may not pay its female employees less or refuse to provide them employment opportunities because of their marital status. Your employer's statements are evidence to support your claim.

In addition, the law presumes that any information an employer solicits pre-employment is used by the employer in its hiring decisions. If an employer or its agents make a representation to an employee upon which the employee reasonably relies, the employee takes or does not take certain action based upon those representations, and the employee suffers damages as a result of the employer's representation, then the employer may be liable to make the employee whole.

You may seek relief from the alleged unlawful discrimination conduct by filing a claim, within a specified time from the last alleged unlawful act, with

(1) the federal Equal Employment Opportunity Commission (EEOC) (within 300 days), the state agency equivalent to the EEOC (within 180 days), or the state court (within two years). A detrimental-reliance or breach-of-contract action may be filed with the state court within six years from the last alleged unlawful act.

Not only legislatures but the courts as well have played a major role in shaping the American workplace. For example, the courts in interpreting legislatures' prohibition against sex discrimination have ruled that such prohibition includes sexual harassment. Similarly, harassment based on one's race, national origin, religion, age, and disability have also been held to constitute unlawful employment discrimination.

The most popular work-related seminars during the past ten years have been diversity training and sexual harassment education and sensitivity. No coincidence exists, but the obvious continues to be ignored. I have presented hundreds of these seminars and find it incredible that many participants are angry at being required to attend these programs. These are the same individuals who act out, are closed-minded, try to get away with as much as possible, and insist that their rights are violated because they cannot bring certain publications to work. These individuals who have nothing to learn are generally those who have much to learn. "A fool thinks he needs no advice, but a wise man listens to others." Proverbs 12:15.

Woman Must Decide Whether to Pursue Sex Discrimination Case

Q. I was an information systems manager until the chairman of the board hired a man to take my place. I was given a choice of working as a programmer and analyst with no pay decrease, or resigning; I chose to stay. However, since that time I have been performing the duties of my old position as well training the individual who replaced me, and have little time to perform my current responsibilities. I voiced my opinion to this man, who is very nice and I have no problem with, but he said I had to train him more in the operations and then I will be able to program.

I know several things about this company, including that they do not like and have no respect for women. The company is owned and controlled by men. The company president does not get along with most people and is extremely volatile. People work in fear of his being in a bad mood, and I have felt his wrath on numerous occasions. Two years ago, one man who used to take the brunt of most of the abuse just packed his belongings and walked out. I want to do the same but cannot because I have a family to support. I keep telling myself that I am a capable person and try not to let the president shake my confidence.

During the past two years I have sought, but have not found, other employment. Do you have any suggestions for me? Do I have legal recourse? Can I quit and collect some sort of compensation?

B. M.

A.   Federal and state antidiscrimination laws prohibit an employer from discriminating against an individual on account of sex. You may possibly have legal recourse against your employer if you can prove that the reason for your transfer (or what actually appears to have been a demotion in job title and responsibilities) was because of your sex. Based on the facts you describe—you are a female replaced by a male, you were demoted in title and authority, and you are responsible for training your replacement and performing your old duties—you may have a prima facie case of sex discrimination. However, from your letter, I can't determine the employer's position on why he transferred you. An employer has the right to transfer a worker to another position for legitimate business reasons, such as the employee's inability to perform a job properly.

Although you may be able to sue for sex discrimination, the practical considerations of filing such a claim must be considered. For example, a lawsuit involves a substantial commitment of time, money, and emotional energy. Your description of the people controlling the company suggests they would surely defend any lawsuit.

Unemployment benefits are provided to people who lose employment through no fault of their own. In other words, if you quit your job because you do not like your employer, you probably will not be eligible for unemployment benefits. However, if you quit your job because your employer has constructively discharged you—demoted you and publicly humiliated you and made the work environment unbearable—you may be eligible.

If you quit your job and file for unemployment compensation, your employer has the right to challenge your entitlement to such benefits. An informal hearing is held before an investigator who will make an initial determination regarding your entitlement to benefits. Either party may appeal the investigator's decision.

In sorting through your options, keep in mind that it is easier to obtain employment while currently employed. Although you have not found another job during your two-year search, you might evaluate the effort you have given to looking for other employment.

In light of your statements that you have little time to perform your job responsibilities and that you expend emotional energy fearing the company president's bad mood, my guess is that you have spent little quality time in conducting a thorough job search. You might redirect your attention by

- Performing only your job duties
- Focusing on your skills and abilities by writing them down
- Networking by informing friends and contacts outside your current job that you are seeking other employment opportunities
- Spending two to three hours each day pursuing a new job

The discipline and energy required to find another job while you are working are substantial; however, the resulting benefits are enormous. By not focusing on the volatile personalities at your workplace and redirecting that energy for your own benefit, you will find you have the ability to perform your job responsibilities as well as take care of yourself. What others say about you does not define you or your capabilities. Take strength from the fact that the company president treats everyone terribly and is not singling you out for special treatment. Follow your determination of obtaining new employment by doing the necessary footwork and being kind to yourself. Examine what you need and based on your strengths, not out of fear, go forward. You will know how to proceed and consequently succeed.

Age Discrimination in Employment Act

Despite the efforts of Congress to prohibit discrimination in the workplace, new forms of discrimination continue to emerge. For example, with several generations now populating the workforce, employment decisions may be biased on the basis of age. Consequently, Congress passed the Age Discrimination in Employment Act of 1967 (ADEA) to prohibit employers from using age as a basis to affect an employment opportunity, benefit, advancement, or termination.

Discrimination Suit May Be Only Option

Q. I am a healthy, 47-year-old married man with children who is currently seeking a new job in the field of computers. My experience spans over 25 years in a number of related job areas. I have a bachelor's degree, as well as a master's degree in my field. I have always enjoyed my work and the people that I've had the pleasure to work with.

Due to a recent takeover of my company, I am now looking for a new position. I recently applied for a job to work with a firm that is based out of state.

After sending my résumé, I visited the firm's home office to interview in person with a number of individuals. I had all the necessary qualifications to fill the position they had advertised for. However, the last thing I was told before leaving was that I did not have enough experience in a particular technical area. Since I was so sure that this had been a perfect fit for someone with my background, I felt that someone's assessment of me must have been wrong. I called the human resources manager and let him know that I could give numerous references to confirm my skills. This did not seem to matter; their minds had been made up.

Looking back on this whole experience, I am now very angry. I believe I was not considered for the position because of my age. Everyone that interviewed me was younger than me. I certainly cannot prove this, but I can prove I had all the qualifications they requested to do the job. Is there anything I can do to have them reconsider me for this position?

W. P.

A.   To ensure equal employment opportunities to all persons regardless of their age, the U.S. Congress enacted the Age Discrimination in Employment Act and the state legislatures have granted similar protections. These laws prohibit employers from discriminating against applicants and employees in hiring, training, compensation, promotion, and other terms and condition of employment on account of a person's age. The protected age group includes people over age 40.

To establish a prima facie case of age discrimination, you as an applicant or employee must prove the following:

- You are over 40 years old;
- You are qualified for the position you desire to hold;
- You were not hired;
- A person substantially younger than you was offered the position.

If you can show these elements, the burden of proof shifts to the employer to prove that it had a legitimate business reason for its employment decision. For example, the person it hired was more qualified for the position. Once the employer meets its burden of proof, the burden shifts back to you to show that the reason offered by the employer was not the true reason.

If you believe you have been unlawfully discriminated against because of age, you may file a claim under the ADEA with the Equal Employment Opportunity Commission within 180 days from the alleged unlawful act. The filing period is extended to 300 days if your state, which it does, has a dual filing agency. You may also file a claim with the state Division on Civil Rights, which is available in your state, within 180 days from the alleged unlawful act, or with the state court within two years of the alleged wrongful activity.

I realize filing a claim is not your preferred choice, but it appears you have few other options available since you have already contacted the employer a second time, without obtaining the desired result. Keep in mind that you probably do not have all the information regarding the basis for the employer's hiring decision, and in fact, there may exist a legitimate business reason. Regardless of whether you take action against the employer, you have the obligation, as does anyone who files a discrimination claim, to mitigate your damages by continuing to actively seek other employment opportunities and document your employment search efforts.

Discrimination exists in large measure out of concern for self-preservation of identity and comfort. For example, I know what it is like to be female, Caucasian, Irish, Catholic, and able-bodied. I have no idea what it is like to be male or Afro-American or Chinese or Islamic or a wheelchair user. In order not to reveal my limited life experiences, as knowledge is power, and to remain comfortable with those characteristics with which I have experience, I will tend to associate only with people who are similar to me. The natural outgrowth of this attitude and lack of education is the creation of barriers and a one-type-of-members-only club in the workplace.

Time for Filing Discrimination Lawsuit Runs Out

Q. I am a white male over 55 years of age. I had worked as a computer and CAT-scanner service engineer for a large company for nearly 15 years. I was the oldest person in the department, since no one over 40 years old was hired.

  During the years after I turned 50, I began to find I was being ever more discriminated against. For example, I could not get a transfer to another position even though I applied for many I thought I was qualified to receive. My e-mails were ever more rarely answered by management, and I was consistently told seniority means nothing in this company. I heard our manager say on a speaker phone he wanted only young, intelligent, aggressive guys for supervisor positions.

My workload was increased, and as it kept happening, my coworkers noticed I was being ostracized and yelled at even more for little things such as going to the bathroom for 15 minutes when I had the flu. I started to lose their support and input, which I needed to do my work. At one point I was given parallel work assignments in different buildings that I could not possibly complete because of the distance between the buildings. I was given impossible tasks.

I started having to work many extra hours every week for which I was not paid. My coworkers realized that the manager wanted me out, and they joined in trying to offend me by saying "Heil, Hitler" to me many times because I am of German descent and I speak German to our German customers and coworkers overseas. I was referred to as an old man who should shut up and leave. I started to tape and write down conversations, as I saw I might need evidence if I would want to seek legal assistance. I asked a company manager about a transfer, and he said, while my tape recorder was secretly turned on, that there is no chance at my age, that it is company policy to harass an older employee out of the company and there is no use for anyone over the hill. He told me about how he was presently harassing a 57-year-old employee.

I sought medical and legal help. My doctor put me on tranquilizers and wrote me off one month for stress. The lawyer did nothing for me, and I had to keep prodding him to do something to negotiate an early retirement. I started to lose my coordination and got into a car accident and was placed on disability. After three months of disability, I went back to work. The harassment continued. Then I was told my department was being relocated to another state. I was denied moving expenses other employees received. I was told to move or leave the company in two weeks whereupon my employment was terminated.

I filed a retaliation claim with the Equal Employment Opportunity Commission (EEOC). The EEOC found for the company in spite of witnesses I could provide and recordings and transcripts of blatant age discrimination. I failed to file a lawsuit within the required time period. I was told later that the EEOC does little to nothing for anyone unless one is a female or a minority.

My question is this: Is there anything I can do? Can I sue the company after three years? Can I support others who have also been harassed or are in court cases against the company? Any advice would be appreciated.

K. W.

A. Individuals such as yourself who believe they have been discriminated against on the basis of age may file a lawsuit pursuant to the federal Age Discrimination in Employment Act (ADEA). As you learned, to file a claim under the ADEA in federal court, you must first exhaust your administrative remedies by filing a complaint with the Equal Employment Opportunity Commission (EEOC). If you fail to file that complaint within the prescribed time period, you are barred from suing in federal court.

The EEOC's purpose and authority are to investigate and enforce several employment laws to ensure that all persons have equal employment opportunities in all aspects of the employment relationship, including hiring, compensation, promotion, and continued employment. The EEOC oversees that employers do not make decisions affecting the employment relationship because of a person's age, race, sex, disability, religion, or other protected classification.

The time period for filing a claim in your state is two years if the complaint is filed with the state Superior Court. If the charge is filed with the state agency equivalent to the EEOC, the time period is 180 days. However, because your state is considered a dual filing state with the EEOC, the time period for filing with the EEOC is increased to 300 days when the complaint is filed with both agencies.

If you believe you were discriminated against in terms of compensation, you have a two-year time period under the wage laws in which to file a claim; or if the company willfully violated the laws regulating wages, the time period is three years.

You sound angry and desirous of teaching your former employer a lesson. You can educate other individuals on how you were treated, and that information can then possibly be used in their lawsuits to show a pattern of unlawful discrimination.

However, it is important not to lose sight of your life's goals and objectives—how you desire to spend your time. You should also ask yourself why you are taking certain action: to get even with the company or to assist other people? Answering these questions requires time and honest self-examination to expose the true motivation. Although the work is not easy, the investment is worthwhile and the results are enormous.

Most rules have exceptions, and the ADEA recognizes that age can affect job performance and the costs of employment benefits. Accordingly, the ADEA provides permissible reasons for discriminating on the basis of age, as explained in the next answer.

Worker May Be Victim of Age Discrimination

Q. I work for a large company that has an apprenticeship program for skilled tradesmen that is under joint company and union control. I applied for a position, and took a written test given to applicants. After a few weeks, I was informed that I scored in the top 30 percent to have a verbal interview. I was told by several people that I scored the highest, and they congratulated me on my new job to come.

A week later, I was told that I was dropped from the list because I, at age 47, was too old. You had to be 45 or younger to be eligible. If so, isn't that age discrimination?

Aren't there laws against this? I would appreciate your reply and comments. F. S.

A. The Federal Age Discrimination in Employment Act (ADEA) and state antidiscrimination laws govern discrimination in employment because of age. These principles apply also to labor organizations. People over age 40 are in the protected group.

However, because age can affect job performance and the cost of employment benefits, the ADEA and state laws set forth some permissible bases for age discrimination:

- Age is a bona fide occupational qualification reasonably necessary to the normal operation of the particular business.
- The discriminatory workplace is in a foreign country and compliance with the law would be a violation of that country's laws.
- The employer is observing the terms of a bona fide seniority system that is not intended to evade the purpose of the law. However, no such seniority system may require or permit the involuntary retirement of any individual, unless the employer complies with an exception that applies to bona fide executives or high-level policy-makers.
- The employer is observing the terms of a bona fide employee benefits plan in which for each benefit or benefits package, the actual amount of payment made or cost incurred on behalf of an older worker is no less than that made or incurred on behalf of a younger worker.
- The employer is observing the terms of a voluntary early retirement incentive plan consistent with the law.

- The employer is discharging or otherwise disciplining an individual for good cause.

These exceptions are narrowly construed. The employer or labor organization has the burden of proving that its conduct fell within one of the exceptions.

From what you have described, the only exception that might apply to your situation is the one pertaining to age being a bona fide occupational qualification reasonably necessary to the normal operations of the particular business. For example, if age would make a person physically unable to perform the essential functions of a job, the employer might legally be able to refuse to hire him for the position because of his age.

I suggest you ask your employer and union representative the specific reason you did not receive the position, as well as the basis for the age restriction. If a legitimate business reason exists for why you did not receive the job, I recommend you ask what other benefits or job opportunities may be available to you now that you have passed the test. You are on the right track in seeking additional information.

The Americans with Disabilities Act

Despite extensive legislation at both the federal and state level, deep-rooted prejudices continue to exist and affect our experiences in the workplace. In 1990 a new classification of protected employees was created with the passage of the Americans with Disabilities Act (ADA). This law prohibits employers from discriminating against, and places of public accommodation from denying full and equal access to an organization's services and benefits, any individual because of the person's disability, record of such an impairment, or perception that the person is disabled. Unlike the other employment laws, the ADA requires employers to take certain affirmative steps to ensure that equal employment opportunities exist or are maintained. (See Chapter 7 for additional details.)

Disabled Must Be Accommodated

Q. For several years I have had a lawsuit in civil court regarding my employer's lack of reasonable accommodations for my disability. As a result of the lack of access, I have fallen six times at work and received injuries exacerbating a disability from childhood. These conditions have made me much more dependent on others.

My case is coming to trial. Now it appears my boss's lawyer wants to put me out on disability leave instead of providing the few accommodations that I need, such as a parking spot close to the office. I do not want to go on disability, as I have always worked to be independent. I only have a year to go to get full pension and health retirement benefits.

Can my employer force me go on disability? With accommodations, I can do my job very well. I thought the Americans with Disabilities Act was to enable disabled employees to keep working, not to exclude them by leaving the workplace inaccessible.

C. S.

A. You are correct about the purpose of the Americans with Disabilities Act (ADA). It was enacted to assist 43 million Americans who are disabled. It forces owners and tenants of places open to the public and employers to provide equal access to all disabled people in the goods, services, and facilities they offer.

The ADA prohibits a covered employer from discriminating against a qualified individual with a disability and requires the employer to make a reasonable accommodation to the known physical or mental limitation of an otherwise qualified individual with a disability, unless the accommodation would impose an undue hardship on the employer's business operations.

A covered employer is one who is engaged in an industry affecting commence and who has 15 or more employees for each working day for 20 or more calendar weeks in the current or preceding calendar year.

Because of the broad range of different types of disabilities, Congress did not seek to define "reasonable accommodation." Rather, the ADA provides that a reasonable accommodation may include making existing facilities readily accessible; restructuring jobs; arranging part-time or modified work schedules; reassigning someone to a vacant position; acquiring or modifying equipment; modifying examinations, training materials, or policies; and providing qualified readers or interpreters for disabled individuals. The list is not exhaustive or mandatory.

From what you describe, it appears your employer's actions are contrary to the ADA's rules. First, your employer has an obligation to make the facility accessible to you. Second, your employer has an obligation to provide you a reasonable accommodation, unless your employer can show that to do so would create an undue burden, which is defined as an action requiring significant difficulty or expense. Providing you with a nearby parking spot does not appear to be unreasonable.

Third, your employer is prohibited from discriminating against you because of a disability. If you are being placed on disability leave when you are still capable of doing your job, it seems you are being treated differently from those who are not disabled. Usually employers want to have their employees at work, not absent and collecting disability benefits.

Continue to stand tall and strong in your position. Maintain your independence and dignity. Keep in the forefront your goal of working until retirement, when you can collect full pension and health benefits. Good luck.

Anger and Unfair Treatment

In addition to the different types of employment discrimination, employment-related lawsuits are often motivated by anger at not being respected, heard, or treated fairly.

Older Worker Says Employer Discriminated

Q. I was employed by a company working at its branch office. When contacted by the company, I was 58 years old with 35 years of experience. The branch office was in the early stages of planning with no fully committed customers, and my job was to manage in its entirety one department of the business. From that point our progress was all positive, and within eight years we moved into larger quarters and were increasing our income monthly and looking upward.

I was informed of my employment termination by the branch manager at a lunch, and my age, 66, was the reason for my being replaced. I was told that "being laid off should not cause hardship, as you have money and can collect social security and unemployment." I was also asked to help my replacement in showing how I handled everyday problems so that a smooth transition would take place, which would be in two weeks.

Everything happened so fast I did not have much I could do but say yes to his terms. If I refused they would fire me, and I would forfeit all accumulated personal time according to company policy.

I think my treatment was unfair and my talents were used to an ungrateful end. Do I have any recourse in this matter?

F. S.

A. I am sorry to hear about the loss of your employment and the frustration and lack of gratitude you are experiencing. The process and timing of filing a claim for age discrimination are that you must first establish a prima facie case, which means you must show (1) you are over age 40 (in the protected group); (2) you were performing your job adequately; (3) you nevertheless were fired; and (4) the employer hired a much younger replacement for you. Once you establish these elements, the burden of proof shifts to your employer to establish that it had a legitimate business reason for terminating your employment. If the employer makes that showing, the burden of proof shifts back to you to prove that the employer's proffered reason is not the real reason but a pretext.

If you believe that your employment was unlawfully terminated on account of your age, you may file a claim with the federal Equal Employment Opportunity Commission under the federal Age Discrimination in Employment Act within 180 days of the alleged unlawful act. In states that have dual antidiscrimination agencies like your state, the filing period is extended to 300 days. In addition, again depending upon the state and in your case, you may file a complaint under the state antidiscrimination law with the state Division on Civil Rights within 180 days of the alleged unlawful act or with the state court within two years of the alleged unlawful conduct. The time period of the alleged unlawful conduct may be interpreted as the day you learned your employment would end.

In deciding to file a lawsuit, keep in mind that the reason for your employment termination must in fact be your age and that you have the ultimate burden of proving such a claim. You understandably feel it is unfair that your employment was terminated and that your work was not appreciated by your employer. However, the employer did compensate you for the services you rendered, and although it may be better to be appreciated for your hard work, such lack of gratitude does not provide the basis for the filing of a lawsuit. Good luck with your decision on whether to seek legal recourse for your employment termination.

Some of the most highly contested and litigated employment cases have a direct correlation to the lack of managerial training, poor communication skills, and negative characteristics, like dishonesty or inconsistency, displayed by both management and nonmanagement employees.

Worker Becomes Target of a Sneaky Supervisor

Q. I have worked for my current employer for the past seven years. Over the past six years I have been given good and very good performance evaluations. During this most recent review I was given an unsatisfactory review. I have proof that this was deliberately done because my supervisor spoke to another worker on my shift and told him my review was purposely done negatively because the company felt I was making too much money for my position and just did not like me.

I have been affected by this both physically and emotionally. I have been to see a doctor for chest pains that were determined to be stress-related and a physiologist for emotional distress. I have since brought the human resource department into this matter. My question is, do I have any recourse for resolving this issue legally? I am thinking of resigning my position because the company has made my working situation unbearable. My self-esteem has been destroyed and my reputation as a good worker tarnished.

D. E.

A.   The conduct you describe was inappropriate, unfair, and understandably upsetting. However, in order for you to have legal recourse against your employer, you must be able to show that you were treated differently because of your age, sex, race, color, religion, national origin, veteran status, marital status, disability, or other similar membership in a protected group.

From your description, there does not appear to be any unlawful reason for how they treated you. If you believe your supervisors were treating you differently because you are a member of one of the protected groups I mentioned, your legal recourse would be to file a complaint with the Equal Employment Opportunity Commission, the state Division on Civil Rights, or the state Superior Court. You would have the burden of proving the existence of the unlawful discriminatory conduct and refuting any evidence regarding the employer's alleged legitimate business reasons for its action.

Should you decide to file a claim against your employer, it requires a tremendous commitment of time, mental and emotional energy, and perseverance. With that in mind, it may not be in your best interest to file a lawsuit.

However, you do have options. For example, your decision to seek the assistance of the human resources department was one. I would recommend that you continue to pursue its assistance and demand answers as well as results. Also, remember that no one has the ability to take away your self-esteem, unless you allow it to happen. If you have any doubts about your skills and talents or you need some reassurance, reflect upon or review your past six years of good and very good performance evaluations.

I would suggest that you not quit your job because it is easier to find employment when you are employed, you may be ineligible to receive unemployment compensation benefits, and being unemployed may create more anxiety and distress in your life. If you have any available vacation, sick, or personal leave, take the time off from work to separate yourself from the situation and give yourself the opportunity to recharge.

If the situation with your supervisors cannot be resolved through the assistance of human resources or other top management, then decide what other employment opportunities are available to you and go after them. Although you are going through a difficult period, keep the focus on treating yourself positively, do not listen to or believe untrue statements, and seek counseling or get involved in a support group or network of friends. Take steps to produce the result you desire.

Other Employment Legislation

The increasing number of discrimination claims and requests for protected classifications, such as sexual preference and parenthood, demonstrate the extent of discrimination lawsuits and the desire for employment security.

Employee Must Work Overtime

Q. Is there any state or federal law that prohibits an employer with thousands of employees from forcing single parents of small children to work overtime or risk suspension if they refuse? A nonmanagement single parent has to work 40 hours plus another 5 hours a week to commute to and from the job, plus another 5 hours unpaid lunch. That is a 50-hour week. It's a large company that could get enough volunteers or could hire more people, but it doesn't. The union that represents these nonmanagement workers is not looking out for these people.

B. B.

A. Your state has no law and there is no federal law prohibiting an employer, based upon size or any other reason, from forcing single parents of small children to work overtime or risk suspension if they refuse.

In general, an employer is free to establish its business needs, including, in a nonunion setting, its employees' work hours and other terms and conditions of employment. There is no maximum number of hours an employee may work, with the exception of child labor and some exceptions based on occupation because of safety concerns. However, companies must pay employees minimum wage and overtime pay for all time worked in excess of 40 hours in any workweek.

Several bills have been proposed in Congress to amend the federal Family and Medical Leave Act. These proposals include giving eligible employees freedom to leave work to participate in or attend their children's educational or extracurricular activities or to accompany the child to routine medical or dental appointments. None of those proposals has been enacted.

As for the union not participating in this matter, it probably can do little until the collective bargaining agreement between it and the employer expires. Employee wages, hours, and other terms and conditions of employment are set forth in that agreement. The terms of the contract must be honored by both parties. Probably the union never negotiated for your overtime concern.

The employer's decision may seem unfair to you, but keep in mind that the employer has different, and often conflicting, needs. The employer's needs must also be considered because it is providing jobs for many people. Bringing in volunteers or new hires may not be economically sound.

Possibly you could speak with your supervisor or human resources department concerning your situation. Many times employees want to work overtime so they can receive additional compensation. Perhaps you could structure a different work schedule, such as working through your lunch hour.

Some changes may be difficult to achieve because of the existence of the collective bargaining agreement. Sometimes management would like to assist individual employees but is precluded from doing so by the terms of the agreement.

Contrary to popular belief, the conglomerates are not the only organizations that must comply with the antidiscrimination laws. The Civil Rights Act and the Americans with Disabilities Act apply to employers with 15 or more employees; the Age Discrimination in Employment Act applies to employers with 20 or more employees. State equal employment laws are stricter than the federal requirements in that they apply to all employers, not just those with 15 or more employees. In essence, if you are in business, the potential for compliance litigation lies in every decision that in any way affects an employee and the workplace.

Avoiding the Lawsuit

Although employers cannot prevent discrimination or employment-related claims from being filed, there are steps employers can take to eliminate certain claims as well as to place the organization in a good defense posture should a lawsuit be filed. The following practices will benefit each organization:

- Communication and training
- Written employment policies
- Effective complaint procedures
- Ways to address employee concerns
- Corrective measures
- Monitoring mechanism

After you have mastered the task of being alert to your behavior and listening to the words you use, the next step is to ask, "How do I create a mutually respectful relationship?" Recall Webster's definition of "relationship" as "two or more things working together." In working together at something new, we generally must start at the beginning. Whether we are building a home, a business, or an idea, we begin with laying a strong foundation so that the project is stable and can weather life's unpredictable storms. As history shows, the institutions and concepts that have stood the test of time have a solid, indestructible foundation. Building a relationship is no different.

The missing ingredients to a good employment relationship are discipline, desire, and practice. Each minute of each day presents another opportunity for practice.

Worker Having Problems with Insurance Coverage

Q. I have a big problem with my job. For over one and one-half years, I have been having problems with my dental plan and getting hurt on the job. Dental was being taken out of my check. One day, I got a toothache, so I called the dental plan to see who the dentist was that I picked. The woman on the phone said I did not have dental, that it was canceled about a month and a half ago. I told her I had my pay stubs to show they were taking out dental. I called my job and told them what happened. They said they assumed that because I gave up my hospital insurance, I did not want dental either. They said they sent me a certified letter stating they were canceling dental. I asked her to show me the letter I had signed and she said she could not find it. My employer gave me back the money it had taken out, and to date they still will not give me back my dental.

Also, I got hurt on the job under hazardous conditions. I had to get boxes from our storage room. All the boxes were piled up against the wall on skids or pallets. As I was getting a box down, my foot was in one of the holes in the pallet. I was trying to hold the boxes so they would not come down and hit me in the face or head. I twisted my wrist, so I went to the nurse. She looked at it and said there was nothing wrong. She refused to write an accident report. For weeks, I have told my supervisor that a certain way I turn my wrist I have pain. Nothing was ever done.

I went to see a doctor who took x-rays. He said that he could not see any broken bones, but he put a splint on my wrist. The next day my supervisor told me I could not work until she talked with administration. Administration got mad that I went to the emergency room without notifying the company. The company made me an appointment with the company doctor for that afternoon. I was told I could not work until I saw the doctor. Then the company canceled my appointment because they said I waited too long to get anything done and said I could go back to work the next day.

Since hurting my wrist, I fell on the job on a wet floor and hurt my left toe, knee, ankle, and wrist again. I had three or four witnesses. The next day, administration made me a doctor's appointment, but I was not satisfied with the doctor and requested to see a different doctor. The company refused.

I feel I am being discriminated against because I complained about my dental insurance. Please, can you give me some advice and help me?

R. G.

A.   I am sorry to hear about the difficulties you have been experiencing with your employment. In regard to the loss of your dental insurance, certain laws regulate under what circumstances and in what manner an employer may terminate an employee's health insurance coverage. For example, if your employer employs 20 or more employees during the preceding calendar year and its business affects interstate commerce, it most likely is obligated to comply with the federal Consolidated Omnibus Budget Reconciliation Act (COBRA). This law specifically provides that an employee must be notified of any loss of health insurance coverage. You may want to confirm that in fact you were sent notification and clarify in person your desires and options concerning your dental insurance coverage. In addition to COBRA, the federal Employee Retirement and Income Security Act (ERISA) regulates the administration and record-keeping requirements of employer-sponsored heath and welfare programs. Again, it is important to speak with your employer concerning this important issue.

As for your wrist injury, you are correct that any work-connected injury or illness is covered by workers' compensation. This insurance program provides coverage for such items as medical treatment, special equipment, and lost wages. In addition to providing coverage for the initial injury, workers' compensation also provides benefits for aggravation of an existing injury.

The purpose of workers' compensation is to provide quick relief and financial security to employees in return for which employees are precluded from suing their employers.

It appears that you provided immediate notice to your employer of both work-related injuries in accordance with your obligations under the workers' compensation law. In most states, including your state, injured employees are not allowed to choose their physician so long as the employer's choice is reasonable. At this point, since you have not received any relief from your employer concerning this matter, you might consider contacting the Department of Labor in your state or an attorney who concentrates on workers' compensation matters.

Communication is the key in every employment relationship. Either the lack of education on behalf of the supervisors or managers with whom you have been interacting or the breakdown in communication appears to be paving the way for a potential lawsuit. It is in everyone's best interest that you receive prompt and competent treatment so that you may work to the best of your abilities.

The examples in this chapter show that most employment discrimination claims are filed because the individual is angry at not being respected, heard, or treated fairly. Although people may not like a certain result, the negative impact is lessened when they are treated with respect, in a fair manner, and with concern for their particular circumstances. Similarly, organizations that provide severance packages or outplacement assistance to employees who have been laid off through no fault of their own after many years of service are generally held in high esteem by the persons being separated, their family members, and coworkers, so long as the delivery of the message was handled properly. Treating someone fairly and with respect is another winning formula of success.

Sensitivity to the needs and interests of others is a universal concept. It requires practice, discipline, and heightened awareness. Several years ago, a company president telephoned me with this concern:

We have a company policy and practice that each December we conduct annual employee evaluations and discuss the reviews. Next week I am scheduled to meet with Sam, one of my vice presidents. He has been informed throughout the year about his poor work performance and the need to improve. Sam's work has gotten worse. We have made the decision to terminate Sam's employment next week. However, we first wanted to get your opinion to make sure there existed no legal problems.

In addition to and probably more important than the legal considerations surrounding the situation were the human factors. After some discussion with the company's president, I learned that Sam had been with the company for five years, had a wife who was not employed outside the home, and had five children. Although the company had legitimate business reasons for its decision to terminate Sam's employment, it was determined to postpone the performance evaluation meeting until after the new year.

Sam was told in January that it appeared he no longer desired to work with the company, its employees, and customers since he had made the decision not to improve his job performance. His employment was terminated. As expected, Sam was upset. However, his distress lessened considerably when he was informed that his last day of employment had been extended a few weeks until after the holidays—out of consideration for him and his family.

The law has many diverse and often conflicting facets. Living the letter of the law is often much different from living its spirit. According to the letter of the law, the company was free to fire Sam during the holiday season. However, termination then would have been devastating to Sam, his family, and employee morale. By taking the time to think through the consequences of its actions, the company created a win-win situation. It lived the spirit of the law—fairness and respect.

The examples in this chapter clearly answer the question of why discrimination lawsuits are filed. Unfortunately, the reasons such lawsuits are filed will continue to exist. The impact of a single incident of treating one individual unfairly can have rippling effects throughout the organization. This time bomb is one of the most explosive areas creating much concern.

The evidence is clear: The federal and state fair employment agencies cannot keep pace with the processing and investigating of complaints alleging unlawful employment action. These agencies, once known for their expediency, are now so backlogged that the American workplace has turned the system on its head. Complaints of unlawful employment action, which at one time took six months to a year to process, now take an administrative agency three to four years to finalize. The federal and state courts are faring no better. As taxpayers and consumers, each of us pays for these employment-related complaints. Accordingly, we must start facing the specific reasons discrimination lawsuits are filed and consider whether justice is being overwhelmed by this avalanche.

Equally as important, if not more so, than having grounds to file an employment discrimination lawsuit is the nonlegal aspect of taking such action. The personal impact of filing or defending against a charge of unlawful employment discrimination is rarely discussed but exacts a heavy toll in stress, uncertainty, consumption of time, nonproductivity, and frustration. Therefore, workers must decide if it is in their best interest to file a complaint, and employers must decide whether to defend against an action or settle the matter. Of course, preventing such claims in the first place is the most advantageous and cost-effective procedure for all parties. Good communication, documentation, uniformity, and consistency in applying employment policies and procedures are powerful tools, as are other winning formulas previously discussed, such as mandatory management training. Even if a complaint of unlawful employment discrimination is filed, the parties at any time have the option to resolve their differences amicably and move forward with their lives. If parties who have been involved in the litigation process take the time to learn the valuable lessons from the road they have traveled, everyone wins. If they don't, life will give them the opportunity to relive a similar experience.

Employment litigation is not simply a discussion of what happened yesterday and how to manage it today. More important, the basis for the lawsuit must be honestly and thoroughly reviewed in order to amend any wrong or perceived unfair treatment or to prevent similar conduct in the future. Continual education and reinforcement of sound business and ethical practices must be consistently applied and practiced in order to uphold the sanctity of the employment relationship. Without this foundation, the obligation to honor the employment commitment will be lost.

These concepts provide the framework for the discussion in the next chapter about employment at-will. The basic premise is that absent an employment agreement, representation, or unlawful discrimination, both the employer and the employee are free to end the employment relationship at any time, for any reason or no reason, with or without notice. This legal principle understandably creates much employee unrest and uncertainty. However, the insights furnished in the next chapter will help all parties live the employment relationship more securely and profitably.

■ five ■

The Much Misunderstood
Employment-at-Will Doctrine

Under current law, many employers seek to protect their interests against employment litigation by clearly stating that the employment relationship is "at will". However, most employees are angry with and dispute what they refer to as the employer's "insensitive labeling." Although the term "at-will employment" has created much hostility and frustration, few individuals understand the term or why it is used. A clear understanding of the employment-at-will doctrine will resolve the unnecessary distrust associated with this misunderstood concept.

In this chapter I explain the common-law origin of the term and why the courts insist upon its continued use in today's marketplace. The nature of the disputes concerning the employment-at-will concept has expanded over the years, almost to the point that the exceptions overshadow the rule. Many of the new bases for enlarging employer responsibility and liability have been premised on what is fair and reasonable in view of all of the facts, and creative employee attorneys have led the way in this trend. To help you avoid the costly consequences of your actions becoming a legal exception to the employment-at-will rule, I examine some of those exceptions and discuss ways to live within the rule.

At-Will Employment Defined

The employment-at-will doctrine was transported to the new world with the English settlers in the seventeenth century and the common law. Throughout much of history, the at-will concept remained intact—a master or employer had the right to fire its servants or employees at any time, for any reason, with no prior notice. The basic ingredients of the master/servant or employer/employee relationship are that the master has a need the servant desires to fulfill in return for the agreed compensation. What many employees fail to recognize about the employment relationship—and herein lies their frustration—is that they have no entitlement to employment, but only the right to be fairly considered for employment opportunities based upon their skills, abilities, and experiences and paid fairly and in accordance with their agreement with the employer for services rendered. After that, the relationship is dependent upon honesty, loyalty, dedication, commitment, hard work, teamwork, and the other characteristics you identified in the list you made in Chapter 1.

Regardless of the type of employment relationship, the employee's primary concern is job security. When the preceding characteristics are consistently practiced, there is less chance of being fired or of having an employee quit without notice. Behind the onerous employment-at-will doctrine lies a simple solution: Honor your commitments and do your job well every day to the best of your ability. Whether your employee quits or you get fired, you will know that you acted appropriately at all times and therefore can find another good or even better employee or employment opportunity.

Some employment terminations do make sense. However, as I said before, happy employees do not quit, and good employees do not get fired. The lists that follow give examples of permissible and impermissible reasons for firing an at-will employee. Note in the list of permissible reasons that no one has been singled out because of sex, race, national origin, religion, age, disability, or other similar protected classification. As I discussed in Chapter 4, such action would constitute unlawful employment discrimination.

An employee-at-will can be fired for

- Wearing a red shirt
- Not listening to national news
- Drinking coffee during work hours
- Writing with a green-ink pen
- Frowning

An employee-at-will cannot be fired for

- Leaving work early when all employees leave work early
- Reporting to the employer or a public body that the employer is or was violating the law
- Filing an employment discrimination lawsuit
- Testifying about the employer's actions before a court of law

- Being of a particular national origin

The questions and answers that follow give added dimension to the employment-at-will doctrine and highlight the contexts in which it does and does not apply.

Firms Have Broad Powers in Hiring, Firing, and Salaries

Q. I worked for a small manufacturing company for the last four years as an inside salesman and earned a salary plus commissions. Six months ago a new general manager gave all employees a document that read, in part:

"This Personnel Policy and Procedures Manual has been prepared to provide employees with information about present company policies and benefits. . . . However, this manual is not a contract or guarantee of employment. The company retains the absolute right to release an employee at any time and for any reason, with or without just cause. . . ."

On the last page you are required to sign the manual, thereby acknowledging your receipt and understanding of its terms.

On the day I was handed the manual, the new general manager asked me three times to sign the manual acknowledgment. At the end of the day I asked the owner of the company, "What if you don't sign it?" The answer was that I would be fired.

Prior to signing that document, I would always meet my draw at the end of the month. A short time after signing, I was advised that my draw was in arrears. I was doing my job, but there were many orders that were not being shipped. A few months later the owner told me that we were about even.

I quit my job a couple of weeks thereafter because I had lost two large accounts due to nondelivery—and the deficit kept growing. I believe that the only way my commissions could have run a deficit so rapidly was because certain orders, for which I did not earn a commission, took delivery priority over my orders.

Is it legal for an employer to change the basis of an employee's pay without first advising the person? Or if my commissions were not changed, does the company have the obligation to pay me because I had done my part by placing the orders and I had no control over the nonshipment? What is my best recourse?

A. M.

A.   If an employer has not agreed with or represented to an employee that he will be employed for a specified period or that the employment will continue unless there exists good reason, an employer has the absolute right to fire an employee at any time, with or without notice, for any reason that is not contrary to law.

Equivalent to the employer's right to fire is the employee's absolute right, absent an agreement to the contrary, to quit at any time, with or without notice, for any reason. Since the time you were hired, the company has had the right to end your employment at any time, for any lawful reason.

The company's statement, commonly referred to as an "employment-at-will" statement, is nothing more than a recitation of its legal rights. Courts in most states have ruled that an employment-at-will statement is an essential component of an employee manual in order to inform and clearly communicate to employees the basis of the relationship.

In response to your question concerning an employer changing an employee's wages or salary, the wage and hour laws require employers to inform employees at the time they are hired and before instituting any change of the amount and method of payment. Whether the company was required to pay your commissions when you had placed the orders even though they had not been shipped depends on how your commission and draw were established.

Most commission salespeople, for example, are not entitled to be paid until the product or service is delivered or rendered to the customer. The facts you describe in your letter do not indicate that your former employer did anything wrong. Maybe you needed to discuss the delivery problems with the owner before you quit your job.

What you are entitled to receive depends on the terms of your compensation agreement with the company. Your best recourse may be to request a meeting, to be held at the company, with the owner, payroll manager, or personnel director to clarify this matter amicably as opposed to filing a complaint with the Department of Labor.

Once employees are hired, they must perform in the manner reasonably expected of them as directed by the employer. These responsibilities are in addition to the unspoken work ethics of trust, loyalty, dedication, and commitment. In return for these services, the employer has the obligation to provide employees the agreed compensation. These basic concepts have not changed.

The confusion that often arises around the employment-at-will statement generally occurs because employees have not been educated on its meaning or, which usually occurs in the majority of cases, employees choose not to hear the reality of their workplace situation. The only changes from the original employment-at-will doctrine are the exceptions the courts have created. When a new client telephones or visits for a consultation, two questions I first ask are, "Does the organization have an employee handbook, or have any pertinent representations been made concerning the nature of the dispute?" I ask these questions because the exceptions to the employment-at-will doctrine include representations, misrepresentations, unwritten employment policies, past practices, employee handbook statements, disclaimers, and whistleblower protection laws.

Many courts, for example, in interpreting the employment relationship, have ruled that when an employer makes a representation to an employee that was reasonable for the employee to rely upon and that in fact the employee did rely upon to his or her detriment, then the employer has an obligation to honor its commitment. The courts have applied this basic legal principle in cases where the representation was made orally, in writing, or by way of the employer's actions.

For example, assume an employer offers an applicant a new job, has him relocate from California to New Jersey, give up his former job, and on his first day of work tells the employee that the organization changed its mind and his services are no longer needed. Something is inherently unfair and wrong in that scenario. In such situations, the courts have required the organization to treat the individual properly so that he or she is not unfairly damaged as the *sole* result of the employer's actions upon which the employee reasonably relied. However, assume the same facts except that the employee has been employed with the organization for eight months, has failed to perform the job duties properly, and has been counseled frequently about the unacceptable job performance. In this case, termination of the employment relationship is not unfair because it was the direct result of the employee's chosen conduct.

People have a sense of fairness in how others are treated. In employment-related litigation, the judge or administrative agency investigator hearing the case often will ask whether the manager or supervisor ever provided the employee direction on how to perform the job properly or counsel the person on what areas needed improvement *before* the employment relationship was terminated. When the answer is no, the result is predictable: If the manager or supervisor never spoke with the individual, how was the employee to know that his or her performance needed improvement? Again, something is inherently unfair about this situation, and when the scales of justice place the unequal power of the employer on one side and the importance of the job on the other side, the scales often tip in favor of the employee.

Communicating the Terms of Employment

As I discussed earlier, communication—speaking, writing, acting, and listening— is essential to the success of all relationships, and the employment relationship is no exception. In this section I highlight the importance of communication in the employment-at-will relationship and provide workplace examples of the four communication skills operating simultaneously in that setting.

Worker Says Reverse Racism, Hairstyle Led to Her Firing

Q. I believe I was fired due to unfair labor practices and possibly reverse discrimination. My employer hired a woman to work in the department I head. She was not an easy person to work with. Many of us found her to be defiant, undependable, lazy, and very uncooperative.

   The other workers in the department complained to me that they were tired of doing her work, so I went to my office manager twice with these complaints, but nothing was done. I was told that eventually she would be let go and I should just tolerate her a little longer.

   One week this black employee came to work with a wild hairstyle. At least one top management representative told her it was inappropriate for our office. I myself laughed and the black employee also laughed and everything was taken in stride. I was not the only employee to make a comment.

   The next day I wore my hair in a different hairstyle, as I frequently do. When some other workers saw my hairstyle, they laughed. No one from management complained, so I went about my business. Then the same top management representative who had told the other employee that her hairstyle was inappropriate asked me if I would change my hairstyle. I complied.

   The next day the black employee told a coworker that I was making a mockery of her by my hairstyle the previous day. She apparently also complained to top management and then left for the day. My office manager called me in and I explained that I in no way intended to make a mockery of anyone, that I believed I was just exercising my right to freedom of choice and that I would never intentionally hurt anyone's feelings.

Later that day I was fired. I feel I was fired for an inappropriate hairstyle. My office manager said "it was not of my ethnicity to wear my hair in that manner."

Is there any recourse here? I know about being an "at-will" employee and that I can be fired for no cause. However, I believe I was fired to avoid a lawsuit or at least extensive trouble from this black employee. Is there anything that could be done about this?

K. M.

A. An employee filing a claim of unlawful employment discrimination has the burden of proving the unlawful conduct. Thus, in order to establish reverse discrimination, you must show that you were similarly situated to the black employee and that the employer treated you differently because of your race.

Your statement that you were fired as a result of your hairstyle is insufficient grounds to make a claim. As a general rule, employers are permitted to determine what constitutes appropriate employee dress and grooming, so long as they enforce the policy uniformly and consistently and the employee's dress or grooming is not based on genuine health, religious, or similar matters.

As for your statement that you believe the firing occurred to avoid a lawsuit, there is no prohibition against this action.

It appears your employer used poor judgment and made the employment situation worse by never responding to the difficulties you and other employees experienced with the problem employee. It also appears the employer elected to take what it perceived to be the easy way out by ending your employment in order to avoid other potential problems of a larger magnitude.

Filing a lawsuit requires an enormous expenditure of valuable time and resources. It seems to me you have already done more than your fair share of investing in this employer. Possibly it is time to invest in yourself and move forward in finding and establishing an employment relationship unlike your previous one. Although you may desire to teach this employer a lesson, what will you gain?

Some people ask if they aren't entitled to a job. How can an employer simply fire an employee for no reason and without any notice? The answer is simple—the same way an employee can quit a job for any reason and with no advance notice. On both sides it comes down to basic values. If people desire to be respected, they will be respectful of others. If people desire honesty, they will be honest. If people desire to be trusted, they will be trustworthy.

When an employer hires an employee, presumably the employer believes the employee is capable of performing the essential job functions and will be a welcome addition to the organization. The prospective employee theoretically accepts the employment offer believing the wages and benefits to be fair and the job fulfilling. Yet often, although by no means the general rule, within six months to two years, the dynamics of the employment relationship may have undergone dramatic changes. The employer may view the employee entirely differently, and the employee's perception of the working environment or day-to-day tasks may also have drastically changed. What happened? Are these not the same parties who freely and knowingly entered into the employment relationship? Neither one forced the other to work together.

No one can possibly provide you job security. Built into every written and un-written job description are the essential requirements of good faith and fair dealing. If you or the organization you work for do not possess these qualities or do not practice these characteristics, you or the organization will have laid the employment foundation on quicksand, and anyone who stands too close will be pulled down as well. Successful people and institutions are built with solid citizens.

Even labor organizations do not file every union member's grievance or arbitration. Of course, certain grievances or arbitrations are filed for political or other reasons, but many are never filed because the grievant lacks the basic qualities of trust, loyalty, dedication, or knowledge. Although unions generally do not espouse this concept, their actions demonstrate that there is no real concept as job security. When workers have stolen time by sleeping on the job or failed to perform their job duties or told a lie, they have freely chosen to no longer work with the organization.

Union Should Stick By Its Commitment

Q. I was discharged from my employment of six years. The discharge was for not reaching my production level. There were some factors why I didn't, in-cluding a change of work procedures and higher standards.

I put in a grievance with my union and waited for an arbitration hearing, which was finally scheduled. I went to the state Department of Labor with my union representative, but the meeting was canceled. Another date was set, and the union paid me for the day plus mileage and tolls.

I went to the union office again, as scheduled. When I arrived, I was met by another union representative, who said something came up and the meeting was again canceled. The explanation this time was unclear. They said that the union was going to send me a check for that day. I lost 10 hours of working time from my current job so I could attend the meeting.

To this day, the union hasn't sent me my money. I have made numerous calls to my union representative, but none were returned. Do I have the right to have an arbitration hearing to state my case in this matter? What is taking so long? I also would like to have the money the union owes me.

P. B

A.   Whether a matter is arbitrable is determined by the terms of the collective bargaining agreement between the union of which you are a member and your employer. The union, as your exclusive bargaining representative regarding your wages, hours, and terms and conditions of your employment, has the right to decide which cases should be submitted to arbitration. The primary factors generally considered by a union in deciding whether to pursue a case to arbitration are the facts of the case, the evidence to substantiate the claim, and the likelihood of success.

The union has the obligation to represent you and all of its members fairly. If you believe the union has failed to represent you fairly concerning your wages, hours, and terms and conditions of employment, you may file a lawsuit in federal district court against the union for such failure.

From what you describe, it appears the union led you to believe that it would pursue, on your behalf, your grievance that your employment discharge was contrary to the terms of the collective bargaining agreement. In that case, the union is obligated to keep this matter moving forward in a timely manner.

If the arbitration hearing needs to be continued, then it is reasonable for the union to provide you advance notice of the rescheduling of the hearing so that you may coordinate your schedule accordingly. You have the right to know exactly what is occurring with your case and your pay. Speak with a union representative who has authority to get answers to your questions, and take all necessary steps to move your matter forward. Follow up your conversations or meetings with letters documenting what steps you have taken and representations made to you by the union. Because the union has represented to you that it will arbitrate your claim and pay your lost wages, it has the obligation to honor its commitment.

Employees are not always the responsible party when employment relationships end. Often the employer fails to provide the employee all of the essential information to perform the job properly, or the manager and the employee have a personality conflict. The list of possibilities is endless. Good communication skills are essential. Both employer and employee alike have an obligation to communicate so that they fully understand the other's perception. Breakdown in communication will eventually destroy the employment relationship.

Fired Worker Seeks Employee Handbook

Q. I was a part-time employee. I started in March and was fired without notice or reason the following February. I am not looking to question their reasons for the firing. I am looking for the employee manual, which in some way shows their procedure in firing, notices, etc. The company is trying to avoid giving me the information.

I was working 50 to 60 hours a week and paid $11 an hour plus overtime for eight hours each day. So even a two-week notice would amount to over $1,000.

I wrote a memorandum to the personnel department requesting the employee handbook. My supervisor called me and stated the book was big and I would not need it. I again requested the book from the main office. The company tried to avoid my request.

The company stated that it does not have an employee handbook and that the field sales manual to which I referred contains only administrative procedure and is used by managers as reference for administrative purposes. I was told that this manual is not distributed to employees, and that if there is any particular information I feel I need, to call.

P. S.

A. I am sorry to hear that you were fired from your employment. As a general rule, absent a contract, collective bargaining agreement, or representation, the relationship between the employer and the employee is at-will. This means that the employer may fire the employee without notice at any time for any reason or no reason so long as the employment termination is not contrary to law. Similarly, the employee may quit his or her job without notice at any time for any or no reason.

Notwithstanding the general principle of at-will employment, the courts have ruled that when employers widely distribute an employee handbook that contains job security provisions, such a handbook, absent a clear and prominent disclaimer, may constitute a contract. Although you are correct in requesting a copy of the handbook, if you never had such a handbook, this important fact may negate your claim that the employee handbook constitutes a contract. However, knowing the organization's policies and procedures and past practices in terminating employment relationships may be useful in determining whether you were treated in a similar fashion.

Your letter indicates that your former employer did respond to your specific request and offered to assist you with any particular information you feel you need. Although you may believe the company will not supply you with the specific information you desire, you may consider calling the company's human resources director and requesting the information, as well as speaking with your former colleagues as to what pertinent information they may know.

This communication may clarify any misunderstanding you have regarding the employee handbook or employment termination procedures. Short of these steps, you have no option to force the company to show you what it does or does not possess by way of employee handbooks, unless you file a lawsuit against the company.

The employee handbook serves many functions for both employer and employee. First and foremost, the handbook sets forth the organization's philosophy and expectations of its employees. In return, the employee receives a document that should serve as a road map for the various questions that arise during the employment relationship.

The handbook should, in addition to addressing the basic concepts of the relationship, expressly state the employer's policy regarding such highly litigated issues as the Family and Medical Leave Act, the Americans with Disabilities Act, and sexual harassment. I recommend to and prepare for clients an employee handbook that covers as many essential details and contingencies as possible to avoid the risk of having courts or administrative agencies interpret an employer's past practices contrary to the employer's expressed corporate policy.

After the establishment of an employee handbook, the next phase is implementation. The best way to meet the objective of having employees understand the policies is to conduct conferences with small groups of employees to review the handbook in detail, with a question-and-answer period for them to comprehend fully any difficult areas of the handbook.

At the end of each session, the employee should sign for the handbook to dispute any later contention that either the material was not adequately explained or the employee was never given a handbook. This simple procedure of having an attendance sheet indicating possession and of explaining policies extensively places employees on notice of the seriousness with which the organization views its policies as set forth in the handbook and the respect an employee should give them.

The final step in proper handbook development is to view it as a living organism. Once it is drafted, employers are tempted to ignore the handbook until presented with litigation. Employers should make revisions to their handbook as warranted to keep current with new statutory requirements and court decisions affecting provisions in their existing handbook.

In this manner not only does the handbook remain up-to-date, but the employees who receive the new revisions appreciate an employer who places an emphasis on maintaining a high standard in employee relations.

Union Members Are Not Employees-at-Will

At-will employment, as that term is legally defined, does not exist in the union setting. The employment relationship that involves a union is governed by a written contract. Most, if not all, union collective bargaining agreements do not contain an employment-at-will clause. Rather, the general termination provision provides that no employee can be fired without "just cause." Although unions proclaim that this protection grants its members job security, the previous discussion on how to protect your job does not support this proposition. In addition, even if you conclude that this language provides job security, do you desire to work alongside an individual whom you know to be lying, cheating, and stealing time from the organization? Wouldn't these actions be detrimental to everyone in the establishment because each person would have to work harder and possibly for less pay?

Smoker Questions Rights at Work

Q. Recently the company I work for enforced a no-smoking policy in any company building; therefore, we must all go outside to smoke. All the union workers have two 15-minute breaks and a half-hour lunch break per day. We are not allowed outside to smoke on our 15-minute breaks, only on our lunch break. Management employees can go outside anytime they feel like it.

When the policy started, the union employees complained to management about the unfair treatment. Management stopped going outside for a while, but now they all go outside again. Is there any legal action we can take on this?

Also, I read an article in the *New York Post* about four months ago stating that President Clinton signed a law or something protecting smokers' rights and that the Food and Drug Administration commissioner issued an order that all smokers were now "federally recognized" drug addicts and that all employers had to provide space in the employment property for smokers. Is this true?

C. K.

A. In the unionized setting, the employment relationship is governed by a collective bargaining agreement. That agreement sets forth the employer's and union employees' obligations with regard to wages, hours, and other terms and conditions of employment. Generally, those matters that the employer and union have not specifically set forth in their agreement or recognized through a past practice are retained by management to regulate. Therefore, if the collective bargaining agreement does not say anything regarding union employees' right to smoke, which it probably does not, there is little that can be done at this time. However, the issue may be raised after the collective bargaining agreement expires and it is time to renegotiate the contract.

It is permissible for the employer to allow management employees to go outside to smoke and not permit this conduct of union employees. Keep in mind that there is a fundamental difference between union and nonunionized employees—the union employees' wages, hours, and terms and conditions of employment are set forth in a collective bargaining agreement; nonunion employees and management employees may establish different terms and conditions for their employment relationship.

In addition, management employees do not receive the same protections or benefits as nonmanagerial employees. For example, most management employees work more than 40 hours a week but are not entitled to overtime pay. Their work schedule depends in large part on projects or events regardless of the time required to complete the work. Most other employees are entitled to overtime pay, and therefore, how they spend their time is important because it costs the employer directly.

In response to your inquiry as to whether smokers are considered addicted to a substance and have certain protections because of this new classification, no law exists at this time clearly granting this protection. The Americans with Disabilities Act and state laws prohibit employers from discriminating against applicants and employees with respect to job application procedures, hiring, advancement, discharge, compensation, job training, and other terms, conditions, and privileges of employment because of a disability. Drug addiction and alcoholism are recognized disabilities under these laws, and certain protections are provided.

However, and more important, these laws do not protect employees who may otherwise be disabled when they come to work under the influence or abuse a substance in the workplace. Therefore, if addiction to nicotine is or becomes a recognized disability, there still may not exist protection for its use in the workplace. Remember that the purpose for which you report to work each day is to perform a service for your employer in exchange for which you receive compensation.

If you believe you are addicted to nicotine, maybe it would be in your best interest to treat it like any other addiction and seek assistance through a physician or 12-step program. This type of action may save your life as well as make your life more enjoyable.

Living, Not Fearing, At-Will Employment

There must be mutual respect for the talent and skills of others on all levels. Human resource managers have been fighting an uphill battle for years to ensure that the organization's human resources—the employees—are of first and foremost importance to the bottom line. Far too often executives focus on the cost of inventory, customer relations, or other external interests and fail to see the value of their own powerhouse—their employees. Management must bring employees into the large vision and mission of the organization so they understand and see their importance. An organization's failure to embrace human resources fully and these basic concepts, in conjunction with proclaiming the relationship to be at-will, has devastating consequences.

As previously discussed, orientation of new employees sets the foundation for the employment relationship. The employer's most powerful first message is that we all the current employees respect the company's resources and expect you as a new employee to do the same. Therefore, the organization is providing you all the necessary information to enable you to do your job properly and let you know what you can expect from the organization in return.

Regardless of industry, each for-profit or not-for-profit organization's primary resource is its employees. Recognition and support of this essential resource are best protected through the establishment of a well-defined human resources or similar department or person. This department or individual is a crucial foundation pillar, without which an organization will not be complete. After a human resource department has been structured, it must make its services known to all employees. This department is the organization's lifeline for employees. Each person has the responsibility to abandon the hard and stead-fast approach that "I have no responsibilities or rights."

Human resources supports and breathes life into the employees and the or-ganization. The department is the liaison between the employee and em-ployer—the mediator, arbitrator, and judge. It trains management; informs em-ployees of their job responsibilities; applies company policy consistently and fairly; pays employees for their services; implements company benefits; en-sures compliance with federal, state, and local employment laws; maintains employee contact and relations; formulates, recommends, and implements employee policies; and provides employee support.

Both managerial and nonmanagerial employees have an obligation to re-spond to and follow the department's guided direction and perform their job duties, at a minimum, in a satisfactory and respectful manner. Conduct and at-titude of employees are guideposts as to whether they desire to work for the organization. Each employee's behavior impacts upon the workplace. There-fore, all employees are responsible for their words and actions.

How do you show that you are an instrument of inspiration? The steps are simple:

1. *Praise all good work.* Of course, we all get busy and caught up in our over-whelming obligations and unexpected tasks and emergencies and a thousand other items. However, I can reassure you that your work environment will be more enjoyable and your responsibilities properly carried out if you provide positive feedback on work well done. This rule applies to all persons, not just management employees. Coworkers providing praise to coworkers instills morale and good relations. How does it feel to receive praise? How often do you receive this gift that has no price tag? How often do you unconditionally give this gift that costs nothing? What are you waiting for? Tomorrow may never come.

2. *Daily feedback.* Performance evaluations are to be completely daily. They are not a formal celebration or execution at the end of the year. There are to be no surprises. When employees are reviewed, they should be able to antici-pate what will be discussed. To help employees better understand their perfor-mance evaluation, have employees evaluate their own performance. This self-examination generally provides assistance in conducting the performance evaluation meeting and assessing the employment relationship as a whole, thereby apprising both parties as to its present and future status.

We all like to know how we are doing and where we fit in—that's human na-ture. Most people appreciate knowing when they are performing a task incor-rectly so they can take corrective steps. Thus, provide employees frequent feedback to educate them on what they are doing well or how they can improve their performance. This type of communication provides employees with the proper tools to perform their work effectively and efficiently as well as to maintain or increase employee morale and respect. Managers and supervisors must meet with and inform employees who are not properly fulfilling their job responsibilities or who are acting contrary to the organization's policies or procedures. Each such meeting should be held immediately after the incident, or as soon thereafter as possible, in order to communicate accurately what has transpired and to demonstrate the importance of the corrective message.

In redirecting employees, management must specifically and clearly delineate what corrective steps need to be taken by an employee who is being disciplined and the possible consequences of the employee's behavior should it persist. Depending upon the occurrence, this meeting need not be formal or should be conducted in the presence of another manager. Similarly, the seriousness or repetitiveness of the behavior will determine the need for the documentation of the occurrence. If documentation is warranted, it should include the date, what was discussed, and who was present at the meeting. Communication with employees about unacceptable job performance is never comfortable. However, employee education and communication are essential to correcting or removing the workplace problem should the employee choose not to address the situation adequately in a timely manner.

One day a client telephoned to inform me that the organization decided to fire a problem employee but first wanted me to review the employee's personnel file to ensure the employer had sufficient documentation before terminating the employee's employment. Following are the pertinent sections (with names changed) of the various memoranda the client sent me; they were written over a seven-month period.

Memorandum 1—A discussion took place between Jill, Hillary and myself concerning Jill's inappropriate and insubordinate behavior. Her behavior was observed by several other employees and visitors. I had recently met with Jill to discuss a similar incident of inappropriate conduct. Due to the nature of this incident, Jill was suspended for three days. Jill is aware that any future incidence will result in termination.

Memorandum 2—A discussion took place between myself and Jill regarding the attached inappropriate comments. She is also aware that calling out to other employees in the hall is unacceptable and disruptive. Jill has been counseled in the past regarding inappropriate and insubordinate behavior. She is aware that any additional concerns will result in termination.

Memorandum 3—Today Jill was given the option of taking lunch at 11:30 a.m. or 1:00 p.m. because other employees were absent. She asked to take lunch at 11:30 a.m. and she was aware that she was to be back by noon. At 12:15 p.m. I saw Jill in the cafeteria and I asked her why she was not back to work. She responded: "I was busy and couldn't leave by 11:30 a.m. What difference does it make anyway." When I told her to return to work, she replied: "I only have a few minutes left." Jill has been counseled in the past and is aware that her behavior is unacceptable. I am waiving any additional suspension. Jill is aware that a future occurrence will result in her termination.

Memorandum 4—Jill has again displayed insubordinate behavior when she changed an assignment given by myself. She did this without my knowledge. Due to the seriousness and frequency of Jill's inappropriate and insubordinate behavior, she, Hillary and myself met on this date. We made it clear the behavior of this type would not be tolerated. Jill understands that any further incidents of this nature will result in immediate termination.

From this documentation, do you think the organization is in a good position to fire Jill? Answer: No. Reason: Each document recites that "Jill is aware that her behavior is unacceptable" and "any further incidents of this nature will result in termination." Do Jill's actions demonstrate that she possesses this crucial information? The courts have ruled that this type of documentation is insufficient; the employee in fact never knew her behavior was inappropriate or when she was going to be fired. Moral: Set a definitive counseling plan or goals to be achieved, and stand by the stated objectives, including employment termination.

Fairness is key to good management. Employees may not always agree with an employment decision, but they do respect an individual who has treated them fairly. Prompt and well thought out responses to employee workplace situations not only can build and maintain employee morale and prevent employment litigation but also can provide a strong defense should a claim be filed.

If you are an employee who has not been provided any feedback, be proactive in your employment relationship. Ask how you are doing, request information about your performance, educate management on your future goals, and seek its assistance in accomplishing your desires. You are a party to this relationship and therefore have a responsibility to participate. Sitting back and complaining is not acceptable. You have not been granted the opportunity to work to provide little or nothing. Such action contradicts what you were hired to do, "work." Rather, you were offered the opportunity because you stated that you were willing, able, qualified, and ready to render a service. Keeping your promise is your obligation and no other person's responsibility.

3. *Role of employee in the organization.* Educate employees on their role in the organization and let them know how their particular work impacts upon the results of a project. For example, employers are well served when they take the time to have employees who are working on a manufacturing line step off the line to experience what happens when they are removed from the operation—there is a gap, the product falls through. The employees can see that each is a crucial component to the entire production.

Employers are also encouraged to periodically walk employees through the entire facility to remind them of the various stages necessary to achieve the end product. Similarly, when a complimentary letter is received from a customer, photocopy the praise letter and circulate it to all employees so that they see the result of their work and feel the glory. Knowing that we are appreciated fosters desire to be appreciative.

4. *Redirect the behavior.* An essential job responsibility of each manager and supervisor is to provide guidance to employees on how they are carrying out their job duties and, when necessary, to demonstrate better methods or new approaches to performing their jobs or approaching their work. Management's obligation is to teach. Although making individuals responsible for their own behavior is uncomfortable, and at times difficult, it has numerous benefits for the individual employee, other employees, the customers, the organization, and the manager and supervisor. To permit people to avoid responsibility for their behavior is counterproductive. The previously quoted memoranda demonstrate the point.

Educate employees on any behavior that has created a problem, explain why the conduct has resulted in a problem, and describe what corrective steps are necessary. Never attack the employee personally. The manager or supervisor's role is to educate and guide employees. The objective of the employment relationship is to work together to achieve a common objective. With that in mind, you can easily see why yelling, blaming, and attacking will never achieve the desired result.

Managers and supervisors who see their roles as dictators who must control actions and take a strong hand will typically take one of two approaches—do nothing because confrontation is uncomfortable, or criticize and blame the employee. Neither approach is workable. Therefore, the employer must give managers and supervisors the proper tools to know how to perform their jobs properly. In essence, the manager's and supervisor's role is be a teacher and provide guidance. However, not everyone is teachable. And remember, no one has the ability to control another human being. Doesn't this frame of reference and approach make life easier? You are not, and cannot, be responsible for another person's behavior unless you have endorsed the conduct. Education of all employees on the employers' policies and procedures serves everyone's best interests.

5. *Documentation.* Employee job performance must be documented. The documentation is to focus on job duties and employees' performance or failure to perform the essential and nonessential job functions. Document transgression of duties or responsibilities at or about of the time of the incident or occurrence. Include the specific details and explicit description of the particular job responsibilities and/or organizational policy or procedure in question and the conduct or behavior that was contrary to what the employer reasonably expected. Also include the names of any other individuals who have direct knowledge of the situation or pertinent documentation. In addition, the preparer and any other management representative should sign and date the documentation.

Equally as important is the documentation of commendable employment performance. Employees need to know that they are appreciated, that their abilities were recognized, and that their hard work contributed to the ultimate success. Furnishing employees positive reinforcement fosters as much, if not more, solidification of the relationship than a pay raise. Failure to acknowledge an employee's golden attributes leads to erosion and eventual collapse of the empire.

Documentation serves several purposes. First, it is a memory refresher for all concerned should the situation arise again and need to be addressed. Second, it provides necessary information to be included on the annual performance evaluation. Third, it evidences the legitimacy of the employment decision, whether it be no raise, a promotion, or employment termination. Include only job-related information on the documentation. The document may be as short as several sentences. It simply needs to describe adequately the details of the particular situation that precipitated the employee meeting and the corrective steps to be implemented or the admirable work. Keep in mind how this document might be used in the future and who is the potential audience. As shown in the memorandums reprinted earlier in this chapter, managers and supervisors frequently state "Any more unacceptable behavior will result in immediate termination." That same statement was repeated in the four memoranda pertaining to the same employee. As with the boy who cried wolf, overusage weakens impact of a warning until it has no effect. It is helpful to have someone else read the document to ascertain another person's perspective, especially when you are creating these types of documents for the first time.

This document that seems so simple and harmless, and to many a waste of time, can have quite an extensive life when they reach some very powerful people, such as the employee's attorney, the judge, and most powerful of all— the jury. Therefore, each manager and supervisor needs to take this job responsibility very seriously.

The question often arises as to whether the employer should have the employee sign the counseling report. There are two schools of thought. Some people believe that an employee may become more upset or angry when asked to sign the report because it creates the appearance of rubbing the employee's nose in the dirt. Others believe that the employee's signature evidences that the counseling session was held and communicates the seriousness of the matter. If the employee refuses to sign the warning, this fact is noted on the document.

Managers and supervisors often are uncomfortable in this counseling or documenting role, or they state they do not have the time. In either case, it is imperative for top management to lead by example. Managers or supervisors who are lax in counseling or documenting employee behavior or performance should themselves be evaluated, counseled, and documented. This investment of time is crucial and cost-effective.

Worker May Be Unable to Get Promotion He Deserves

Q. I am a white male government employee looking for a promotion to the next technical grade level. I do not feel I am being fairly evaluated by my supervisor on my ability to perform my job. Furthermore, I feel I am being purposefully neglected by my supervisor in support of his own interests.

   Coworkers and other supervisors have told me they feel I should receive a promotion. I feel this is not only unfair to me but also to some of my coworkers. I am one grade lower than some individuals whom I direct and coordinate on a project. In addition, I have held a position normally performed by those who are two grade levels above where I am now.

   I have talked to my supervisor about my promotion several times. He, in his short time of less than a year, has cited a few things he would like me to improve on: provide monthly status reports and keep him up-to-date with weekly conversations. However, despite these few administrative shortcomings, he has stated I am technically qualified to receive a promotion. In his opinion, he has stated, I could be "next" in line within the department. I have provided the status reports and sat down with him on a weekly basis, providing information to him and asking his opinions on certain situations, both of which have been satisfactory with his requirements. In addition, he has never once responded with concern or inquiry toward any issues I have provided to him.

Whenever I have inquired about a promotion, the answers and possibilities have always been elusive. He was not willing to commit to a date to review my status toward a promotion and stated it may not be a good time to go for a promotion due to the competition.

My supervisor does not want to make waves with his superiors. If he supports my promotion, he needs to confront his superiors. This is further compounded, since the organization is currently under an overhead shortage. Promotions would cut into that overhead our organization receives as a result of the man-hour rate our organization charges for services.

So my question is, under these circumstances, how does one go about convincing his superiors that he is deserving of a promotion and would benefit the organization? Is there any way to claim a supervisor is negligent or has purposefully done wrong to benefit himself, legally or otherwise, when the benefit is more political than monetary or career-enhancing?

J. K.

A.   Unfortunately, there is no legal remedy for the frustrating situation you describe, unless you fall within one of the employment-at-will exceptions: a representation that you relied upon to your detriment; a contract or a collective bargaining agreement; a decision based upon a protected classification such as your race, age, sex, or disability; or an act or inaction contrary to civil service requirements or law.

Although it seems unfair, an employer is free to make employment decisions based upon internal politics, unreasonable expectations, or another reason, as long as it is not in violation of one of the listed items. The law does not provide a remedy for every wrong.

You seem to have a realistic understanding of the different factors impacting your supervisor's inaction in supporting your promotion. From your description, it appears—and this is important to keep in mind—that his decision has nothing to do with you or your abilities and has everything to do with him and the general workplace environment. Clearly, and likewise important for your consideration, your supervisor's words do not match his actions. His conduct communicates that you will not, in the near future, receive that promotion you desire and are otherwise eligible to move into.

Therefore, in determining your course of action, keep in mind that you are not capable of controlling or forcing your supervisor to take an action he does not want to take. This pursuit on your behalf will result in further frustration. Accordingly, decide what factors are within your control. For example, educate your supervisor's superiors on your abilities and valuable contributions to the organization, or seek other employment opportunities. Although the situation you describe is unfair and you recognize it as such, look at what options you have available to you, gain the insight of persons you respect, and then make your decision based upon those factors that you can influence, are in your best interests, and take you in the direction you desire.

Retaining Power

Taking care of yourself through use of good communication, being your best, and looking for ways to improve how you live your life are stellar ingredients for breeding success. No one has the ability to usurp your power when your daily brew is in mixing these essential elements. Although life may not hand you the desired result, the quest is always what you can learn from the situation and how you can make life better. Continuing to improve your life from where you currently stand will add dimension to your well-being and to those around you. Here is an example of an at-will employee refusing to be a victim of life's circumstances.

Employee Questions Whether Her Rights Were Violated

Q. Due to moral and ethical issues, I submitted my resignation to my superiors in mid-October, effective mid-November. After four years and seven months, I wished to leave the agency with some dignity. However, I would later pay for verbalizing my feelings in my superior's presence, who was allowed to sit in a support meeting and hear staff complaints, mine included.

After the staff meeting, my superior, who is also the cofounder and associate director of the agency, called a meeting to inform all that she was taking over my job. She also stated that she wanted to know who was on board and for those who were not to get off. From that time on, I was invisible. I was no longer allowed to interact with staff or outside agencies, or make any decisions regarding my job. I was told that two days in-house was sufficient and I could use that time to find myself another job.

Four days before my resignation date, I received a call from my superior informing me that I was not needed on the job at all. She further stated that there was no need for me to return and to stay out until my resignation. I somehow feel as though my rights as her employee have been violated, but I am not quite sure just how. Can someone just walk in and take your job because you work for them? Why was I not allowed to work until my resignation date?

L. W.

A.   As a general rule, an employer has the right to terminate an employee's employment for any reason at any time, with or without notice. There are certain exceptions to this employment-at-will rule: An employer cannot fire an employee for an unlawful reason, such as the employee's sex, age, race, color, religion, marital status, veteran status, sexual preference, or disability; nor can an employer terminate the relationship in retaliation for an employee's claim or testimony in such matters as a workers' compensation or discrimination action; nor may an employer discharge an employee contrary to an agreement between them.

No exception appears to apply to the facts you describe. Rather, it appears that your superior was angry with what was stated during the staff meeting and as a result chose to end the relationship when she had everything in place. Just as you had the right to resign, so did the employer have the right to select your last day of employment.

It is understandable that you would be upset with how your employment relationship ended, especially when you were respectful by providing three to four weeks' advance notice of your resignation. However, your superior did provide you time to find another job. Your job ended only four days sooner than the date you selected, and you still achieved your goal of resigning with some dignity.

As you can see from the previous chapters, every facet of the employment relationship is connected, and every essential employment tool works in perfect harmony. Using your positive characteristics on a daily basis and refusing to be a victim will not only serve you well in the employment-at-will or just-cause relationship but will also protect you against one of the most uncomfortable workplace situations—sexual harassment, the topic of the next chapter.

six

Sexual Harassment in the Workplace

In educating employees throughout the country on sexual harassment in the workplace, I ask the seminar participants what they think makes a good employment relationship. Most individuals have no instantaneous response. After some deliberation, a few employees provide their insight—respect, communication, good wages, teamwork. When I ask this same group of individuals what makes a bad employment relationship, I readily receive numerous responses with descriptive adjectives.

I then ask the participants how many people have ever been a party to or have heard the following statement: "Jane just has no sense of humor. She got all upset when I was telling that joke on sexual relations." Unfortunately, most people respond in the affirmative. Although most people are tired of hearing about sexual harassment in the workplace, especially after the President Clinton and Paula Jones case, the sentiments of the United States Supreme Court in June 1998 are similar to my audiences' reply to the joke on sexual relations. In a landmark decision, the Court in *Faragher v. City of Boca Raton,* 524 U.S. 775 (1998), stated, "[e]veryone knows by now that sexual harassment is a common problem in the American workplace." In light of this statement, the large number of sexual harassment cases with large jury awards, and the infiltration of these lawsuits in the school systems, there exists a real need to understand the importance of this subject matter.

The most critical aspect is that plaintiffs always name at least two parties as defendants in a complaint of sexual harassment. Most persons think of the employer as being potentially liable. However, they fail to realize that an employer that does everything required of it under the law is not liable. That leaves the individual who precipitated the lawsuit by engaging in the harassing conduct. Most people are shocked to learn that this individual may be personally accountable for his or her behavior. Thus, it is imperative for all employees to understand fully their obligations concerning workplace interactions, what their behavior in the workplace is communicating, and how certain conduct negatively affects coworkers.

Supreme Court Justice Stewart stated in *Jacobellis v. Ohio*, 378 U.S. 184 (1964), that he could not define pornography, "but I know it when I see it." Sexual harassment, in essence, is evaluated similarly. Whether certain conduct or behavior constitutes sexual harassment is determined from the perspective of the person who is the target of or is observing the behavior. The perception of the alleged harasser is irrelevant. In addition, the fact that the alleged harasser did not intend to offend another person is of no consequence; lack of intent is no defense to a claim of sexual harassment.

Most individuals believe sexual harassment has more to do with people looking for a pot of gold than a remedy for an illegal and immoral act. The primary question is, "How many zeros are at the end of the jury award?" Regardless of how you feel about the subject, statistics reported by the federal Equal Employment Opportunity Commission (EEOC), the administrative agency authorized to enforce this area of the law, reveal that the American workforce is still in great need of education and sensitivity training concerning sexual harassment in the workplace. During the 1990s, the number of sexual harassment charges filed with the EEOC more than doubled, and the monetary damages (not including awards through litigation) topped $50 million (Table 6.1)

These numbers are startling. For those individuals who believe that too much focus is already placed on sexual harassment in the workplace and that nothing further is required, the numbers demonstrate otherwise. In addition, the EEOC numbers do not include other costs associated with employee absenteeism, poor employee morale, stress, tension, and low productivity within the entire workforce.

The New Jersey Supreme Court in 1993 was one of the first states in the country to provide detailed guidelines regarding workplace sexual harassment. In that case, *Lehmann v. Toys 'R' Us, Inc.*, 132 N.J. 587 (1993), the court stated, "[t]he most important tool in the prevention of sexual harassment is the education of both employers and employees." The court provided employers guidance on how to prevent sexual harassment claims: "In light of the known prevalence of sexual harassment, a plaintiff [employee] may show that an employer was negligent by its failure to have in place well-publicized and enforced anti-harassment policies, effective formal and informal complaint structures, training, and/or monitoring mechanisms." Unfortunately, little changed during the next five years, except the increase in the number of sexual harassment complaints.

TABLE 6.1   Sexual harassment charges filed with EEOC,
1990–1999

	Number	Percent filed by Males	Damages (millions)
1990	6,127	8.0	$7.7
1991	6,883	8.0	$7.1
1992	10,532	9.1	$12.7
1993	11,908	9.1	$25.1
1994	14,420	9.9	$22.5
1995	15,459	9.9	$24.3
1996	15,342	10.0	$27.8
1997	15,889	11.6	$49.5
1998	15,618	12.9	$34.3
1999	15,222	12.1	$50.3

SOURCE: www.eeoc.gov/stats/harass.html (updated annually).

All employees, independent contractors, partners, and executives need to understand their responsibility with respect to sexual harassment in the workplace. Every citizen pays for the inappropriate behavior, charges of unlawful conduct, the investigation of the complaints, and astronomical damage awards through higher taxes, increased consumer costs, poor productivity, and individual damage.

Sexual Harassment Defined

What is sexual harassment? We read and hear about it on a regular basis in the news and elsewhere. We know sexual harassment exists. Have you ever given much thought to what is sexual harassment? The courts have ruled that there are two types of sexual harassment. The first is quid pro quo sexual harassment. This type of unlawful behavior occurs when a manager, director, or someone in a position of authority who has the ability to affect the employment relationship makes sexual behavior or sexual conduct an explicit or implicit term or condition of employment. For example, when job benefits are promised or withheld in exchange for or in an attempt to gain sexual favors, unlawful sexual harassment has occurred.

The second type of sexual harassment, which we hear more about, is the hostile work environment. The courts have defined this unlawful behavior as unwanted or unwelcome sexual conduct that is severe or pervasive and that a reasonable person would determine creates an uncomfortable work environment. For example, such conduct includes sexual advances, innuendos, derogatory sexual comments or jokes, or touching.

When a complaint of sexual harassment is filed, the allegations are viewed from the perspective of the gender of the plaintiff (or complainant), though a standard of "reasonableness" applies. Accordingly, if a female files the complaint, the allegations are viewed from the perspective of the reasonable female. If a male files, the allegations are considered from the viewpoint of the reasonable male. What perspective is "reasonable" is determined by the jury, and in most cases each juror can identify with the plaintiff , either through personal experience or that of a relative or friend. This personal understanding of disrespect and abuse of power has precipitated the enormous jury awards.

Most individuals are under the false impression that the person who is the object of sexual harassment must inform the alleged harasser that his or her behavior is offensive or unwelcome before a complaint of sexual harassment can be filed. Nothing could be further from the truth. The courts operate on the premise that each person has the responsibility to treat all persons with courtesy and respect and that no one has the obligation to educate others about their behavior. This assumption of a prior warning is also inaccurate because a person does not need to be the target of sexual harassment in order to file a complaint. For example, assume you and I get together everyday to exchange sexual and promiscuous jokes; neither of us is offended. However, Joe and Mary, who work in the next cubicle, overhear our conversations, and both are very offended by our jokes. Both Joe and Mary may file a sexual harassment complaint.

Many employees become angry when they learn about the far-reaching effects of sexual harassment. However, therein lies the answer—workplace sexual harassment has far-reaching effects. These same employees respond that Joe and Mary shouldn't be so sensitive or should get up and move or wear earplugs. Again, the emphasis is misplaced. The focus needs to be on the individuals engaging in the non-work-related offensive conduct, not on the persons seeking to fulfill their job responsibilities. Another common complaint from employees as a result of the proliferation of sexual harassment lawsuits is, "I can't open my mouth in the workplace today for fear of getting sued, or I should quit my job and become a monk." However, there is still much to talk about in the workplace without the concern of offending another individual or buying a lawsuit. For example, a male coworker tells a female coworker that she "looks nice." Is there anything wrong with that statement? Unanimously, the management and nonmanagement employees I have educated have stated that on a scale of 1 to 5, 1 being defined as definitely not sexual harassment, have rated this statement as a 1. Here's another example: A male supervisor tells a female subordinate that she "looks attractive." Again, unani-

mously the rating has been a 1 or 2. I can't say it enough: The key to any successful relationship is common courtesy and respect.

Sexual harassment often is difficult to define because we all come from different backgrounds, have different life experiences, and have different interpretations of behavior. Therefore, the heightened awareness of how my behavior may impact upon another individual is even more critical in the area of
sexual harassment. For example, some individuals come from a background
where they communicate through touching. However, other persons are very
offended by any type of touching. Again, the common denominator must be
what is in the best interest of the *other* person, or how can I communicate so
the *other* person can receive my message? Stated another way, am I treating
others the way I desire to be treated? These simple and basic values keep you
respectful of the other person's needs.

The courts recognize that we are human beings and therefore make mistakes.
Accordingly, in most instances, a one-time incident of unwelcome behavior of a
sexual nature will not constitute sexual harassment, unless that one-time incident is outrageous and severe. In general, the courts and administrative agencies
look to whether there is a pattern or practice of unwelcome sexual conduct that
makes the workplace hostile or uncomfortable. No one fact or number of incidents is key; rather the courts and administrative agencies consider all the circumstances in determining whether sexual harassment existed.

Communication again plays a key role in preventing an uncomfortable
work environment. It will always serve the individual and the organization
well to inform the alleged harasser or the individual's supervisor or someone
else in management of the offensive conduct in order to make clear that the
behavior is not acceptable and corrective action is needed. In addition, the
person filing the complaint of sexual harassment has the burden of proving
the alleged unlawful conduct. Therefore, if you have made someone in management aware that certain behavior is offensive and the conduct continues,
the sexual harassment charge becomes more egregious because the opportunity to cure the situation has been given and ignored.

A common question raised by employees is how many of the sexual harassment complaints filed have no merit. Unfortunately, there are no statistics to
provide an answer, but because human nature is imperfect, the number of frivolous complaints is sizable. The realistic concern of thwarting groundless claims
needs to be paramount by ensuring that employees are properly trained and
that all complaints be taken seriously, investigated immediately, and, when necessary, a remedy provided. Anyone found to have filed a false claim of harassment has violated the basis of the employment relationship and should be im-

mediately discharged. Because sexual harassment complaints often involve one person's word against another's, proving falsity of the charge is difficult. False claims have a devastating impact upon the alleged harassers, their family members, and coworkers. In situations where individuals have been wrongly accused, they are greatly disadvantaged in trying to disprove something that never transpired. Because it is next to impossible to disprove a negative, those falsely accused are usually unable to clear their name and reputation. The fear of a revengeful complaint sends a powerful distrusting message rippling through the organization, leaving everyone wondering whether coworkers or superiors are who they represent themselves to be or can be trusted.

A growing and difficult area of sexual harassment law involves determining whether the conduct was consensual or unwelcome. These cases fall into two categories. In the first type, a group of employees gather during lunch hour and regularly exchange sexual comments and innuendos. Everyone participates in these conversations. If one employee decides to file a complaint of sexual harassment, the individual must show that the very conduct he or she was actively engaging in was unwelcome. In most circumstances, the courts deny the claim based on the determination that the behavior was welcome. In contrast, assume the employees gather at lunch and only one employee is making the statements, but everyone is laughing at them. In that situation, the courts have held that the teller of sexual jokes engaged in unlawful sexual harassment because mere laughter is generally not considered active participation.

If peer pressure is bad in children, it is worse in adults. People laugh because they are uncomfortable, they do not know what to do, or they do not desire to stand out, so they go along with the group. The moral is that laughter does not necessarily indicate that others are in agreement with or enjoying the behavior. Although some employees maintain that it is unfair to hold them to an unrealistic and conflicting standard when they have no basis for knowing that their actions are being interpreted as harassing, most people understand what is acceptable and unacceptable workplace behavior. The fact that they have engaged in conduct that is not work-related and is disrespectful makes them accountable for their decisions. Keep in mind that sexual harassment is not limited to the telling of jokes or other verbal exchanges. Rather, sexual harassment can take a variety of forms, including touching, pinching, repeatedly brushing against another's body, patting, grabbing, written words, and pictures.

The lunchroom scenario raises another important dimension of sexual harassment. Employees are on their own time, but they are still on the employer's premises and therefore must behave accordingly or pay the consequences. A similar situation exists when employees hang pornographic materials in the lockers provided by the employer to store the employees' property. Two questions: First, can pictures alone be found to be sexually harassing? Yes, pictures, without any other action, have been found to constitute sexual harassment. Second, are the lockers personal and private to the individual employee? No, the employer owns the lockers, and the lockers are part of the work environment. Many employees insist they can bring to work whatever they desire. They believe any restriction on this personal liberty is a denial of their freedom of speech. However, the simple question takes us back to basics: Why does one go to work? Stated another way, on what basis is a paycheck earned? Even more to the point, why would you bring something to work that you know may be offensive to others? Again, courtesy and respect need to be taught, practiced, and modeled.

Another frequent area of sexually harassing behavior occurs at the annual holiday party when the mood is festive and the alcohol is flowing. Even though this event is held away from the workplace, the employer has sponsored the event for the employees' benefit. Therefore, the rules of the workplace control. Similarly, the law of the employment relationship also governs the employer-sponsored baseball, bowling, or similar leagues or activities.

Some employees assert that it is unrealistic to expect such good behavior in the workplace when we are constantly exposed and in fact bombarded by such sexual acts and contamination outside of the work environment. Again, people have free will and the ability to choose what type of environment they will expose themselves and their family to and how they will treat others. If your choice is to watch pornographic films and bring what you have seen into the workplace, you may also elect to lose your employment opportunity. Your enjoyment of pornography does not mean that others desire to participate in the same entertainment. Accepting and respecting people's differences and the purpose of the workplace are essential in maintaining a healthy employment relationship. The facts remain the same: Why are you being paid, and what commitment did you make at the time you accepted the employment offer?

An example of liability involved an employee who tried to interrelate his personal interests with those of the workplace when he placed a pornographic photo (which was more offensive to men than it was to women) on top of his toolbox. When the employer received complaints from the employee's coworkers, the employer responded that it could do nothing because the employee owned the toolbox and he needed his tools to perform his essential job functions. The coworkers filed a sexual harassment complaint. The court found the employer and employee liable on the basis that the pornographic photograph constituted sexual harassment and that when the toolbox came into the workplace it was transformed and became part of the work environment.

The second category of cases involving the issue of whether conduct is consensual versus unwelcome encompasses some of the ugliest claims because they delve into the personal lives of the parties and the human tragedy that often strikes others as well. These cases involve workplace dating. Although workplace dating has caused many casualties, statistics reveal that the majority of marriages began with workplace romances. When I ask participants at my seminars whether it is sexual harassment for a male supervisor to ask a female subordinate for a date, the majority respond that it could be, but more information is needed. Managers and supervisors must recognize that they stand in a position of authority with the ability to affect the employment relationship of a subordinate and that their actions can be misconstrued. To safeguard against these types of lawsuits, some employers have implemented formal antidating policies, while the majority of employers strongly and unofficially recommend the same. An even greater number of employers have issued a dress code policy as a result of the increasing number of sexual harassment complaints.

Managers and supervisors are held to a higher standard regarding their behavior toward a subordinate in the workplace because of their ability to affect the subordinate's employment conditions and opportunities. This distinction is so important that the United States Supreme Court has mandated employers to train their managers and supervisors about what is sexual harassment and how to respond properly to a sexual harassment complaint. The failure to provide this training may be evidence of the employer's lack of reasonable care in maintaining a healthy and safe work environment and may result in liability. In *Faragher v. City of Boca Raton*, 524 U.S. 775 (1998), the United States Supreme Court held: "Recognition of employer liability when discriminatory misuse of supervisory authority alters the terms and conditions of a victim's employment is underscored by the fact that the employer has a greater opportunity to guard against misconduct by supervisors than by common workers; employers have greater opportunity and incentive to screen them, train them, and monitor their performance."

The courts recognize to a large extent that employers, like the rest of us, have no ability to control or dictate another human being's behavior. Consequently, if employers take reasonable, precautionary steps against sexual harassment by establishing and distributing a sexual harassment policy, instituting an effective complaint procedure, educating employees on what is workplace sexual harassment, investigating employee complaints, and remedying any workplace harassment, there will be no employer liability. In order to motivate employers to be proactive in this extremely sensitive area and reduce the number of workplace harassment cases, the Court in *Faragher* ruled that when there is no tangible employment action, such as loss of a promotion, taken against an employee and the employer has exercised reasonable care to prevent and correct promptly any sexual harassment behavior, if the employee has been unreasonable by failing to take advantage of any preventive or corrective opportunities provided by the employer or to avoid harm, the employer may seek dismissal of the employee's sexual harassment lawsuit.

Employer's Responsibility of Providing Mandatory Training

In addition to managers and supervisors understanding what type of behavior is sexual harassment, equally as important is for them to know how and in what manner to respond to a complaint of sexual harassment. These individuals are on the front line and therefore are usually the first to observe or receive a complaint. Because they speak for and on behalf of the organization, they must be prepared to address that "common problem [of sexual harassment] in the American workplace" by being given the tools to perform their jobs properly. As the next example demonstrates, most employees do not know the legal definition of discrimination or harassment, but they do not like how it feels. And although employees know what discrimination and harassment feels like, they do not know how to respond to these difficult situations. Therefore, employee training is an essential component of doing business.

Most employment laws seek to balance employees' concerns and employers' interests. Not surprisingly, however, employees and employers believe that the law provides them little protection. Typically, the law is not the problem, but rather how individuals treat one another. As in any relationship, communication and respect are key if employers and employees are to work together to resolve their workplace problems.

Dealing with Harassment on the Job

Q.   I believe I am being sexually harassed at work. However, I do not know how to deal with this issue and would appreciate some guidance.
     V. S.

A.   How to deal with sexual harassment is extremely difficult, especially when the attitude flows from the company's top level of management. However, top management often is unaware of the conduct and must be made aware of it.

     If you believe you are being sexually harassed, I recommend you first find out to whom within your organization you can voice your concerns. Discuss with that person the type of treatment you have been receiving and what changes need to be made.

Employers are advised to take these concerns seriously. Understanding and attempting to work with the employee is crucial. If your employer refuses to listen to and work with you, you may voice your problems in a civil complaint. Employers are also advised to educate their managerial and supervisory employees on what their responsibilities are under the sexual harassment law.

Unfortunately, most employees receive little or no training in this area, even though they are charged with administering these laws on a daily basis. Consequently, the lack of education often results in poor employee morale and lawsuits.

The courts have ruled that there are two distinct types of sexual harassment—quid pro quo and hostile work environment. Quid pro quo sexual harassment occurs when an employer (or supervisor) implies or states that if an employee refuses sexual demands, he or she will be terminated, receive unfavorable performance reviews, be passed over for promotions, or suffer other adverse employment consequences. Hostile work environment sexual harassment, by contrast, occurs when an employer, fellow employees, or outside third party harasses an employee because of his or her sex to the point that the working environment becomes "hostile." Because harassment based upon a protected classification (e.g., sex, race, religion) is considered unlawful discrimination, an employee who believes he or she is being treated unfairly may pursue the same options applicable in discrimination cases: file a complaint with the state fair employment practices administrative agency, the state court, or the EEOC.

Companies should have designated individuals to whom disgruntled employees may discuss their concerns. Providing employees the opportunity to be heard and attempting to work with them usually avoids litigation. However, an amicable result cannot always be reached, and the employer needs to document the situation, any action taken, and the reasons for the action.

In deciding how to proceed, ask yourself what in the end you desire to achieve, keeping in mind that in most cases no one wins in litigation.

In addition to training managers and supervisors, employers are well served by training all their employees on what is workplace sexual harassment because an employer's liability is determined to a large extent by the degree of reasonable care the employer exercised in addressing this "common problem in the American workplace." Any one of the following thought processes may cost the organization hundreds of thousands or millions of dollars, and these experiences are well documented: Employees often are unaware that their behavior is offensive or may constitute sexual harassment; employees believe they need to be informed that their behavior is harassing or offensive before a sexual harassment complaint can be filed; employees believe their actions are innocent and do not harm; employees think they can say and do anything they desire without repercussion; employees believe that management does not care or does not take an aggressive stand on such "trivial" matters as sexual harassment.

Would an employer exercise reasonable care by taking preventive steps if the unsafe work condition was a leaking gas pipe, broken glass, handling of dangerous substances, or the removal of toxic waste? Absolutely. The unsafe condition is known, and the solution available. Likewise, sexual harassment in the workplace is an unsafe condition and will not simply disappear on its own. Education against the toxic substance protects the organization and its most valuable assets—individual employees who may be harmed by the conduct or individual employees who may be personally liable because they simply do not know any better.

Unfortunately, the existence of sexual harassment in the workplace gives new dimension to an employer's basic responsibilities. Employers must teach employees how to work together and respect one another. As discussed earlier, without these two essential ingredients, no relationship can exist, let alone survive or be profitable. Approximately 35 percent of the employees who have attended my sexual harassment educational and sensitivity training seminars believe that a male employee leering and gawking at a female coworker is acceptable workplace conduct. However, when asked how it feels to be stared at, everyone said "uncomfortable." Because of the liability attached to these claims, can you as an organization, manager, supervisor, or nonmanagerial employee afford not to be educated in this area of employee relations?

Basic guidelines to protect employees and the organization concerning workplace sexual harassment are simple:

1. Have a written sexual harassment policy and disseminate it annually to all employees.
2. The policy must define sexual harassment and outline an effective complaint procedure.
3. Provide annual training for all current and new management and nonmanagement employees.
4. Address any and all employee concerns regardless of whether an employee may not desire to file a formal complaint.
5. Immediately investigate the complaint, within forty-eight hours of its receipt, no excuses.

6. Should any harassment be found to exist, implement corrective measures. The courts will not accept anything less than the removal of the harassment from the workplace.

7. Monitor the workplace continually. Managers and supervisors must constantly be aware of what is occurring within and around the work environment or employer-sponsored events.

Because job performance often requires employees to interact with persons outside the employment structure, it is easy to understand that sexual harassment liability does not exist solely within the confines of the particular organization or only among its employees. Rather, sexual harassment may occur when employees visit customers or other persons outside the organization or when outside third parties visit the organization. When such behavior occurs off the work site or from an outside third party (for example, a visitor, vendor, employee from a different organization, or independent contractor), employees have the same rights as if they were in their own work environment being harassed by a coworker. Therefore, employers must clearly communicate in their sexual harassment policies and training programs that employees are to inform their supervisor or other management representative, and/or the individual harasser, that the outside party's conduct is unacceptable and that remedial action is needed. Employers have limited ability to take direct action against third-party offenders but usually have some way to communicate to them that their behavior will not be tolerated. These options include educating offenders' employers, refusing to use the services of the offenders or their employers, or denying offenders access to your facility. Organizations that fail to take the necessary steps to address the situation for fear of losing the business relationship often pay more than the value of the business dealings.

In addition to employers being accountable for workplace harassment against their employees by coworkers, superiors, and outsiders, The United States Supreme Court in 2000 declined to review the decision of a lower court that ruled employers may be liable for racial harassment of its independent contractors by the acts of its employees. In *Danco, Inc. and Guiliani v. Wal-Mart*, 178 F.3d 8, 16 (1st Cir. 1999), the court stated:

[t]o make out a hostile work environment claim, the plaintiff must show not only a contractual relationship, but also two further elements: (1) that the plaintiff was exposed to comments, jokes, or acts of a racial nature by the defendant's [employer's] employees; and (2) that the conduct had the purpose or effect of interfering with the plaintiff's work performance or created an intimidating, hostile or

offensive working environment. In addition, the defendant [employer] will ordinarily only be liable for harassment by low-level employees if management level employees knew or should have known about it.

Harassment based upon an individual's membership in a protected group such as race, national origin, age, veteran status, disability, or religion is just as unlawful as sexual harassment. Thus, training of employees should extend beyond sexual harassment to encompass these forms of harassment as well. The legislatures and the courts have told and continue to tell us that we need to learn how to work together. Most of us have no special training on how to get along with people different from us, and because we are so poorly equipped to deal with this vital component of life, we need to learn or the courts will extend liability.

Employee Feels Harassed Because She Won't Pierce

Q. Last week my daughter called to ask my opinion regarding what she felt was harassment. She works as a saleswoman in a jewelry department. The sales manager recently started offering ear piercing for those customers who request it.

My daughter refused to do anything that requires the rendering of a traumatic injury to anyone's body parts, no matter how applied. Her supervisors and other coworkers keep hounding her about her refusal. What recourse does she have?

B. S.

A. Webster's defines "harassment" as "to annoy persistently." The law acknowledges that there are different degrees of harassment. For example, the criminal code of conduct defines certain types of harassment as criminal acts, and depending upon the severity of the behavior, the conduct has varying degrees of punishment. In addition, the civil code of conduct also defines other, lesser forms of behavior as harassment.

With respect to the work environment, there are also different forms of harassment, the most publicized of which is sexual harassment. However, harassment based upon a person's race, religion, national origin, sexual preference, age, disability, veteran status, marital status, or other protected classification is just as illegal as sexual harassment. Illegal harassment is conduct that is unwelcome, severe, or pervasive and creates what a reasonable person would call a hostile work environment.

From what you describe, it is unclear whether your daughter has a genuine religious belief behind her refusal to pierce any person's body part. If this is the situation and she can prove the genuineness of her belief, such behavior by her supervisors and coworkers may constitute unlawful harassment. If she does not fit into one of the protected classifications, her legal recourse is limited.

An employer mandating that employees adhere to the company's policies or insisting that employees perform their essential job functions does not constitute unlawful harassment. Rather, employees at the time they accept a job offer commit to performing the job duties to the best of their ability. Employees who disagree with the job responsibilities or do not want to perform in the manner expected by the employer have the option of seeking another job.

Beyond the legal ramifications, no one has the moral right to disrespect another human being. Perhaps it may be in your daughter's best interest to tell her supervisor or another person in management that she does not care for how she is being treated and seek a resolution.

The course material for sexual harassment education must be delivered in a uniform manner to avoid a legal challenge by plaintiffs' attorneys who are increasingly creative in seeking to invalidate an employer's policy and training. The current trend in such litigation is to employ an expert on sexual harassment training to evaluate the course material provided to employees for inconsistencies in content, presentation, implementation, and investigation and for insufficient information and inaccurate representation. To combat this legal strategy, the employer should ensure that its sexual harassment trainer has impeccable credentials in the areas of experience, education, and reputation.

This training is critical for several reasons. First, employees must be taught by a person well educated in the field so that they receive accurate and complete information. Second, real-life examples of what conduct is and is not sexual harassment must be contrasted to show the differences and range of inappropriate workplace behavior. Third, employees must be given the opportunity to ask questions of someone equipped to provide answers. Fourth, the consequences of unlawful sexual harassment must be clearly and specifically explained concerning the harm it causes the victim, the organization, and the harasser. Failure to provide these safeguards has left many employers liable on the finding that their training was insufficient to meet their legal obligation to educate their employees.

Most American workers have completed their formal schooling by the time they enter the job market. Accordingly, the workplace is the only forum available to provide compulsory education. Because the courts are expanding liability for workplace sexual harassment, employers and employees must be proactive in this area in order to safeguard the organization and its most valuable assets—its employees.

The courts also are imposing liability for sexual harassment on educational institutions. The United States Supreme Court in *Davis v. Monroe Organization Board of Education et al.*, 526 U.S. 629 (1999), held school boards liable for student-on-student sexual harassment in specific instances. The EEOC issued "Sexual Harassment Guidelines for Educational Institutions" to address student-on-student sexual harassment as well as student harassment of school employees or third parties. The EEOC identified three steps that educational facilities not currently in compliance must implement: First, institutions must create an employee sexual harassment policy that defines sexual harassment and what steps are to be followed should employees believe they are being sexually harassed; this policy would also address teacher-student sexual harassment. Second, institutions must establish a student-on-student sexual harassment policy that gives clear guidelines for educators and staff. Third, the policies must be implemented by training all personnel. Preferably, all students would also be given formal education on this important subject matter so that they will be well equipped should this inevitable behavior touch their lives.

In *Davis,* the Court noted that teachers occupy a special role in student development: "The maintenance of discipline in the schools requires not only that students be restrained from assaulting one another, abusing drugs and alcohol, and committing other crimes, but also that students conform themselves to the standards of conduct prescribed by school authorities." This language mandates that school authorities impose a standard of conduct that includes providing an environment free of sexual harassment, similar to the standard imposed upon private and public employers.

The Court concluded in *Davis* that recipients of federal education funding are properly held liable in damages only when they are deliberately indifferent to sexual harassment, of which they have actual knowledge, that is so severe, pervasive, and objectively offensive that it can be said to deprive the victims of access to the educational opportunities or benefits provided by the school. The Court focused on the control issue in the academic setting:

> In these circumstances, the recipient retains substantial control over the context in which the harassment occurs. More importantly, however, in this setting the Board exercises significant control over the harasser. We have observed, for example, 'that the nature of [the State's] power [over public school children] is

custodial and tutelary, permitting a degree of supervision and control that could not be exercised over free adults.'. . . *The ability to control and influence behavior exists to an even greater extent in the classroom than in the workplace* (emphasis added).

As more lawsuits are filed against school boards, the academic curriculum will soon include such topics as harassment and diversity.

Conducting an Investigation

In medicine, the first person requested to remedy the situation is the doctor. In the same manner, the first person sought out by the complainant to assist in remedying workplace sexual harassment is the supervisor. If the sexual harassment complaint is handled properly, the complaining employee will not file a lawsuit, and employees will be aware of what the employer will and will not tolerate. This result will lead to a workplace environment free of tension between employees and management. Too often employees' chief complaint concerning management is its failure to respond to employees' concerns. In the area of sexual harassment, failure to respond will result in a lawsuit.

Knowing when sexual harassment occurs and how to process the complaint internally will determine to a large extent the outcome of any future litigation. In today's litigious society, employees sue not only their employers but also their managers and supervisors because of their ability to affect the employment relationship and workplace environment. This means that each manager and supervisor is a potential litigant in a sexual harassment complaint. If you use the tools in this book today, you can prevent the litigation of tomorrow. Therefore, it is crucial for supervisors to know how to conduct a proper investigation and for employees to be aware of what they can reasonably expect in an investigation.

A key factor courts examine in determining liability of an organization and its representatives is the immediacy of the investigation. The closer in time an organization responds to a claim of sexual harassment, the more likely the chance of avoiding liability, since the employer is viewed as having fulfilled one of its primary duties by conducting a timely investigation.

Proper documentation is essential in conducting an investigation. The documentation created is not prepared ultimately for the organization but rather for the plaintiff's attorney, the judge, and the jury. Because the investigation and documentation can prevent liability or determine large jury awards, many organizations are retaining outside firms experienced in these matters to conduct the investigation. The retention of a neutral third party serves several benefits. First, the employer ensures itself that the investigation will be handled promptly, consistently, and competently. Second, employees view outside investigators favorably because they are perceived to be nonbiased; employees have less fear of retaliation; and there is a sense that confidentiality will be maintained because the investigator is not present daily in the workplace. Third, having an outside investigation relieves managers and supervisors of this job function, which is a task they usually resent. Consequently, their investigation may not be as thorough or complete as it needs to be, which exposes the employer to liability.

The Fair Credit Reporting Act (FCRA) has been interpreted by the Federal Trade Commission (FTC) to apply to investigations by third parties of workplace misconduct, including investigations of sexual harassment. Consequently, the FTC requires strict compliance with the FCRA. Under the FCRA, with limited exceptions, the employer must obtain the report subject's consent before procuring an investigative consumer report, and the employer must provide the employee a copy of the investigation report prior to an adverse action. Both the American Bar Association and the Society for Human Resource Management have opposed the FTC's interpretation of the FCRA. Amendment of the FCRA legislation is now before Congress.

When employers receive a complaint of sexual harassment, they must respond to the situation, not react. Certain actions are not advisable, such as transferring the complainant to another work station or position. Such conduct has been held to constitute unlawful retaliation. Rather, upon receipt of a harassment complaint, managers or supervisors should, if possible, stop what they are doing and take the time to meet privately with the complaining employee. If meeting immediately is not possible, schedule a mutually convenient time within the next twenty-four hours.

When conferring with employees in these situations, ask open-ended questions such as who, what, where, when, and how. Get such a complete description of employees' complaints that by the end of the meeting you feel as if you were present during the complained-of conduct. Take detailed notes during the meeting and obtain specific quotes as to what was said and what occurred. Ask if there were any witnesses. Find out what action employees desire the employer to take. The more information you receive, the better you and the organization will be able to respond to these sensitive situations.

Near the conclusion of the meeting, repeat back to employees your understanding as to what they have reported to you. Then document in your notes that you reiterated to them your understanding of the situation and they informed you your understanding was accurate or you made the necessary changes. Inform employees that everything you have discussed is confidential and that they are not to discuss the matter with other employees, that the matter will be immediately investigated, and that if they have any further problems or need anything, to come see you immediately. Employees often request that no one be made aware of a complaint or at the very least that the alleged harasser not be informed of who complained, but you cannot give such a guarantee. You can, however, represent that the matter will be kept as confidential as possible.

At the conclusion of the meeting, give employees a copy of the employer's sexual harassment policy and note this fact in your documentation. The purpose of again distributing a copy of the policy is to support employees further so that if they have additional questions or concerns they may also consult the official policy. Provide employees reassurance and be empathetic. Employees need to know that they are supported by the organization. It is not your role to make a conclusion or form an opinion at this point as to whether sexual harassment occurred. Rather, your responsibility is to gather all of the necessary data so an informed assessment can be made.

Managers and supervisors charged with investigation responsibilities usually have many questions about the employee meeting. For example, can another management representative be present when I meet the employee so that I can protect the organization and myself by ensuring I get all the pertinent information? Having another person present raises several concerns. First, complaining employees have come to you in most circumstances because they are comfortable speaking with you. Generally, people speak more freely and openly one-on-one, especially when discussing such a sensitive topic as sexual harassment. Second, you may be inviting to the meeting the very person with whom there exists the problem, either directly or indirectly. Even if you tell employees in advance that you'd like to have a certain person participate in the session, placing your interest over theirs may greatly reduce the amount or type of information you receive, thereby unnecessarily prejudicing the investigation.

Can I tape-record the meeting? Again, people speak more freely and openly when they can engage in a personal conversation without any electronic devices. The addition of a recording device often creates an unnecessary tension that may inhibit employees and consequently block the flow of information. Remember, the investigation will be based on your understanding of the situation. If you need more information or you have additional questions, you may simply meet with an individual again. Regardless of who eventually conducts the investigation, such as human resources or an outside investigator, each management employee must be prepared to participate in this initial phase of gathering the pertinent facts.

Should I have complainants read the notes I have taken and sign the document? There are two schools of thought here. The first group believes that the investigation takes shape based upon the employer's understanding of what transpired as set forth in these initial notes. Determination of whether the employer acted reasonably in conducting the investigation is also based upon these notes. Therefore, having complaining employees read and sign the notes may be immaterial, since the employer's perspective of how it responded and why it acted in a certain manner governs the investigation and, if applicable, the remedy imposed. As a precautionary measure, this group advocates repeating to complainants the employer's understanding as to what has been communicated during the meeting and noting the same in the documentation. This group questions that complaining employees can read the supervisor's handwritten notes. Most of us have difficulty reading our own penmanship, especially when we are writing quickly in an attempt to record all the data or when using personal shorthand, so we shouldn't require others who may be completely unfamiliar with our handwriting and who are experiencing stress and tension to figure out what has been written. In addition, most persons feel uncomfortable signing something they have not prepared or have had no opportunity to revise or place in their own words.

The second group believes it is important to have complaining employees sign the document so they cannot later recount a different version of events. In addition, a signature adds credence to the validity of the complaint in that employees will think twice about filing a false complaint if they are required to sign the initial investigation notes. Moreover, it ensures that all the pertinent details have been made part of the lead investigation document.

An alternative to both positions may be to ask complaining employees to prepare a written statement and sign it. However, this request cannot be a mandate, nor may it be a substitute for the employer's responsibility to obtain the information. If you ask employees to prepare a written statement, advise them you need it within the next day or two, the sooner the better, because you will immediately begin to investigate the matter.

Can I have employees who are complaining of sexual harassment write everything down and then schedule a time to meet when they finish the report? The courts have ruled that the employer, not the employee, has the obligation to immediately conduct an investigation as to what occurred. This responsibility cannot be delegated. To wait and meet with employees after they have made a written report may be too late. In addition, employees might not think of all the necessary information to include on the report. Again, a personal one-on-one meeting is the recommended course of action.

It cannot be stressed enough that documentation is the key component in the investigation. In keeping with that theme, at the end of the meeting with the employee, as well as all future meetings with anyone interviewed as part of the investigation, immediately rewrite your notes. This practice serves several purposes. First, most of us are incapable of recording everything verbatim. Rewriting your notes immediately, or within a relatively short time thereafter, will help you to recall and record other details discussed during the meeting, thereby creating a better document and consequently a more thorough and accurate investigation. Your notes are the linchpin of the investigation and therefore must be as detailed and specific as possible.

The next persons to be interviewed are any witnesses. In meeting with witnesses, it is crucial to make them aware of the confidentiality of the situation. A certain amount of detail must be revealed in order to solicit the desired information, but you must divulge *only* those particulars that are necessary. As with complainants, ask open-ended questions to get a feel for the work environment, the general work history of the department, or section in question and make other similar inquiries to gain perspective on how the employees work and interact.

In speaking with other management representatives, do not discuss the fact that a sexual harassment complaint has been filed or the details of the complaint. Respect in a relationship includes respecting confidentiality. I have received far too many complaints concerning how often supervisors talk among themselves about the personal matters of their subordinates that were disclosed on a confidential basis. Respect is required at every turn, no excuses accepted. Breach of confidences breeds disrespect for the gossiper.

At the end of your meeting with witnesses, reiterate your understanding of their knowledge and rewrite your notes. If you later learn that an employee has disclosed details discussed during the meeting—for example, only you and that employee possessed the information—such conduct constitutes insubordination and should be disciplined accordingly. Failure to take an aggressive stance in protecting the integrity of the process will erode employees' confidence in using the complaint procedure.

You speak with alleged harassers last so that you are armed with as much information as possible before the meeting. Undoubtedly, alleged harassers will have many questions as well, so you need to be prepared. However, you need to take the lead and ask the questions; at this point in the process you are not there to answer questions. That time will come later, if necessary. These background data are also critical so that you know what questions to ask and can see the truth or falsity of the information you possess. If alleged harassers become hostile or angry and refuse to speak with you, advise them that it is in everyone's best interest to have a full and accurate understanding as to what transpired, for if they refuse to speak with you, you must reluctantly conclude that the allegations are true because nothing has been offered to the contrary. Inform these individuals that you are not there to judge; you simply desire to know the facts and are in the process of seeking all pertinent details. Never accuse these individuals of having committed any wrong. Again, your role is as fact-finder. After the necessary data have been gathered, then the conclusions can be made. If they say they will not speak with you without their lawyer present, you may inform them that no attorneys are invited into the employment relationship. This matter involves the employer and its employees.

As you did for complaining employees, give alleged harassers a copy of the organization's sexual harassment policy. Keep in mind that these individuals also have rights, and the rights of both parties must be taken into consideration and evaluated at all times so as not to intrude upon anyone's rights. This challenge is a true balancing act. At the conclusion of the meeting, advise these individuals of their confidentiality obligations. Reiterate what you have discussed to ensure you have an accurate understanding, and rewrite your notes as close in time to the meeting as possible, preferably immediately afterward.

After all known persons possessing firsthand personal knowledge regarding the allegations of sexual harassment have been interviewed, it is time to review all the documentation that has been assembled as part of the investigation and make a determination based upon this information as to whether sexual harassment occurred. In evaluating this information, it is advisable to make findings of fact from the data gathered. This process will force you to review all of the information gathered and often will lead to the conclusion naturally. In assessing the specific details, never lose sight of the obvious information, such as where the alleged act of sexual harassment occurred, the size of the room, the time of day of its occurrence, and the ability of others not named as witnesses to hear or see. All of these details add credence to the truth or falsity of the claim, and in those difficult "he said, she said" situations, may give the ultimate answers.

Careful review of the facts will lead to a well-founded determination of whether sexual harassment occurred. Because you will need to work with one or two other trusted management representatives throughout this process in getting their feedback and thoughts, it is important that the final decision concerning sexual harassment also be made collectively. Again, old adages have stood the test of time because they provide assistance—"two heads are better than one."

After the decision has been made concerning whether sexual harassment occurred and, if necessary, what disciplinary action needs to be imposed to remedy the situation and to prevent any further occurrence, the decision needs to be communicated to the complainant and alleged harasser. I cannot emphasize the importance of this closure enough. Each party needs to know how life will be going forward. Accordingly, the employer must provide direction. It is advisable to meet individually with the complainant and alleged harasser and advise each of the employer's determination and general basis for its action. This decision should also be confirmed in a short memorandum to each employee. It is not required or recommended to inform witnesses of the employer's decision, as their role was limited to furnishing information. The employer's decision is to be and remain confidential, and all documentation must also be maintained in a confidential manner.

As with other life experiences, it is best to prevent a problem before it occurs. In the case of sexual harassment, the Supreme Court has made it clear that employee training is not only a reasonable preventive step but is mandatory for all supervisory employees. Once this training is in place, management knows what to look for and how to correct inappropriate workplace conduct. These educational programs present the opportunity to all employees to use and improve upon their communication and empathy abilities. These characteristics will serve the employer and its employees well not only in the context of preventing sexual harassment but also in complying with the Americans with Disabilities Act (ADA), which I discuss in the next chapter. Because of the numerous types of disabilities and an employer's affirmative obligations under the ADA, what you have learned in this chapter gives you a strong foundation for understanding the ADA.

seven

The Americans with Disabilities Act

The Americans with Disabilities Act (ADA) was enacted in 1990 to assist 43 million Americans who are disabled. The ADA applies to covered entities such as employers and labor organizations; government services and programs; owners, tenants, and operators of commercial facilities and places of public accommodation; and providers of telecommunications. In this chapter I define the basic terms of the ADA and explain, in the context of the employment setting, the protections the ADA provides, why the law was passed, what conduct is prohibited, what affirmative obligations are imposed on employees and employers, and the practical application of the law's stringent requirements. Included are examples of typical workplace situations that show how the law applies and highlight the types of claims filed and disabilities most often cited in litigation.

Many of us fortunately are able-bodied and able-minded. Consider, though, the following scenario: While you are walking to your car after work or walking home from a friend's house, an out-of-control car jumps the sidewalk and hits and throws you 100 feet. You survive but with permanent injuries, including the loss of your ability to walk and use of your writing hand. Now the ADA has meaning in your life. Everyone—able-bodied or disabled—needs to have respect for the differences, abilities, and feelings of others. We may look different on the outside, but we're very much the same on the inside.

The ADA, unlike any other employment law, is proactive because it forces applicants, employees, and employers to talk, work together, seek solutions, look at differences, accept differences, and produce extraordinary results. A disabled individual may perform a job differently from someone able-bodied, but if the desired result is or can be achieved, the law prohibits employment discrimination.

Not all physical and mental differences are classified as disabilities. In addition to the ADA regulations defining what the law does not protect, the courts have given guidance in this area. In this chapter I describe the legal threshold to receive protection under the ADA, areas that clearly are not granted security, and questions still to be answered by the courts. As with any well-intentioned remedy, abuses of the ADA exist. The day the ADA was signed into law, a disability activist group filed a lawsuit against the Empire State Building because of its alleged nonaccessibility to disabled people. Therefore, I also address misunderstandings about the ADA and provide an outline of what to watch for concerning potential abuses of the law's protections and how to defend against such claims.

Compliance with the ADA will require many people to review and evaluate their current practices, and in some cases, to make changes. Reflection and change can be debilitating or rejuvenating, depending upon an individual's perceptions. The discussion here should assist you in easing that process and provide insight on how to enhance employment relationships, customer relationships, employee opportunities, and organizational profits.

The employment laws are designed to serve each working citizen. These laws are viewed from the perspective of those for whom the particular law was enacted to protect. The following example examines the ADA from a disabled person's perspective.   •

Depression May Have Led to Firing

Q. I had been working for an employer and was unceremoniously laid off. The reason I was given was for a change in personnel. The new general manager was recently promoted from sales manager. As a sales manager, he interviewed me for a possible position as a sales assistant. It would have been a promotion. During the interview, he asked me why I had so many sick days (not above the allotted amount). I responded that I suffered from depression, which caused me to miss so many days. I informed him that I had a change in medication recently and was feeling much better. I responded that I would not miss work and would give a 100-percent commitment to the position.

Well, a few weeks went by, and he hired an outsider for the sales position. I approached him to ask him why I was not promoted into the position, and he would not give me an answer. A few weeks later, I was terminated. I feel I was dismissed because I revealed to the general manager that I suffered from a mental illness. Do you think I have a case against this company?

R. P.

A.   The Americans with Disabilities Act (ADA) and state law prohibit employers from discriminating against applicants or employees in hiring, compensation, training, promotions, benefits, discharge, or any other term or condition of employment because of an individual's disability.

A disability includes any physical or mental impairment that substantially limits one or more of an individual's major life activities. A mental impairment includes any psychological disorder such as emotional illness, organic brain syndrome, and specific learning disabilities. Major life activities include caring for oneself, performing manual tasks, walking, seeing, hearing, speaking, learning, and working.

From what you describe, you are protected by the ADA and state law. However, the fact that you are protected does not necessarily mean that you have a claim against the company. To substantiate a legal action against the employer, you have the burden of proving that you were denied the promotion or that your employment was terminated because of your disability.

Your employer took two independent actions regarding your employment status—the potential promotion and the employment termination. As for the promotion, you must ascertain whether you were qualified for the position and the reasons the other individual was hired. If the other individual was more qualified than you for the sales assistant position, then the employer had a legitimate business reason for its decision that was unrelated to your disability, and its actions were lawful. If your depression was the reason for the decision, then your employer's conduct would be in violation of the ADA and state law.

Use a similar analysis to determine the reason for your employment termination. For example, if you were laid off because of economic reasons or fired because of poor job performance, then the employer had a legitimate business reason for its decision and consequently did not act contrary to your rights. On the other hand, if its action occurred because of your disability or some fear associated with your condition, then you would have a claim against the company.

To decide how to proceed, you need to gather more information and honestly review all the facts surrounding the company's decisions before you can properly and fully assess whether you have a claim against the company.

Empathy

A first step in ADA compliance is for employers to take affirmative action in overcoming and eliminating any negative attitudes toward disabilities in the workplace. Empathy is a valued and admired quality because of the wisdom and insight it provides. For example, if you are one of the fortunate nondisabled Americans and therefore cannot truly understand what it is like to be disabled, close your eyes and bring to mind how you felt when you broke your arm, sprained your ankle, lost your glasses, or had shampoo in your eyes and you desired to use both hands, walk without assistance, see where you were going, or find the soap you had dropped. In those simple examples, most of us feel frustrated, anxious, impatient, and without direction. Take the time to recall such an experience. Was it uncomfortable or painful? Did it create a sense of loss, helplessness, fear, or uncertainty? Perhaps it instilled gratitude for your abilities, relief in knowing your condition was not permanent, or ingenuity in finding a new approach to accomplish your goal. For individuals protected by the ADA, their abilities are important, their experiences are permanent, and their method in achieving the desired end must be considered.

To gain perspective on the ADA, practice the following action plan:

1. Step into the shoes of another. "I complained that I had no shoes until I saw the man who had no feet."
2. Respect your own abilities.
3. Respect others' abilities.
4. Be a role model for common courtesy.
5. Offer assistance to those in need.
6. Accept that tasks can be performed in a variety of ways.
7. Demonstrate understanding.
8. Learn from others.
9. Show how humility breeds success.
10. Invite differences.

During one of my ADA educational seminars, a woman raised her hand and reported the following:

I have worked for this organization for fifteen years. During my entire employment I have always felt left out. It was not until today in hearing your ADA presentation that I feel comfortable to let my coworkers know that I have a hearing loss in my one ear. If people don't speak within the range of my good ear, I don't hear them. I believe I have been perceived as standoffish or that I don't want to do my share of the work. In fact, often I can't hear what has been said or I don't even know that someone is speaking to me. I have felt too embarrassed to say anything about my disability.

The room was silent for several seconds. Someone finally spoke:

I've worked with Sally for many years and never knew she couldn't hear me. I remember several times approaching her from behind and asking her to assist me with a project that had an immediate deadline. Sally never answered me. I just thought that she didn't want to help and that she wasn't a team player.

Someone else spoke:

I always believed Sally thought she was better than the rest of us and didn't want to associate with us. I had no idea she felt lonely and left out or that she would even want to have lunch with anyone who works here.

How often do you judge without having all the pertinent information? I was riding the escalator in Penn Station during evening rush hour when suddenly there was a lot of commotion and shoving. I grabbed the handrail as I started to fall off the escalator step into the person behind me. As I caught myself, the elbow of the man pushing behind me went into my ribs. I saw that a woman who was trying to get on the escalator was blind. I shouted to the man who was pushing, "Sir, sir, the woman is blind!" He stopped pushing. Are you in a hurry too?

We all have heard the stories about people who have abused the protections of the various employment laws. Unfortunately, these people do exist. But why give them an opportunity to abuse you or your organization? In most situations, if you do the right thing every minute of every day, you will not provide them the door through which they need to walk to attack you. For example, shortly after the ADA was enacted, an alleged blind woman with a seeing-eye dog visited local retailers in her neighborhood. She entered the stores with her dog, which was on a five-foot leash, and browsed the aisles. Upon seeing the dog, the store employees approached the woman and informed her that she needed to leave immediately as no dogs were allowed in the store. When she reported that she was blind, they retorted that she did not appear blind and escorted her to the store exit. She returned to the store thirty minutes later with two police officers as her witnesses; this time she had her dog on a harness that is generally associated with seeing-eye dogs. She again reported that she was blind and had a right to bring her seeing-eye dog into the store. As further proof, she showed the store employees an identification card that stated her dog was a trained seeing-eye dog. They still refused her access to the store.

As you might guess, the woman sued the retail stores and their owners. Regardless of the true state of the woman's condition, these lawsuits could have been avoided with some simple steps.

1. Learn your responsibilities under the ADA.
2. Be open.
3. Treat others as you desire to be treated.
4. Investigate before assuming the wrong facts.
5. Seek guidance.
6. Find mutual agreement.
7. Create an inviting atmosphere.
8. Ask questions.
9. Be honest.
10. Be flexible.

Your responsibilities under the ADA depend upon the particular situation. Although this is not the preferred, clear-cut answer, the ADA makes it clear that a blanket rule is not possible because every disability is different and therefore requires different considerations. Not every situation on the surface presents itself as an ADA matter, when in fact it may have ADA implications. Following is such an example, which also shows the importance of the ten steps to avoid an ADA claim.

Nonsmoker May Have Legal Recourse

Q. This letter is in regard to my recent layoff from my position of 13 1/2 years as a secretary. I would appreciate any help you can give me regarding this situation, as I feel I was discriminated against for being a nonsmoker.

The building in which I worked sustained a fire. My boss and I relocated to temporary offices and then our permanent office. After about a day, I realized that the building was a smoking building. I have been in a nonsmoking building for my 13 1/2 years. I brought this to my boss's attention, and all he could say was that he could not move again because he had incurred a lot of expenses with this fire.

I was getting sick every day from the smoke. I could not understand why I was getting the smell of the smoke when I was sitting up in the front of the building all by myself in the reception area, and these smokers were toward the back of the building. It seemed that every time the air conditioner went on, it would pull the smoke and bring it up to the vent that was right above my head. I brought this to my boss's attention, and he said he would talk to the owner of the building. I even went out to get an air purifier and used it, but it did not help. I would spray some deodorant spray just so that I could breathe better. I would come home and cry because I just did not feel well. I also had to pass these smokers whenever I had to go to the ladies room or put postage on mail or run copies.

I then brought a fan from home and started using it. Another employee complained that my peach-smelling deodorant made her sick. The owner of the building told me I had to turn off my fan and get rid of the spray. To make a long story short, my boss laid me off because the owner of the building told him that I would not be able to use my fan or the spray anymore, and he did not want me to get sicker. I feel I was discriminated against because I am a nonsmoker. I only had five more years before I retired. I lost out on a raise and substantial bonus. I became depressed. I still cannot believe I lost my job due to a woman who is not concerned about her health or the health of her tenants. Do I have any legal rights?

G. K.

A.   I commend you on your efforts and positive expenditure of energy in attempting to find solutions to the problem.

The federal Occupational Safety and Health Act (OSHA) requires employers to provide a safe and healthy work environment. It appears that this basic requirement was not met in your case. It also appears that this building has what is commonly referred to as sick-building syndrome in which the ventilation system causes occupants to become sick. In such circumstances the landlord may also have obligations to make certain repairs.

Youe state Supreme Court has held that each employee has a common-law right, in addition to a statutory right, to work in a safe and healthy work environment. In *Shimp v. New Jersey Bell Telephone Co.*, 145 N.J. 516 (1976), the court ordered the employer to eliminate the hazardous workplace conditions that were created when an employee was exposed to her coworkers' secondhand smoke. The court's decision supports your position: "The evidence is clear and overwhelming. Cigarette smoke contaminates and pollutes the air, creating a health hazard not merely to the smoker but to all those around her who must rely upon the same air supply. The right of an individual to risk his or her own health does not include the right to jeopardize the health of those who must remain around him or her in order to properly perform the duties of their jobs. The portion of the population which is especially sensitive to cigarette smoke is so significant that it is reasonable to expect an employer to foresee health consequences and to impose upon him a duty to abate the hazard which causes the discomfort."

In addition, the Americans with Disabilities Act and state law specifically require an employer to reasonably accommodate an employee who is disabled and otherwise qualified for a particular job. Employees who have a breathing condition or severe allergies to smoke have been found to have a disability, and the employer has been ordered to accommodate them so they are not exposed to secondhand smoke. These laws are enforced by the federal Equal Employment Opportunity Commission and the state Division on Civil Rights.

Employees injured as a result of being exposed to secondhand smoke also may file a workers' compensation claim. The state Workers' Compensation Act provides compensation, including medical and monetary relief, for work-related injuries and illnesses.

In addition, your state has a smoking law that requires employers with 50 or more employees who do not have a smoke-free workplace to have a written policy designating smoking and nonsmoking areas in order to respond to the very concerns you describe.

As you can see, you have several options available to you in contacting the various agencies that enforce these laws and the Department of Health or filing a complaint with the state Superior Court. First, consider some primary questions: What are your goals? Do you desire to be re-employed in your former position by taking the necessary steps to file a complaint and begin a lawsuit? Do you want to communicate with and educate your former employer about its obligations in order to resolve the matter amicably. Do you want to seek other employment opportunities? Evaluate what is most important to you, what is in your best interest, and proceed accordingly. You are obviously an intelligent and creative individual, so use your talents to support your goals. Good luck and keep the positive energy flowing.

Disability Defined

The ADA employment section has two essential requirements. First, it prohibits covered employers from discriminating against qualified individuals with a disability in regard to job application procedures, hiring, advancement, discharge, compensation, training, or other terms, conditions, or privileges of employment. Second, the ADA requires covered employers to make reasonable accommodations to the known physical or mental limitations of otherwise qualified individuals with a disability, unless the accommodation would impose an undue hardship on the operation of the employer's business. A covered employer is one who is engaged in an industry that uses or places services or goods into the stream of interstate commerce and who has 15 or more employees for each working day in each of 20 or more calendar weeks in the current or preceding calendar year. Although the ADA does not cover all employees, many states have fair employment laws that contain requirements similar to the ADA's, and they cover all employers in that particular state regardless of size.

The term "qualified individual with a disability" means a person "who with or without reasonable accommodation can perform the essential functions of the job he or she desires or holds." "Disability" means "(1) a physical or mental impairment that substantially limits one or more of the major life activities of such individual; (2) a record of such an impairment; or (3) being regarded as having such an impairment." As you can see, or maybe have experienced, these terms are extremely broad and at times difficult to apply. Accordingly, the ADA places enormous responsibility on an employer that must comply with the law while simultaneously maintaining the organization's interests.

In determining whether an individual is protected by the ADA, each "disability" classification must be evaluated separately. In the first definition, the ADA regulations contain three elements: (1) "physical or mental impairment," (2) "substantially limits," and (3) "major life activities." The ADA regulations define "physical or mental impairment" as "[a]ny physiological disorder, or condition, cosmetic disfigurement, or anatomical loss affecting one or more of the following body systems: neurological, musculoskeletal, special sense organs, respiratory (including speech organs), cardiovascular, reproductive, digestive, genito-urinary, hemic and lymphatic, skin, and endocrine." It also includes "any mental or psychological disorder, such as mental retardation, organic brain syndrome, emotional or mental illness, and specific learning disabilities."

Most temporary conditions such as a pregnancy or broken leg, personal characteristics such as eye or hair color, and personal traits such as poor judgment or quick temper are not considered impairments protected by the ADA. In evaluating whether an individual is disabled, the ADA regulations state that the following factors may be considered in making the determination: "The nature and severity of the impairment, the duration or expected duration of the impairment, and the permanent or long-term impact or result from the impairment."

Next, "substantially limits" means the person is "unable to perform a major life activity that the average person in the general population can perform, or is significantly restricted as to the condition, manner or duration under which an individual can perform a particular major life activity as compared to the condition, manner or duration under which the average person in the general population can perform that same major life activity." "Major life activities" include "caring for oneself, performing manual tasks, walking, seeing, hearing, speaking, breathing, learning and working." When working is the "major life activity" in issue, a special definition of "substantially limits" applies: "Significantly restricted in the ability to perform either a class of jobs or a broad range of jobs in various classes as compared to the average person having comparable training, skills and abilities. The inability to perform a single, particular job does not constitute a substantial limitation in the major life activity of working." Whether an individual's condition substantially limits a major life activity is determined on a case-by-case basis. Therefore, communication is key.

In *Sutton v. United Airlines, Inc.*, 527 U.S. 471 (1999), the United States Supreme Court held that "[t]he determination of whether an individual is disabled should be made with reference to measures that mitigate the individual's impairment, including, in this instance, eyeglasses and contact lenses." The facts in this case involved two job applicants who sought the position of global pilot. They were both severely myopic; each applicant's uncorrected visual acuity was 20/200 or worse in her right eye and 20/400 or worse in her left eye, but with corrective lenses was 20/20 or better. The employer informed the applicants that they did not meet the company's minimum vision requirement of uncorrected visual acuity of 20/100 or better.

The Court stated: "A person whose physical or mental impairment is corrected by medication or other measure does not have an impairment that presently 'substantially limits' a major life activity. To be sure, a person whose physical or mental impairment is corrected by mitigating measures still has an impairment, but if the impairment is corrected it does not 'substantially limi[t]' a major life activity." The Court further noted that there were other positions for which the applicants were qualified, such as regional pilot and pilot instructor.

An example of the second type of disability—"a record of" a physical or mental impairment—is someone who has had a heart attack, cancer, or similar condition. The discrimination usually occurs based on the subjective concern or fear that the impairment will reoccur or that an injury will result based on the prior impairment. Even if the employer has objective evidence that the condition will more than likely reoccur, the ADA prohibits the employer from taking adverse employment action based on the disability. For example, the employee is immensely overweight, smokes, regularly drinks alcohol, does not exercise, has high blood pressure, worries, is anxiety-ridden, and has had a heart attack. He is next in line to be promoted. However, the position to which he would be promoted is highly stressful, and the employer fears the individual would have another heart attack. Does the employer have an obligation to provide the promotion, or does it have an obligation to safeguard the individual, his coworkers, the organization, and its customers and therefore promote someone else to the stressful position? Answer: The ADA prevents the employer from denying the promotion opportunity notwithstanding that the employee has had a heart attack and refuses to take care of himself.

The third type of disability,—"being regarding as having" a physical or mental impairment—is to provide protection to individuals who are "rejected from a job because of the 'myths, fears and stereotypes' associated with disabilities." The United States Supreme Court in *Sutton* stated that "[t]here are two apparent ways in which individuals may fall within this statutory definition: (1) a covered entity [the employer] mistakenly believes that a person has a physical impairment that substantially limits one or more major life activities, or (2) a covered entity mistakenly believes that an actual, nonlimiting impairment substantially limits one or more major life activities." For example, in the *Sutton* case, the applicants argued that the employer's vision requirement was impermissible because the employer mistakenly believed that they were unable to perform the work of global airline pilots due to poor vision and that the belief was based upon myth and stereotype.

Because one type of covered impairment is cosmetic disfigurement, employment decisions made on the basis of a person's facial disfigurement or severe overbite may give rise to an ADA action. The *Sutton* Court stated:

> [b]y its terms, the ADA allows employers to prefer some physical attributes over others and to establish physical criteria. An employer runs afoul of the ADA when it makes an employment decision based on a physical or mental impairment, real or imagined, that is regarded as substantially limiting a major life activity. Accordingly, an employer is free to decide that physical characteristics or medical conditions that do not rise to the level of an impairment—such as one's height, build, or singing voice—are preferable to others, just as it is free to decide that some limiting, but not substantially limiting, impairments make individuals less than ideally suited for a job.

Following are criteria of how the ADA defines "discriminate":

- Limit, segregate, or classify applicants or employees in a way that adversely affects them because of their disability;
- Participate in a contractual or other relationship that subjects a covered employer's applicants or employees with a disability to the discrimination prohibited by the ADA;
- Use standards, criteria, or methods of administration that have the effect of discriminating on the basis of disability or that perpetuate the discrimination of others who are subject to common administrative control;
- Exclude or deny equal jobs or benefits because of the known disability of individuals with whom qualified individuals are known to associate;
- Not make reasonable accommodations when no undue hardship can be demonstrated;
- Use standards, tests, or other selection criteria that screen out or tend to screen out individual with a disability or classes of individuals with disabilities when it cannot be shown that the criteria are job-related or consistent with business necessity;
- Fail to select and administer tests to ensure applicants and employees who have a disability that impairs sensory, manual, or speaking skills that the test results accurately reflect the factors the test purports to measure.

Because there are so many different types of disabilities with varying needs or requirements, it is imperative for the employer and employee to meet and discuss what will achieve everyone's objectives. The courts have consistently made it clear that whether a person has a disability protected by the ADA, and if so, what reasonable accommodation can be made is an individualized inquiry. Failure to have an open conversation about the disability of someone who is otherwise qualified for the position may be costly to both parties. Here is one such example:

Disabilities Require an Open Discussion

Q. I am writing to you for advice to see if my husband was discriminated against and harassed. Sometime in July or August my husband advised his supervisor that in the fall he would have trouble arriving to work on time and that he would have to leave early to be home before dark. We live quite a distance from where my husband worked.

The supervisor advised my husband to bring a note from his doctor and everything would be okay. My husband did this and everything was fine from September to November, when my husband was told to see the company doctor. When my husband went to the company doctor, he put my husband on restricted duty. The duty was permanent and included no night driving. He could work only during daylight hours and had to return home before dusk.

When the supervisor received the company doctor's restriction, the company suspended my husband for one day with no pay because he arrived at work at 9 a.m. He then was suspended for a total of four or five days with no pay because they said he was late for work. They would not let him leave early to be home before dusk. He received a final warning which stated if he was late after the last suspension, he would be fired.

My husband had to stay in a rented room near to his work and was gone from the family six days a week. This was very devastating for all of us. My husband is legally blind. After a month of this arrangement, my husband went out on disability, as he did not want to get fired. My husband has worked for this company for 12 years. Could this company do this with these doctors' orders?

E. P.

A.   The Americans with Disabilities Act (ADA) prohibits employers with 15 or more employees from discriminating against disabled persons who are qualified to perform the essential job functions of the position they desire or hold. When an employer knows that an applicant or employee is disabled, it has the obligation to provide the person a reasonable accommodation if such an accommodation is necessary to enable the individual to perform the essential job duties.

Because of the numerous types of disabilities and jobs, Congress did not define "reasonable accommodation." Rather, it listed examples of different types of employment accommodations, such as job restructuring, part-time or modified work schedules, or acquisition or modification of equipment or devices. An employer, however, is not required to provide a reasonable accommodation if to do so would create an undue hardship on the employer.

To determine what options are available in ascertaining whether a reasonable accommodation can be made, the employer and employee must discuss the different possibilities and their impact on the overall business structure. From what you describe, it does not appear that your husband and his employer had any communications regarding his need or his desire for a reasonable accommodation.

The facts are insufficient for me to say whether your husband may have a claim under the ADA. Note the possibility that his failure to report to work on time because of his driving restrictions would disappear if the family lived closer to his place of employment. The family domicile decision is within your and your husband's control and is not the responsibility of the employer.

Perhaps you and your husband simply desire to have his work schedule changed. How that goal can be accomplished so that he can still perform his job responsibilities needs to be discussed. I suggest that your husband contact the human resources department or upper management to make them aware of the situation. When possible, it is in everyone's best interest to work at reaching a win-win solution.

Employer's Obligations

The ADA protects only qualified individuals with a disability—that is, individuals who, with or without a reasonable accommodation, can perform the essential functions of the job. The employer's judgment is considered in determining which functions of a job are essential. If an employer has prepared a written job description before advertising or interviewing an applicant (see Chapter 3), the EEOC, state civil rights agencies, and courts will give credence to this description as to the position's essential functions. Although the ADA does not require employers to develop or maintain written job descriptions, such documentation is a useful employment tool as a "blueprint" that provides objective guidance during the hiring process and employment relationship and serves as documentary evidence should a discrimination claim be filed.

In preparing written job descriptions, employers should carefully determine which functions of a job are essential. The standards and criteria that should be included in the job description are required education, work experience, physical demands, mental requirements, environmental conditions, safety concerns, skills, licenses or certifications, psychological factors such as judgment, ability to work under pressure, or interpersonal skills and other demands. Applicants and employees must be treated uniformly and fairly and on the basis of their individual merits and not upon preconceived notions relating to the requirements of a job or an individual's ability to perform them. The next example demonstrates the value of properly outlining employer policies and employee responsibilities.

Disabled Employee Unable to Perform Essential Job Functions

Q. Can an employee on workers' compensation be terminated from his or her employment because corporate policy states that the employee must return to work within a specified time period after taking a leave of absence due to a work-related injury or illness?

B.J.K.

A. The state workers' compensation statute does not regulate how long an employer is required to keep open a disabled employee's position. If an employee is not physically, mentally, or emotionally capable of reporting to work and performing the essential job functions expected of him or her, an employer is not obligated to hold the employee's position open indefinitely.

The Americans with Disabilities Act grants protection to a "qualified individual with a disability" and requires employers to provide a disabled person a reasonable accommodation, unless to do so would create an undue burden. A reasonable accommodation may include extending a leave period, if the employer is covered by the law and the employee comes within the definition of disability. Each situation must be examined individually.

Most employers will keep an employee's job open for some minimum duration while the employee is on a leave of absence. However, the employer also has the obligation to its other employees and its customers to maintain its business operations and cannot have an open-ended leave policy.

To determine whether a particular job function is essential, the initial inquiry is whether the employer actually requires employees in the position to perform the function the employer asserts is essential, and if so, whether removal of such a function would fundamentally alter that position. The qualification standards must be job-related and consistent with business necessity. In order to define a job's core requirement, the employer must know why the position exists, how the job fits into the overall company structure, and the end result that is expected to be achieved. Because each individual possesses different abilities or methods to accomplish a specified result, the ADA prohibits employers from discriminating against disabled employees if they can achieve the desired goal but through a different mechanism. In making this determination, an employer may ask about an applicant's or employee's ability to perform the essential job requirements and is prohibited from inquiring into the person's disability.

To have a true understanding of a job for which a description is being prepared and what it entails, place yourself in the shoes of the person required to perform the job functions and work through his or her daily activities. It is advisable to have another person review the job description for a second point of view and clarification. All documentation generated in creating the job description should be destroyed so that only one final product exists. A substantial amount of time and thought is required in order to prepare a thorough and workable job description. However, the benefits support this investment. The job description will assist the employer and employee in defining the parameters of their working relationship, from hiring to compensation to promotion to, if necessary, termination of the relationship.

The second major component of the ADA employment section is the employer's affirmative obligation to provide reasonable accommodation for a known disability, unless to do so would create an undue burden. To determine what constitutes a reasonable accommodation in any particular situation, the employer must have open communications with the applicant or employee, because there is no set definition. Just as the term "disability" is extremely broad with limitless possibilities, so too does "reasonable accommodation" have infinite interpretations.

The ADA provides that a "reasonable accommodation" may include making existing facilities readily accessible; restructuring jobs; arranging part-time or modified work schedules; reassigning a person to a vacant position; acquiring or modifying equipment, modifying examinations, training materials, or policies; and providing qualified readers or interpreters for disabled individuals. The list is not exhaustive or mandatory. Reasonable accommodation also includes physical access to the employer's establishment as well as to locations outside of the work site where the employee may be required to travel on behalf of the employer or in response to an employer-sponsored event. For example, the employer is having a holiday or retirement party at a local restaurant. The gathering will be held on the second floor, but the establishment does not have an elevator. One of the employer's employees is a wheelchair user. Does the employer have an obligation to find another location for the celebration? Is one option to carry the disabled employee up the stairs? Can the employer merely ascertain whether the employee will be at the party, although no other employees must give a definitive answer about attending?

Although the employer may have no control over the restaurant's ADA compliance, it does have the ability to find a restaurant or other location that does comply with the ADA. Yes, the employer must find another location. No, the employer cannot opt for carrying the employee up the stairs. No, the employer cannot require the employee to provide an answer about attending the party. Yes, ADA compliance makes good business sense. Because an employer cannot ensure that all aspects of an outside facility are in ADA compliance, I recommend that an employer entering into a contract for a banquet function designate, in writing, who is responsible for ADA compliance and any resulting liability if there is a violation. The ADA does not specify who is responsible in these situations, nor does it prohibit the parties from designating ADA liability.

As you can see, the employer and employee must determine what accommodation is reasonable based upon the particular facts of each individual case. Therefore, it is useful to view "reasonable accommodation" as intangible and nonthreatening, with the understanding that often there is no "right" answer. This approach will make ADA compliance easier and possible because employers and their managers and supervisors will be able to discuss and identify the various options available. In short, "reasonable accommodation" is a means by which to assist people with disabilities by exploring alternative ways to reach the common end of creating a relationship in which both the employer and employee profit.

An employer's obligation to provide accommodation arises when the employer either knows or should have known of an individual's disability. An employer must provide only a reasonable accommodation, not the best accommodation or even the accommodation requested by the disabled person. However, as a practical matter, it is important to remember that disabled individuals have lived with their disability and therefore have invaluable experience as to how they may best be able to perform the essential job functions. In addition, the employer's efforts to accommodate a reasonable request provides tremendous support for employee morale and for the disabled employees, their coworkers, and their associates. It is never good employee or public relations to be known for not honoring a simple request, let alone requests from disabled individuals that will help them perform their job duties.

Reasonable accommodation does not mean an employer must modify the essential job functions. However, employers may find themselves in a quandary when an employee's performance declines as a result of a disability. Open discussion with employees is a crucial factor in complying with the reasonable-accommodation obligation. The employer, when possible, should reach agreement with disabled individuals and then document the reasonable accommodation or basis for the reasonable-accommodation decision to demonstrate the employer's good-faith effort to comply with the ADA. Disabled individuals should be required to sign the documentation as evidence that they are in agreement with the accommodation furnished. The cost of providing reasonable accommodation cannot be passed on to the disabled individuals. In many situations, experience has shown that a reasonable accommodation can be provided at relatively little expense.

An employer is not required to provide an accommodation if it would impose an undue hardship on the organization. The ADA defines an "undue hardship" as

an action requiring significant difficulty or expense, when considered in light of the following:

1. The nature and cost of the accommodation needed;
2. The overall financial resources of the facility involved;
3. The number of persons employed at the facility;
4. The effect on resources and expenses or the impact the accommodation would have on the operation of the facility;
5. The overall financial resources of the covered entity;
6. The overall size of the covered entity's business with respect to the number of employees;
7. The number, type, and location of the facility;
8. The type of operation of the covered entity, including the composition, structure and functions of the work; and
9. The geographic separateness and administrative or fiscal relationship of the facility in question to the covered entity.

Determining Eligibility

On the issue of whether an individual is physically or mentally able to perform the essential job functions, the ADA is explicit concerning medical examinations, the purpose of such tests, and when they may or may not be conducted. Three basic time periods control whether a medical examination is permissible by an employer and the type of medical examination: preoffer (pre-employment), postoffer (pre-employment), and the employment period. During the preoffer period, or before a job offer is extended, an employer may not require a job applicant to take a medical examination, respond to medical inquiries, discuss the nature or severity of a disability, or provide information about workers' compensation claims. Pre-employment drug or alcohol testing is not considered a medical examination as long as the only information revealed is the use of illegal drugs or alcohol.

During the postoffer period, or after a conditional job offer has been extended but before the applicant has begun to work, the employer may make the job offer conditional on the satisfactory result of a medical examination. However, this medical examination is valid only if all those entering the same job categories are subject to the same requirement, regardless of disability, and the required confidentiality of medical records is observed.

The EEOC, the administrative agency authorized to enforce the ADA employment provisions, has provided extensive guidance on this issue, as set forth in the following publications. In its *Technical Assistance Manual,* the EEOC states that

> [t]hese postoffer medical examinations do not have to be job-related or consistent with business necessity. However, if an employer uses criteria that screen out employees with disabilities as a result of such examinations, the exclusionary criteria must be job-related, consistent with business necessity, and such that performance of the essential job functions cannot be accomplished with reasonable accommodation.

The EEOC in its *ADA Enforcement Guidance: Preemployment Disability-Related Questions and Medical Examinations* provides that

> [a] job offer must be "real" for the employer to be able lawfully to ask disability-related questions or require medical examinations. A job offer is real if the employer has evaluated all relevant non-medical information that it reasonably could have obtained and analyzed before giving the offer. If the employer can show that it could not reasonably obtain and evaluate all non-medical information at the preoffer stage, the offer still would be considered "real." In addition, an offer will be considered "real" if the employer can demonstrate that it needs to give more offers to be able to actually fill vacancies or reasonably anticipated openings.

In its *Technical Assistance Manual,* the EEOC further states that

> [a]n employer must comply with the ADA when removing people from the pool of applicants to fill actual vacancies. It must do this by notifying an individual orally or in writing if his or her placement into an actual vacancy is in any way adversely affected by the results of a postoffer medical examination or disability-

related question. If the individual alleges that a disability affected his or her placement into an actual vacancy, the EEOC will carefully scrutinize whether the disability was a reason for an adverse action. In making this determination, the
EEOC will determine whether the medical examination was job-related and consistent with business necessity.

Also set forth in the *Technical Assistance Manual* is this EEOC provision:

> After an employer has obtained basic medical information from all applicants
> who have been given conditional offers in a job category, it may ask specific in-
> dividuals for more medical information if the follow-up examinations or ques-
> tions are related to the previously obtained information. In certain industries,
> such as air transportation, applicants for security and safety-related positions are
> normally chosen on the basis of many competitive factors, some of which are
> identified as a result of a postoffer preemployment medical examination. It is not
> the ADA's intent to prohibit an employer from choosing an applicant on the ba-
> sis of factors identified as a result of a medical examination conducted after an
> offer of employment has been made, but before the offer has been confirmed,
> provided the results are not used to screen out qualified individuals with disabil-
> ities on the basis of a disability.

During the employment period, or once an individual becomes an employee, different rules apply to when and why the employer may require
medical examinations. The EEOC, in its *Technical Assistance Manual,* states
that

> [u]nder certain circumstances, the ADA permits employers to require medical ex-
> aminations of employees after they begin to work. For instance, under the ADA,
> employers may make inquiries into the ability of an employee to perform job-re-
> lated functions. However, employers may not make inquiries or require a medical
> examination of employees regarding the existence, nature or severity of the em-
> ployee's disability, unless the examination or inquiry is shown to be job-related
> and consistent with business necessity. A medical examination or inquiry may be
> considered job-related and consistent with business necessity under the ADA
> when, for example:
>
> - an employee is having difficulty performing his or her job ef-
>   fectively;
> - an employee who is injured, on or off the job, becomes ill or
>   suffers any other condition that meets the ADA definition of

disability, wishes to return to work, and an examination is necessary to determine whether an accommodation is necessary or whether the individual can perform the essential job functions, with or without accommodation, without posing a health or safety threat that cannot be reduced or eliminated by reasonable accommodation; or

- an employee requests an accommodation, and an examination is necessary to determine whether the employee has a disability covered by the ADA and to identify an effective accommodation.

Worker Fired After Failing Random Alcohol Testing

Q. I am writing in reference to being terminated by my former employer. I voluntarily entered an inpatient alcohol treatment program in October and in February of the following year and completed both programs satisfactorily and returned to work at full status.

I was employed for almost 10 years and was a good employee and always got favorable evaluations. However, due to insurance problems with my outpatient provider, I could not afford to go to all the counseling that I needed. As a result of this, I relapsed and drank a large quantity of alcohol one night in November. I drank until 11 p.m. that night and went to work the next morning at 7 a.m. My name was randomly chosen from the computer for mandatory drug and alcohol testing about 9 a.m. I failed the Breathalyzer and was given an immediate 14-day suspension.

My concern is that I feel I have been discriminated against because other employees have failed the Breathalyzer or drug screen, or both, and were given the chance to go to a rehabilitation program and were not terminated. My contention is that voluntarily going into rehab for alcohol, which the company says is protected, worked against me because if I never would have sought help on my own, then I would have only been suspended for 14 days and asked to go to an alcohol rehab.

According to a book I read about the Americans with Disabilities Act, an employer may not discipline an employee for the same conduct more severely than others have received. I believe that I was disciplined more severely than my fellow employees, and was also discriminated against because the company is in the midst of downsizing its staff and I happen to be a white male who was neither management nor in the union.

J. N.

A. The Americans with Disabilities Act (ADA) prohibits an employer from discriminating against a qualified individual with a disability. Alcoholism is considered a disability under the ADA. However, this prohibition does not limit an employer's right to require employees not to be under the influence of alcohol at the workplace.

In fact, the ADA further states that an employer may hold an employee who is an alcoholic to the same qualification standards applied to other employees, even if any unsatisfactory performance or behavior is related to the alcoholism.

The ADA does provide that an employer may not discriminate against individuals because they have successfully completed or participated in a supervised rehabilitation program. However, this is not your situation. Your employer granted you two leaves of absence to attend a rehabilitation program and at the conclusion of each returned you to full status. It was your own actions, regardless of the reason for your relapse, that resulted in your employment termination.

Generally, an employer should treat its employees similarly, and your former employer did that. You, like the other employees, were granted a leave of absence to attend a rehabilitation program. The fact that you attended voluntarily does not change the result or show a different treatment.

It appears that you desire to find some reason other than your drinking upon which to blame your loss of employment opportunities. Your employer's downsizing and your status as a white male who is neither management nor in the union are irrelevant. The fact that you drank a large quantity of alcohol after having attended two alcohol rehabilitation programs is what is important. Maybe this unfortunate result will have a positive ending in allowing you to see and accept your drinking problem so that you can live a better life. The choice is yours.

Employer's Defenses and Liabilities

An employer may expect the same quality and quantity of production or standard of care from a disabled employee as it does from a nondisabled employee. Similarly, an employer is not required to hire or continue to employ a disabled individual who poses a direct threat to the health or safety of other individuals in the workplace. Employers and employees need to understand the fine line between a disability protected under the ADA and a medical condition that compromises everyone's work.

Employer May Fire Worker Who Has Had Frequent Absences

Q.   I was fired from my job, working for a doctor, which I had had for three years. I have asthma that usually gets bad about twice a year and occasionally requires hospitalization for at least a week. This past year, I was admitted to the hospital for an asthma attack, and two days after admission an emergency appendectomy was done. After discharge I was still in pain. After seeing several doctors, I was told to have a laparoscopy, but it could not be scheduled until the following month.

Just before I went back, the doctor whom I worked for called me at home and told me that I was missing too much work and he was thinking about hiring someone else. He said my work was excellent and had no problem at all with me except my absences. I told him I would need four days off for my laparoscopy and then everything should be taken care of. He agreed, but told me if I was out sick anymore, there would be problems.

I had the surgery. A month went by and everybody in the office came down with bronchitis, one at a time. They all were out of work for at least a week while they had this. Needless to say, I ended up with bronchitis also. I went to my physician, who told me to stay out of work for at least a week or until my fever broke. I spoke to the office manager and told her I would be coming back to work on Monday. She agreed and on Sunday the doctor called me at home and told me he had had enough and that I was fired.

I feel I was entitled to severance pay, and I would like to know where I stand with this on legal ground. I am also entitled to pay for two sick days, which was never paid to me. I got fired for having legitimate medical problems.

All physicians kind of stick together. What is going to happen anytime I have a prospective employer and he would like references from his friend? I kind of feel like the last seven years of my life have been a waste. Where do I go from here?

P. H.

A.   I am sympathetic to your situation and can only imagine the distress you must feel, especially because your illnesses and consequently your absences from work were out of your control. Although you may have some protection under state law and the Americans with Disabilities Act because of your disability—the asthma, not the bronchitis—your employer appears to have complied with his responsibilities of providing you additional time off for your surgery.

From the facts you state, it appears your employment was terminated because of your inability to be at work and perform the services for which you were hired, not because of your medical problems. Just as your medical condition was beyond your control, it was also beyond the control of your physician employer. You know how frustrated you were with the entire situation. Think how he felt, and think of the feelings of your coworkers and patients who had to handle the consequences of your absences. A company may reasonably expect its employees to report to work, and when they fail to do so, the employer has the right to end their employment.

In regard to your question on severance pay, your state has no law that obligates an employer to offer severance pay. Without a past practice or representation that you would receive severance pay, there exists no legal obligation. Similarly, an employer is not required to provide paid sick leave. The employer may establish any policy outlining under what circumstances employees will receive pay when they miss work because of sickness. Many employers have a policy of not paying employees for unused sick time upon the termination of their employment. If you are unsure of your former employer's policy, you might want to telephone the office and ask about it.

I would also suggest you call your former employer and specifically ask him whether you may use him as a reference and, if so, what he will say. During that conversation, remind him what he said to you about being an excellent employee. If he will not provide a favorable reference, maybe there is another employer you can contact. You have been in this profession for seven years, but only three years with your immediate former employer.

Life is a process, filled with opportunities from which we learn. No time is wasted unless you choose not to learn from your experiences. I am certain that if you sat down and listed what has occurred in your life during the past seven years, you would be amazed at how your life has grown. Keep a positive attitude; it greatly impacts the quality of your life.

The ADA prohibits an employer from disclosing an employee's medical information. In fact, all medical information is to be kept separate from the employee's personnel file and marked and maintained in a confidential manner. There are three exceptions to the general confidentiality rule. An employer may disclose an employee's medical condition to (1) managers or supervisors on a need-to-know basis; (2) first-aid and safety personnel if the disability might require medical treatment; and (3) government officials who are investigating a complaint. Often in talking among themselves, managers and supervisors speak of confidential matters regarding the employees they supervise.

This behavior not only may violate the law but also communicates disrespect for another person's privacy and well-being. Such communication is unwarranted gossip and demonstrates the supervisor's inability to uphold a position of authority honorably.

Disability discrimination claims are extremely costly from the humanitarian point of view and financially. Employer awareness of its ADA obligations in not discriminating and in providing a reasonable accommodation may prevent lawsuits. Employers have the obligation to post in an accessible format to applicants and employees a notice of their rights under the ADA. Individuals who believe their employer or prospective employer has violated the ADA must exhaust their administrative remedies by filing a charge of unlawful employment discrimination with the EEOC within 180 days of the alleged unlawful act. Available remedies include hiring, reinstatement, back pay, interest on back pay, lost benefits, front pay, injunctive relief, and such other equitable relief as a court may deem just and proper. The prevailing party may, within the court's discretion, be awarded reasonable attorney fees, expert fees, and costs of suit. Employers who act with malice or reckless indifference to applicants' or employees' ADA rights may also be liable for punitive damages. Depending on the size of the employer, compensatory and punitive damages are limited as follows:

- $50,000 for employers with at least 15 but fewer than 101 employees in each of 20 or more calendar weeks in the current or preceding calendar year;
- $100,000 for employers having at least 101 but fewer than 201 employees during the relevant period;
- $200,000 for covered employers having at least 201 but fewer than 501 employees during the relevant period; or
- $300,000 for covered employers having 501 or more employees during the relevant period.

The following list, compiled by the EEOC, identifies the most common alleged disabilities upon which an ADA claim is filed:

1. Back impairment
2. Depression
3. Diabetes
4. Heart
5. Anxiety

6.   Hearing impairment
7.   Vision
8.   Cancer
9.   Manic depression
10. Epilepsy

What do each of these conditions have in common? Think about it. Review the list again. The answer cannot be seen at first. That is it! The disability cannot be seen. How important is it then that you not act until you have all the necessary information to proceed? I have discussed numerous examples of how knowledge and sensitivity can win the day. As with every employment law, you cannot prevent a claim from being filed under the ADA. However, unlike any other employment statute, the ADA makes it immensely important that you have concrete evidence in knowing and resting easy that you did what was right and necessary, or one day it may be *you* who needs a little assistance.

——————— ■ eight ■ ———————

The Family and
Medical Leave Act

Most employment laws are enacted for the protection of employees, prohibiting prescribed conduct and, in most circumstances, placing the responsibility on the employer to take certain affirmative steps. However, the Family and Medical Leave Act (FMLA) is not all one-sided and requires employees to take specific steps in order to enjoy the protections of this law. Therefore, it is in employers' and employees' best interest to understand their rights as well as their obligations.

Many states have laws similar to the FMLA. When the FMLA and state law conflict, the more generous law controls. However, the federal law and most state laws do not require employees to specify the statute under which they are asserting the right to take a leave of absence. Therefore, in order to know which law is applicable, the employer must initiate a discussion with the employee on that issue and document the conversation. Equally as important, all managers and supervisors must be familiar with the requirements of both laws before preparing a family and medical leave policy and making employment decisions concerning these employee protections. If an employer desires, it may always grant more rights than those provided by federal or state law.

The FMLA was enacted in 1993 to allow "eligible employees" to take up to 12 workweeks of unpaid leave in a 12-month period for (1) the birth of a son or daughter and in order to care for such son or daughter; (2) adoption or foster care placement of a son or daughter with the employee; (3) to care for the employee's spouse, son, daughter, or parent who has a serious health condition; or (4) the employee's own serious health condition that makes the employee unable to perform one or more of the essential functions of the person's position. The law also grants eligible employees job security in the event a leave of absence is needed for one of these events and requires an employer to continue the employee's health benefits during the FMLA leave.

Covered Employers

Employers whose activities affect interstate commerce and who employ 50 or more employees for each working day during each of 20 or more calendar workweeks in the current or preceding year must comply with the FMLA requirements. For the purposes of counting the number of employees, any employees, including part-time employees, who are on the employer's payroll for every day of the week counts for that week.

In joint employment relationships, only the primary employer is responsible for giving the required notices, providing FMLA leave, and maintaining health benefits. Factors considered in determining who is the "primary employer" include the authority/responsibility to hire and fire; to assign/place the employee; to make payroll; and to provide employment benefits.

Temporary or leasing agencies are usually the primary employer in the situation where another company has retained an employee's services for a limited time or specific project. Employees who are jointly employed by two employers must be counted by both employers for assessing employer coverage, regardless of whether the employee is maintained on both employers' payroll. Job restoration is the responsibility of the primary employer. However, the secondary employer must accept the employee returning from FMLA leave if it continues to use the services of the primary employer and the primary employer chooses to place the returning employee with the secondary employer. The secondary employer must comply with FMLA requirements.

Who Is Eligible for FMLA Leave?

Only those employees who meet all three of the following criteria are eligible for FMLA leave.

1. The employee has been employed by the employer for at least 12 months;
2. The employee has been employed for a least 1,250 hours of service during the 12-month period immediately preceding the commencement of the leave; and
3. The employee is employed at a work site where 50 or more employees are employed by the employer within 75 miles of that work site.

The employer must determine that an employee who requests an FMLA leave meets each of the three criteria. Failure to make this assessment may expose the employer to an unnecessary discrimination lawsuit based upon the different treatment of its employees. Calculation of whether the employee has worked 1,250 hours includes only the actual hours worked, including overtime; absence from work for sickness, vacation, or personal time is not counted because it is not time worked. The time an employee furnished services to a secondary employer while employed by a temporary or leasing agency is included in determining whether an employee is eligible for FMLA leave.

The requisite 12-month work period need not be consecutive months. For example, if an eligible employee resigns, then is subsequently rehired, the employee's period of previous service must be used in determining whether that employee is eligible for family and medical leave. However, only those hours worked during the previous 12-month period will be credited toward the 1,250-hour requirement. Therefore, it is possible that because of the length of time the individual was not employed, the employee may fail to meet the requirement of having worked at least 1,250 hours during the previous 12-month period.

The FMLA requires covered employers to keep records regarding the dates and hours a leave is taken, documents related to any dispute about the designation of a leave period, notices to or from employees relating to the leave, documents related to leave policies, employee premium payments, and medical certifications. The employer is required to keep these records for a minimum of three (3) years. Because of the sensitive nature of these records and in accordance with the ADA mandates, all FMLA documentation must be treated and maintained in a confidential manner and kept separate from the employee's personnel file.

Employee Entitlements

For the first two of the four grounds for an FMLA leave—the birth of a son or daughter and to care for such child and the adoption or foster care placement of a son or daughter—such leave must be taken within 12 months of the child's birth or placement. This leave may commence, if necessary, before the birth or placement for prenatal care or because the employee is unable to work or leave is necessary for the adoption or placement to proceed. The employee's child need not be sick for the employee to qualify for leave? Further, the leave is available to both men and women. However, if a husband and wife are both eligible for FMLA leave and work for the same covered employer, their leave may be limited to a combined total of 12 weeks during any 12-month period when the leave is for the birth, adoption, or foster care placement or to care for the employee's parent who has a serious health condition.

The third type of FMLA leave—an eligible employee's request to care for a spouse, child, or parent who has a serious health condition—applies even when the employee is not the individual's primary caretaker. The FMLA regulations provide that

> The medical certification provision that an employee is "needed to care for" a family member encompasses both physical and psychological care. It includes situations where, for example, because of a serious health condition, the family member is unable to care for his or her own basic medical, hygienic, or nutritional needs, or safety, or is unable to transport himself or herself to the doctor, etc. The term also includes providing psychological comfort and reassurance which would be beneficial to a child, spouse or parent with a serious health condition who is receiving inpatient or home care.

The FMLA is interpreted broadly to encourage employees to attend to the family unit when illness strikes one of their members. However, courts have found that an employee merely "visiting" a parent with a serious health condition does not qualify for FMLA leave.

How would you respond to the following scenario?

> Employee requests vacation time to take newborn baby to visit grandmother out-of-state. Employer denies request because employee has no accrued vacation. A week later the employee calls work and reports she is taking her baby to the pediatrician. The next day the employee calls and leaves a message that she will not be in that day. On the following day the employee calls in sick. The employer learns that the employee's absence from work was to visit her grandmother and fires the employee. The employee sues the employer alleging it violated the FMLA.

Was the employee's absence in this situation within one of the FMLA's qualifying reasons? In this case, the court ruled that the FMLA does not provide leave to a parent who desires to take a vacation and just so happens to take her child with her. Further, the court stated that to permit an employee to retroactively assert that her absence was an FMLA leave would violate the legitimate interests of the employer to manage its workplace and employees in a fair, reasonable, and efficient manner. To safeguard against a fraudulent FMLA leave, an employer may request a health care provider's certification as to the serious health condition status of the employee's spouse, child, or parent, or the employee.

The following example demonstrates the importance of asking questions to ensure full compliance with the FMLA.

Determining If Leave Act Applies May Not Be Easy

Q. I am the human resources manager of a company that is required to comply with the Family and Medical Leave Act. I understand that an eligible employee is one who has worked for the company at least 12 months and a minimum of 1,250 hours during the preceding 12 months. In determining whether an employee meets the eligibility requirements, must the 12 months be consecutive?

Recently, an executive employee requested a reduced leave schedule, 2 to 3 hours leave two days a week, under the act, to receive chemotherapy treatments. His position is exempt from the wage and overtime provisions of the wage and hour law. However, the wage and hour law prohibits an employer from reducing an exempt employee's salary by less than a full day; otherwise, the exempt status will be lost.

Must the company grant this executive employee 12 weeks of reduced leave and still be required to pay this individual his full salary even though he is not working full days? The company is also concerned that this individual's medical treatment will extend beyond 12 weeks. Is the company required to provide additional time off to enable the employee to continue in his treatment?

T. B.

A. As you correctly note, an eligible employee under the Family and Medical Leave Act is one who (1) has been employed by the employer for at least 12 months; (2) has worked a minimum of 1,250 hours in the 12 months preceding the leave; and (3) works at a facility where there are at least 49 coworkers employed within 75 miles of the workplace. An employer covered by the act is one whose activities affect interstate commerce and who employs 50 or more people for each working day during each of 20 or more calendar workweeks in the current or preceding year.

The 12 months of the employment period need not be consecutive. Overtime hours are included in calculating the minimum number of hours. Employees exempted from the overtime provisions of the Federal Fair Labor Standards Act (the federal wage and hour law), like the executive employee in your question, are presumed to have worked 1,250 hours during the previous year if the company has no record of the number of hours worked.

In regard to your second question, the federal wage and hour law states that deductions of less than a full day may not be made from an exempt employee's salary if that status is to be maintained. However, the FMLA regulations provide an exception. If an employee works less than a full day under a reduced work schedule or intermittent leave falling under the act, the employer may pay the exempt employee only for the hours worked without the employee losing his exempt status, so long as the employee meets the definition of eligible employee and the leave is for a protected reason.

The law does not obligate employers to provide any more than 12 weeks of leave because of a serious medical condition affecting the employee or his family member, or the birth, adoption, or placement of the employee's child.

However, your last question comes within the parameters of the Americans with Disabilities Act (ADA). The ADA applies to employers with 15 or more employees on each working day in each of 20 or more calendar weeks in the current or preceding year. This law requires employers to make reasonable accommodations regarding the physical or mental limitations of an otherwise qualified person, unless the accommodation would create an undue hardship on the employer's business operations. A reasonable accommodation includes a modified work schedule or additional leave. Thus, an employer's FMLA obligations may end, but ADA responsibilities may begin. Therefore, the company should have a family and medical leave policy that is flexible to accommodate an otherwise qualified employee with a disability. Each situation must be evaluated individually.

The increase in the number of employment laws has made managing the employment relationship more difficult. The FMLA, like other employment laws, cannot be read in a vacuum but must be understood and applied as a whole. In addition, it must be read in conjunction with the state family leave act, the workers' compensation law, the federal Employee Retirement Income Security Act (ERISA), and the Consolidated Omnibus Budget Reconciliation Act (COBRA), to name a few.

The FMLA allows the 12 weeks of leave to be used on an intermittent or reduced basis when medically necessary, except when the leave is taken for the birth, adoption, or placement of the eligible employee's child. In the latter cases, the employee may take intermittent or reduced leave only if the employer agrees. An employee may take such a leave in increments of one hour or less depending upon how the employer's payroll system accounts for absences or leaves. "Intermittent leave" is leave taken in separate blocks of time due to a single qualifying reason, rather than for one continuous period of time. A "reduced leave" is a leave schedule that reduces an employee's usual number of working hours per workweek or per workday. Employees needing intermittent or reduced leave must attempt to schedule their leave so as not to disrupt the employer's operations. In addition, an employer may assign an employee to an alternate position with equivalent pay and benefits that better accommodates the employee's intermittent or reduced leave schedule.

Difficult to Take Family Leave on an Intermittent Basis

Q. I have a question concerning the federal Family and Medical Leave Act. I will be needing to leave 1.5 hours early one day a week to get my children to the therapist. May I apply 1.5 hours from the bank of available family leave for this time out?
    K. S.

A. In order to be granted a reduced leave schedule or intermittent leave under the FMLA, an employee must pass through a series of statutory requirements and procedural hoops, including the following:

- The leave must be "medically necessary" for a "serious health condition."
- The employee must make a reasonable effort to schedule the treatment so as not to "disrupt unduly the operations of the employer."
- The employee must give at least 30 days' notice to the employer.

Under the first requirement, the term "medically necessary" has been interpreted to mean that the employee's doctor appointment cannot be routine; the employee must have an urgent reason for visiting the doctor on a particular date and time.

A "serious health condition" has a rather lengthy legal definition. It includes inpatient care in a hospital, hospice, or residential medical care facility; a period of incapacity of more than three consecutive days and any subsequent treatment; any period of incapacity due to or treatment of a chronic serious health condition; a permanent or long-term incapacity due to a condition for which treatment may not be effective; or any period of absence to receive multiple treatments.

Regarding the employee's duty not to "disrupt the operations of the employer," the courts want to see a cooperative effort between the employer and employee. The legislative history of the FMLA states that its goals should be implemented in a manner that accommodates the legitimate interest of employers. Leave taken under the law may not be taken intermittently or on a reduced leave schedule unless the employee and the employer agree to such an arrangement.

The final requirement of notice is self-explanatory. If employees have a need for foreseeable leave, they must give 30-day notice of the leave request. If the leave is not foreseeable, the courts examine the facts and circumstances of each case to determine if there was "practicable notice" provided the employer. "Practicable notice" has been defined as the first available opportunity the employee has to alert the employer of the leave; the employee must attempt to contact the employer to give notice of the impending leave.

In sum, the courts examine each case under the three-prong approach I have outlined. Thus, you will need to ascertain whether you meet these requirements as well as speak with your employer concerning them.

Under the FMLA regulations, an employer can calculate the 12-month period during which the employee takes leave by any one of four methods: (1) the calendar year; (2) any fixed 12-month period (e.g., the employer's fiscal year, or the 12-month period beginning on the employee's "anniversary" date); (3) the 12-month period beginning with each employee's first FMLA leave and, thereafter, with each FMLA leave that occurs after the preceding period; or (4) a rolling period whereby each employee's remaining leave entitlement would be any balance of the 12 weeks not used in the preceding 12 months. An employer must choose one method and apply it uniformly to all employees. If the employer fails to select a method, employees may choose whatever method is most beneficial for them.

Family Leave Act Does Not Require Work-Shift Changes

Q. My son's wife had a mastectomy, and she requires at least six weeks of chemotherapy and radiation treatments. My son works the midnight shift for a public agency. He is using his sick leave and vacation time to be with her. She is afraid to be alone at night. My question is this: Is he entitled to a day-hours job?

   J. R.

A.   The federal Family and Medical Leave Act requires employers, including public agencies, to provide eligible employees up to 12 weeks of unpaid leave of absence because of a family member's serious health condition. To be eligible, your son must have been employed by the employer for at least 12 months, must have worked a minimum of 1,250 hours in the 12 months preceding the leave, and must work at a location where his employer employs at least 50 workers within 75 miles of that site.

A "serious health condition" means a physical or mental illness, injury, impairment, or condition that involves inpatient care in a hospital, hospice, or residential medical care facility or continuing treatment by a health care provider. The employer may require the employee to furnish a health-care provider certification to substantiate the leave request. The 12 weeks of leave may be used on an intermittent or reduced basis because of the employee's or the employee's family member's serious health condition, where medically necessary. However, employees need to schedule this type of leave so as not to disrupt the employer's business operations.

Although this law requires employers to grant eligible workers a leave of absence in circumstances such as you describe, it does not mandate that employers temporarily change an employee's work shift. However, your son might speak with the personnel department to see if he could work the day shift temporarily. Perhaps he knows someone who works the day shift who would be willing to switch shifts. I suggest that your son explain the reason for his request. He is in a difficult situation, and most people, if possible, would want to help or may know someone else who could assist him in achieving his objective.

Serious Health Condition

The regulations that follow will assist employers in determining when an employee's absence is due to a "serious health condition" of the employee or the employee's family member and therefore may be designated as a leave pursuant to the FMLA. In applying these general principles, keep in mind that each situation is fact-specific, and thus the employer must evaluate the reason for each employee's absence on a case-by-case basis.

The FMLA defines "serious health condition" as a physical or mental illness, injury, impairment, or condition that involves inpatient care in a hospital, hospice, or residential medical care facility or continuing treatment by a health care provider. The FMLA regulations more specifically define "serious health condition" as a situation that comes within one of the following categories:

1) Inpatient care in a hospital, hospice or residential medical care facility or any subsequent treatment in connection with such inpatient care. For example, an employee's overnight stay in a hospital for pneumonia would be considered a serious health condition.

2) Continuing treatment or supervision by a health care provider. This category includes any one or more of the following:

(i) A period of incapacity (i.e., inability to work, attend school or perform other regular daily activities due to the serious health condition, treatment therefor or recovery therefrom) of more than three (3) consecutive calendar days, and any subsequent treatment or period of incapacity relating to the same condition, that also involves:

(A) Treatment two or more times by a health care provider, by a nurse or physician's assistant under direct supervision of a health care provider, or by a provider of health care services (e.g., physical therapist) under orders of, or on referral by, a health care provider; or

(B) Treatment by a health care provider on at least one occasion which results in a regimen of continuing treatment under the supervision of the health care provider.

(ii) Any period of incapacity due to pregnancy, or for prenatal care.

(iii) Any period of incapacity or treatment for such incapacity due to a chronic serious health condition. A chronic health condition is one which:

(A) requires periodic visits for treatment by a health care provider or by a nurse or physician's assistant under direct supervision of a health care provider;

(B) continues over an extended period of time (including recurring episodes of a single underlying condition); and

(C) may cause episodic incapacity such as asthma, diabetes or epilepsy.

(iv) A period of incapacity which is permanent or long-term due to a condition for which treatment may not be effective. The employee or family member must be under the continuing supervision of, but need not be receiving active treatment by, a health care provider. For example, Alzheimer's, a severe stroke or the terminal stages of a disease.

(v) Any period of absence to receive multiple treatments (including any recovery therefrom) by a health care provider or by a provider of health care services under orders of or on referral by a health care provider. For example, restorative surgery after an accident or other injury or where medical intervention or treatment is necessary to prevent the likely result of incapacity, such as chemotherapy, radiation, physical therapy or dialysis.

A written job description is highly valuable in determining whether employees have a "serious health condition" that makes them unable to perform one or more of the essential functions of their position. The FMLA relies upon the ADA's definition of "essential job functions" in evaluating an employee's condition. An employer may have the employee's doctor fill out a certification supplied by the employer that lists the specific job functions the employee is responsible for performing. The employer should request, with the written permission of the employee, the physician's assessment of the employee's abilities to carry out the assigned duties in light of the employee's condition. Or the employer may simply provide a statement of the employee's essential job functions in requiring a certification from the health care provider. If the physician determines that the employee is able to perform the essential functions of the position, the employee is not eligible for FMLA leave. However, if the physician determines that the employee cannot carry out any one of the job's essential functions, the employee is entitled to FMLA leave.

Voluntary or cosmetic treatments that are not medically necessary are not "serious health conditions" under the FMLA regulations, unless inpatient hospital care is required. For example, orthodontic work or acne treatment is not covered. However, restorative dental surgery after an accident or removal of cancerous growths is covered. In addition, treatment for allergies, stress, and substance abuse would qualify if the conditions of this section are met, whereas routine physical examinations would not.

Mom Fired While Caring for Child

Q. My workplace problem began when I decided to take time off from my job to care for my infant. After maternity leave, I went back to work. One day when my child was eighteen months old, I encountered my babysitter walking along the street and was in a state of shock; all along she was leaving my child to go out and run errands. My baby stopped eating and was acting very strange. She would only smile at me, and would only eat for me, and that meant staying awake most of the night and day.

I explained everything to my boss, and he decided I should go out on family leave. After I was out of work 5 to 6 weeks, he changed his tune and said I must come back to work the next day. That was impossible—what would I do with my baby, just as I was getting her back into shape and trusting strangers again? I cried, "Please do not fire me, please give me more time to get my situation in order." The company had someone filling in for me with no problem. In fact, they had this girl as an extra sales rep, and I believe forced me out to give her my territory at a lower rate of pay.

When I did not show up the following day, I received a letter of termination. Even though I did not have medical records of my child being ill, she was still ill mentally. Today, she is healthy, and I believe it is because I stayed home and reassured her that everything was okay. I also believe what this company did to me is totally against the law. I know my child is the most important thing in this world, but having a job you truly love is also very rare. I was an excellent employee and also was one of the top in the division in sales. Now I am collecting unemployment benefits, which is very depressing, and looking for jobs in the newspaper is a downer. Please let me know more about the family leave law, and if it would be worth it for me to fight this company or a waste of my time.

L.M.H.

A.   The federal Family and Medical Leave Act and your state's family leave law were enacted to balance the demands of the workplace with the needs of families and to promote the stability and economic security of families. Thus, employers covered by these laws must provide eligible employees up to 12 workweeks of leave in any 12-month period in certain circumstances. In your case, the leave would have been to care for a son or daughter who had a "serious health condition."

The term "serious health condition" means an illness, injury, impairment, or physical or mental condition that involves inpatient care in certain types of facilities or continuing treatment by a health care provider. "To care for" a family member includes the individual's psychological well-being. But the other statutory requirement, that the family member have a "serious health condition," must also be met.

Although you desired a leave of absence to care for your child, your request probably does not come within the statutory protections of a leave based on her "serious medical condition." As you state, you had no medical documentation, and thus it sounds as if your daughter was not in a hospital or under the care of a health care provider. Employers are required to provide their employees notice about their rights and obligations under this law. I don't know whether this occurred, but if you had been given the necessary information, perhaps you would have obtained the medical documentation if your child was in need of the medical attention. However, absent a serious health condition, the family leave laws would provide you no protection.

The law does not provide a remedy for every unfairness or injustice. It is unfortunate that you did not have open and thorough discussions with your boss or perhaps with someone in the human resources department to evaluate the situation and determine available options. That would be a responsibility of both parties.

It does not appear to be in your best interest to pursue a claim against your employer. However, you do have some other, more positive avenues to pursue. First, you state that you are an excellent employee, and that you liked your job. Therefore, it may be worth your while to pay a personal visit to your former employer to educate or remind the decisionmakers of your excellent skills and valuable contributions to the company, and ascertain whether they need someone with your abilities. Second, if your former employer has no current openings, ask for job leads and a letter of recommendation. Third, use your excellent sales skills in selling your most important commodity—yourself. Fourth, get out and network in seeking other employment opportunities; most jobs are found by word-of-mouth.

When you get down, remember that you gave yourself and your daughter the most priceless gift—your time when she was in need.

Health Care Provider Certification

To substantiate the employee's FMLA leave eligibility, an employer has the right to require its employees to furnish a health care provider certification within fifteen (15) calendar days of the employer's request, unless it is not practicable under the particular circumstances. If the employee fails to submit the certification in a timely manner, the employer may delay the commencement of the employee's leave. An employer must give written notice to the employee of the health care provider certification requirement, but an employer's verbal request to an employee to furnish any subsequent medical certification is sufficient. The U.S. Department of Labor has created a Certification of Health Care Provider form to be used specifically for documenting FMLA absences. This form, which can be reproduced, is a good compliance tool and should be used each time the employer has reason to believe that an absence qualifies as a FMLA leave. If another form is used, it cannot solicit information beyond what is requested in the government form and, in all instances, only information relating to the condition precipitating the need for the leave may be required.

When the employee has furnished a completed and signed certification, the employer may not request additional information from the employee's health care provider. However, the employer's health care provider may contact the employee's health care provider, with the employee's permission, in order to clarify and verify the medical certification. If there is reason to doubt the seriousness of the health condition after receipt of the certification, a second medical opinion can be required at the employer's expense. The employer may designate this health care provider, so long as the individual's services are not regularly utilized, employed, or contracted by the employer, unless the employer is in a location with limited health care access.

If there is a disagreement between the first two opinions, the employer can require a third medical opinion. The third medical opinion, also at the employer's expense, must be from a physician who has been agreed upon by both the employer and the employee. As I have emphasized so much in this book, full and open communication is essential in maintaining a healthy employment relationship, and it is particularly applicable to the FMLA regulation governing the selection of the health care provider to furnish the third medical opinion. That regulation states that if the employer does not make a good-faith attempt to reach agreement with the employee concerning the mutual selection of a health care provider to furnish a third medical opinion, then the employer is bound by the first certification. And if the employee refuses to act in good faith, then the second medical opinion shall control. When mutual agreement has been reached, the third medical opinion shall be determinative.

If the employer chooses to have a second or third medical opinion, it cannot delay or deny the employee's FMLA leave and corresponding benefits. Rather, the employer has the obligation to honor the leave request until a final determination has been made. In addition, the employer must furnish to the employee, if requested, a copy of the second and third medical opinions and reimburse the employee or family member for any reasonable out-of-pocket travel expenses incurred to obtain the medical opinion. An employer cannot require an employee or family member to travel outside normal commuting distance to obtain the medical opinion.

How would you respond to the following situation?

> The employee requested and was granted FMLA leave based upon a doctor's certification that he had bronchitis. The employee did not return to work on the scheduled date. A day later the employee telephoned the employer and reported that he was now getting treatment in Mexico and his new doctor would be in touch with the employer. The employer gave the

employee eighteen days to return to work. The employee failed to call in or report to work. Two weeks thereafter, the employee's new doctor faxed a note to the employer stating that the employee was unable to work because of irritable bowel syndrome, hernia, and ulcer and that he needed another six weeks of rest. The employer sent a letter to the employee at the address shown on the company's records, although it believed him to still be in Mexico, requiring him to report for a second medical examination. The employee did not report for the examination.

May the employer terminate its relationship with the employee? Yes, the employer may discharge the employee because of his refusal to cooperate with the employer's request for a second medical opinion. In addition, the employer could have made this request when the employee informed the employer that he was being treated by a doctor in Mexico. In this case, the court noted that the FMLA regulations do not specify how notices are to be sent to employees concerning a second medical opinion. However, an employer's reliance on an employee handbook, collective bargaining agreement, or other similar policy is acceptable.

When the employee requests FMLA leave in advance of the leave date, the employer has a greater ability to assess the situation fully in determining the existence of a serious health condition. However, when the employee is absent from work without any advance warning, the employer's task in determining how the leave should be classified is more difficult. The FMLA regulations require the employer to designate whether the employee's absence is an FMLA leave and to notify the employee in writing that the leave time will be classified as FMLA leave. When the employer does not have sufficient information to make such a determination, it should *immediately* make further inquiry of the employee, not a third party, about the reasons for the leave. It is critical to address this leave designation with the employee for a variety of reasons, including the fact that, with only one exception, the leave designation cannot be made after the employee returns to work. The FMLA regulations state that any dispute as to whether the leave qualifies as FMLA leave should be resolved through discussions with the employee.

Consider another example:

An employee has not made an FMLA leave request but has been absent from work for more than three (3) calendar days for reasons other than vacation, jury duty, or similar factor. Still no one hears from the employee. Who has the obligation at this point?

The employee has the primary responsibility to make contact. However, to demonstrate concern for the employee and safeguard the employer's interest, so does the employer. On the fourth calendar day (a "serious health condition" means being incapacitated for a period of more than three consecutive days), the employer should either notify the employee in writing that he or she is considered to have resigned voluntarily in accordance with its established policy, or call the employee and ascertain the basis for the absence.

What happens in the next real-life example?

> Employee calls her employer to inform it that she would be absent from work because she was in a lot of pain and did not know when she would be able to return to work. The employer never heard from her again until she filed a lawsuit alleging that the employer violated the FMLA when it discharged her.

Did the employer's actions violate the FMLA? In this case, the court ruled that the employee had failed to furnish the employer sufficient notice upon which it could make an informed decision that the employee needed or was requesting FMLA leave. Therefore, the employer's discharge of the employee did not violate the FMLA.

The Two-Business-Days' Notice Requirements

When the employer has concluded that an employee's leave is an FMLA leave, it must *immediately* or within two business days notify the employee, in writing, that such designation has been made. Specifically, the FMLA regulations read as follows:

> (i) Where the employee does not give notice of the need for leave more than *two business days* prior to commencing leave, the employee will be deemed to be eligible if the employer fails to advise the employee that the employee is not eligible within *two business days* of receiving the employee's notice.
>
> (ii) Once the employer has acquired knowledge that the leave is being taken for an FMLA required reason, the employer must promptly (within *two business days* absent extenuating circumstances) notify the employee that the paid leave is designated and will be counted as FMLA leave.
>
> (iii) If the employer requires paid leave to be substituted for unpaid FMLA leave, or that paid leave taken under an existing leave plan be counted as

FMLA leave, this decision must be made by the employer within *two business days* of the time the employee gives notice of the need for leave, or, where the employer does not initially have sufficient information to make a determination, when the employer determines that leave qualifies as FMLA leave if this happens later.

(iv) If the employee was absent for an FMLA reason and the employer did not learn the reason for the absence until the employee's return (e.g. where the employee was absent for only a brief period), the employer may, upon the employee's return to work, promptly (within *two business days* of the employee's return to work) designate the leave retroactively with appropriate notice to the employee.

(v) In most cases, the employer should request that an employee furnish a certification from a health care provider at the time the employee gives notice of the need for leave or within *two business days* thereafter, or, in the case of unforeseen leave, within *two business days* after the leave commences. (Emphasis added.)

The U.S. Department of Labor has created an Employer Response to Employee Request for Family or Medical Leave form. This form may be reproduced and is also a good tool to document compliance with the law.

Contrary to the belief of many employees, an employee cannot choose how to designate a leave of absence. An employer has an obligation to apply its employment policies uniformly and consistently, and therefore, all leaves that qualify for FMLA leave must be designated as such. This consistent application of the organization's FMLA policy will uphold employee morale, and if a claim is filed, it will present a defense against such action.

In addition to employers providing notice concerning FMLA leave, employees also must furnish their employer notice of the need for FMLA leave. An employee's notice requirement is at least 30 days in advance of the leave, or in the event of an unforeseeable leave, as soon as practicable. If an employee cannot provide a reasonable excuse for why 30 days' notice was not provided, an employer can delay the employee's leave until 30 days after notice was given. A number of judicial decisions have addressed the responsibility of employees to notify their employer of the need for FMLA leave. These court rulings have consistently held the employee responsible for giving the employer adequate notice. Consequently, the adverse employment action taken against the employee for failure to provide the requisite notice has been determined not to constitute a violation of the FMLA.

Continuation of Employee Benefits

When eligible employees qualify for FMLA leave, the employer must maintain their health benefits during their absence. In addition, the employer must maintain all other employment benefits that have accrued before the employees' leave. The FMLA defines "employment benefits" as "all benefits provided or made available to employees, including life insurance, health insurance, disability insurance, sick leave, annual leave, educational benefits and pensions, regardless of whether these benefits are provided by a practice or written policy of an employer or through an 'employee benefit plan.'" With respect to the continuation of health insurance, the employer must continue to make its contributions to employees' health insurance premiums. To the extent that the insurance plan also requires employee contributions, employees on leave must continue to make those payments. An employer cannot require employees on leave to pay their share of the medical premium prior to the time when employees not on leave must make such payments.

The FMLA regulations state that

[I]f the FMLA leave is substituted paid leave [i.e. sick or vacation time], the employee's share of premiums must be paid by the method normally used during any paid leave. If the FMLA is unpaid, the employer has a number of options for obtaining payment from the employee. The employer may require that payment be made to the employer or insurance carrier, but no additional charge may be added to the employee's premium payment for administrative expenses. The employer may require employees to pay their share of the premium payments by any of the following ways:

(1) Payment would be due at the same time as it would be made if by payroll deduction;

(2) Payment would be due on the same schedule as payments are made under COBRA;

(3) Payment would be prepaid pursuant to a cafeteria plan at the employee's option;

(4) The employer's existing rules for payment by employees on "leave without pay" would be followed, provided such rules do not require prepayment (i.e., prior to the commencement of the leave) of the premiums that will become due during a period of unpaid FMLA leave or payment of higher premiums than if the employee had continued to work instead of taking leave; or

(5) Another system voluntarily agreed to between the employer and the employee, which may include prepayment of premiums (e.g. through increased payroll deductions when the need for FMLA is foreseeable).

In order to apply any one of these methods fairly, the employer must inform its employees, in advance, by written notice of its requirements concerning continuation of health benefits. If employees are late in paying their contribution, the employer cannot terminate health coverage, unless the premium is still outstanding following a 30-day grace period. Whenever employees fail to make their medical insurance contribution by the initial due date, the employer must inform them, in writing, that medical coverage will be terminated for nonpayment on a specific date. The employer should consider sending the letter to employees by regular mail as well as by certified mail, return receipt requested, to have confirmation of its delivery.

If the employer terminates an employee's medical insurance, the FMLA requires the employer, upon the employee's return to work, to restore the employee's health insurance to the preleave coverage. The employer cannot require the employee to meet any qualification requirements, such as a waiting period or medical examination. The employer can recover its share of the insurance premium for unpaid leave as long as the employee fails to return to work for a reason not covered under the FMLA. Similarly, if the employee returns to work for less than 30 calendar days and then resigns, the employer may still recoup its costs. If the leave was paid leave, use of sick time, or workers' compensation while on FMLA leave, the employer cannot recover its premiums.

An employer has no obligations concerning continuation of health benefits if it does not sponsor the plan and the employees purchase individual policies from an insurer. In order to come within this exception, the employer must satisfy the following criteria:

- No contributions are made by the employer;
- Participation in the program is purely voluntary;
- The employer's involvement with the program is limited to making its employees aware of the program without endorsing the plan, collecting premiums through payroll deduction, and remitting them to the insurer;
- The employer receives no consideration beyond administrative fees; and
- The health insurance premium does not increase upon employment separation.

Reinstatement Requirements

The law is clear that upon return from FMLA leave, an employee is entitled to be placed in the same position the employee held when the leave commenced, or to an equivalent position with equivalent benefits, pay, and other terms and conditions of employment. Ordinarily, an employee will be restored to the same position the employee held prior to the FMLA leave, with the same pay and benefits, if the position remains available. However, an employee who is unable to perform an essential function of the position because of a physical or mental condition, including the continuation of a serious health condition, has no right to return to the same position or another position.

In order to deny an employee restoration to employment, an employer must be able to show that the employee would not otherwise have been employed at the time reinstatement is requested. For example, an employer would have the burden of proving that an employee would have been laid off during the FMLA leave and therefore would no longer be employed. In balancing the employer's and employee's interests, the FMLA regulations state that "an employee has no greater rights to reinstatement or to other benefits and conditions of employment than if the employee had been continuously employed during the FMLA leave period." An employer remains free to operate its business in accordance with its organizational objectives and interests, so long as its decisions are not based on the fact that an employee has requested or taken FMLA leave.

An employer may also require fitness-for-duty certification in order to verify that employees are able to return to work. This certification must relate only to the particular health condition that caused an employee's need for the leave. This documentation is important to protect employees and the organization and merely confirms that returning individuals are able to perform their essential job functions without injury. If the employer informs employees that they are required to provide a fitness-for-duty certification upon their first day back to work and an employee fails to present the requested documentation, the employer may delay restoration until the employee submits the certificate. Employees who fraudulently obtain FMLA leave have no protections under the FMLA.

Key Employees

An employer may deny reinstatement to "key employees" if such action is necessary to prevent "substantial and grievous economic injury" to the employer's operations. The FMLA regulations state that the test is whether the restoration will cause the damage, not whether the employee's absence will result in injury. The FMLA defines a "key employee" as one who is paid a salary and "is among the highest paid 10 percent of all the employees employed by the employer within 75 miles of the employee's worksite." The FMLA does not define "substantial and grievous economic injury." The regulations merely state that the "standard is different from and more stringent that the 'undue hardship' under the ADA."

The "key employee" exception is meant to protect the employer's business operations based upon the employee's unique position within the organization and high salary level. As with the other employment laws, applying a specific section is dependent upon the totality of the circumstances. The "key employee" exception depends upon a variety of factors, and no one fact in particular is controlling. For example, what is the person's particular role in the establishment? What are the business needs at the time of the key employee's FMLA leave? What are the employee's responsibilities in relationship to those business needs? What are the business time constraints? What is the impact upon the organization if it were to bring the key employee back when someone else has been assigned to perform the key employee's job duties? What are the costs to the employer to pay such a high salary to more than one individual to achieve the needed result?

In order to invoke protection for not reinstating a key employee, the employer must give written notice to the employee, either in person or by certified mail, as soon as the decision not to reinstate has been made. The FMLA regulations provide that the "notice must explain the basis for the employer's finding that substantial and grievous economic injury will result, and, if leave has commenced, must provide the employee a reasonable time in which to return to work, taking into account the circumstances, such as the length of the leave and the urgency of the need for the employee to return. An employer who fails to provide such timely notice will lose its right to deny restoration, even if substantial and grievous economic injury will result from reinstatement."

The FMLA regulations further provide that "[i]f an employee on leave does not return to work in response to the employer's notification of intent to deny restoration, the employee continues to be entitled to maintenance of health benefits and the employer may not recover its cost of health benefit premiums. A key employee's rights under the FMLA continue unless and until the employee either gives notice that he or she no longer wishes to return to work, or the employer actually denies reinstatement at the conclusion of the leave period." The employer's decision to deny restoration, along with the reasons for its decision and the employee notice, should be clearly documented. In applying the FMLA, it is important to remember that a covered employer never has the right to deny FMLA leave to an eligible employee who has a protected reason for a leave.

Notices

Every employer covered by the FMLA is required to post and keep posted on its premises, in conspicuous places, a notice explaining the FMLA's provisions and providing information concerning procedures for filing a complaint. Also, if the employer has written policies, such as a handbook, information concerning the FMLA must be included in the handbook or other documents. If an employer's workforce is composed of a significant number of workers who cannot read and write English, the employer must provide information about the FMLA in a language in which the employees are literate.

In order for employees to be fully aware of their rights and responsibilities concerning the FMLA, the employer must clearly delineate these protections and obligations in a written format and distribute the information to all employees. The policy should be as detailed as possible to give everyone a common understanding of the expectations. The employer's failure to furnish this information may result in lack of understanding by employees, inconsistent application of the FMLA procedure, and employment litigation. A clearly written, well-informed policy will enhance the employment relationship, prevent misunderstandings, and support the employer's enforcement of its employment policies and practices should an adverse employment action occur or a claim be filed.

An employer may require that employees on FMLA leave report periodically on their status and intent to return to work. This personal contact, as in every relationship, is essential. Employers are encouraged to include in their FMLA policies the following information:

> Any employee who takes a leave of absence is required to keep the personnel manager apprised of his or her condition by calling and personally speaking with the personnel manager, or other designated management representative in his or her absence, once a week to inform the personnel manager of your status and expected return-to-work date. Employees must personally call and speak with the personnel manager or his or her designee. Notifica-

tion by family members or friends or leaving a message on voice mail or speaking with any other individual at the organization is not acceptable. Failure to adhere to these requirements may result in the loss of benefits and/or employment.

When employees first leave the employment setting for any length of time, the normal reaction is for them to feel uncomfortable for a number of reasons. First, they are out of sync with an established schedule they previously maintained. Second, they are not conversing with the same individuals on a daily basis. Third, they are uncertain about what is transpiring in the workplace and about their job responsibilities and job security. However, after employees have been out for two or three weeks and have adjusted, they become comfortable with this new routine and sense of freedom. Now the absence does not seem so bad and in fact often is welcomed. Therefore, regardless of why employees are absent, it is imperative to keep them committed to the relationship.

Collective Bargaining Agreement

The FMLA expressly defers to collective bargaining agreements that provide greater FMLA protection. However, employee rights under the FMLA may not be waived by an employment benefit program or collective bargaining agreement. Nor can employees waive their FMLA rights.

Negotiating the terms of an FMLA leave policy is a mandatory subject of bargaining because it impacts upon employees' terms and conditions of employment.

Educational Institutions

In order to address the needs of students in elementary and secondary schools, the FMLA includes a special provision that governs the leave of persons employed principally as instructors in such schools or agencies. The FMLA regulations define "instructors" as "those whose principal function is to teach and instruct students in a class, a small group, or an individual setting. This term includes not only teachers, but also athletic coaches, driving instructors, and special education assistants such as signers for the hearing impaired. It does not include, and the special rules do not apply to, teacher assistants or aides . . . counselors, psychologists, or curriculum specialists." The number of employees is irrelevant for the purposes of determining whether an educational institution is an employer covered by the FMLA.

For educational instructors who request intermittent or a reduced leave schedule for planned medical treatment of themselves or a family member such that the leave would constitute more than 20 percent of their working time during the overall leave period, the school or agency has a choice: In addition to granting the leave as requested, the school or agency may require such employees either (1) to take leave for periods of a particular duration not to exceed the duration of the planned treatment or (2) to transfer to an equivalent position that better accommodates the requested leave for which they are qualified.

In addition, the school or agency has the right under the FMLA to require instructional employees on leave to continue the leave until the end of the academic term under the following circumstances: If the leave will begin at any time before the last 5 weeks of the academic term, the school or agency may require employees to continue their leave until the end of the term if (1) the leave will last for at least 3 weeks and (2) the leave will be completed within 3 weeks from the end of the term. If, however, the leave is for other than employees' own serious health condition and it starts within the last 5 weeks of the academic term, the school or agency has the right to require employees to continue their leave until the end of the term if the leave is (1) greater than 2 weeks and (2) will be completed within 2 weeks of the end of the term. Finally, if the leave is for other than employees' own serious health condition and it starts within the last 3 weeks of the academic term, the school or agency may require employees to continue their leave until the end of the term so long as the leave is greater than 5 working days.

In applying this section, a school may not have more than two academic terms per year. Also, if the leave entitlement of instructors who are forced to take leave through the end of an academic term is exhausted during the leave, the school must continue their health benefits throughout the leave and restore employees to an equivalent position when the term ends. If employees are required to take additional leave than what they originally requested under either of the preceding two sections, only the leave needed counts towards their 12-week entitlement; the remaining time is not charged.

Enforcement

Employees who believe that an employer has violated the FMLA may file a claim and seek injunctive and monetary relief. An action must be filed within two years of the alleged violation. Actions based on a knowing violation of the FMLA, however, may be brought anytime within three years of the alleged violation. An employer is prohibited from discriminating against, interfering with, restraining, or denying employees from exercising their rights under the FMLA. Employees may institute an action for violations of the FMLA in state or federal court or file a complaint with the U.S. Secretary of Labor. A complaint filed with the Secretary of Labor may be filed in person, by mail, or by telephone with the Wage and Hour Division, Employment Standards Administration, U.S. Department of Labor. The Secretary of Labor is empowered to investigate and attempt to resolve complaints made about violations of the FMLA as well as file suit on behalf of an employee.

There are two situations that generally result from an employer's violation of the FMLA: The employer terminates employment of employees once they go on leave, or employees continue working against their will. Employees may recover damages for either unlawful act. If the first situation occurs, employees may recover damages equal to any wages, salary, employment benefits, or other compensation they have been denied or have lost. Under the second scenario, employees may recover any monetary losses they have sustained, including but not limited to the cost of providing care up to the amount equal to 12 weeks of their wages or salary. Employees also recover interest on the awarded sums in either circumstance. The court may also award attorneys fees, expert witness fees, costs of suit, and injunctive relief, such as employment, reinstatement, and promotion. In addition, damaged employees are entitled to recover "liquidated" damages equal to the amount of compensatory damages plus interest, unless the employer can demonstrate that its violation was in good faith and that it had reasonable grounds to believe that it was not violating the FMLA.

FMLA and the Americans with Disabilities Act

Because the FMLA and the ADA have different and often conflicting mandates, it is essential to know the requirements of both laws. For example, in regard to the ADA's requirement that employers provide a reasonable accommodation to an individual with a known disability who is otherwise qualified for the position, the EEOC has stated in its *Technical Assistance Manual* that

> Flexible leave policies should be considered as a reasonable accommodation when people with disabilities require time off from work because of their disability. An employer is not required to provide additional paid leave as an accommodation, but should consider allowing use of accrued leave, advanced leave or leave without pay, where this will not cause an undue hardship. . . .

A uniformly applied leave policy does not violate the ADA because it has a more severe effect on an individual because of his/her disability. However, if an individual with a disability requests a modification of such a policy as a reasonable accommodation, an employer may be required to provide it, unless it would impose an undue hardship.

The EEOC's position is that an employer should consider providing employees who have taken an FMLA leave and are still "disabled" at the end of the leave the opportunity to take additional leave beyond the 12 weeks as a reasonable accommodation under the ADA. However, under what circumstances this extension will be permitted and how the extension is applied must be done in a uniform and consistent manner to avoid exposing the organization to a discrimination lawsuit. For example, before making this option available, the employer must determine that an individual fits the ADA's definition of "disabled."

Worker Says Disability Led to Job Loss

Q. I have a severe vascular problem. I cannot stand, walk, lift, etc. My employer makes you work on your feet, which caused me to be permanently and irrevocably disabled. I went on family leave. My employer had me sign a paper saying that the organization makes allowances for the handicapped and/or disabled. When I tried to come back to work, the organization said no more light duty and that my employment was terminated since I was impaired.

P. E.

A. The federal Family and Medical Leave Act (FMLA) grants eligible employees a 12-week leave of absence for a variety of reasons, including to care for the employee's own serious health condition.

While the employee is on leave, the covered employer must maintain the employee's health benefits in the same manner as before the employee commenced the leave. Upon returning from the leave, the employer is to restore the employee to the same position the employee held prior to the FMLA leave, with the same pay and benefits, if the position remains available, or to an equivalent position with equivalent benefits, pay, and other terms and conditions of employment. However, the employee has no right to return to the same position.

In addition to the FMLA, the federal Americans with Disabilities Act (ADA) prohibits covered employers from treating disabled employees who are otherwise able to perform their essential job functions differently in the terms and conditions of their employment. The employer may also be required to provide reasonable accommodation to employees with a known disability to enable them to perform their essential job duties. Although the term "reasonable accommodation" is not specifically defined, it includes, by way of example, part-time or modified work schedule, job restructuring, reassignment to a vacant position, and making existing facilities readily accessible. However, an employer is not obligated to change its business operations or a job's essential job functions to accommodate disabled employees, or to make reasonable accommodation if to do so would be an undue burden.

Many states, including your state, have fair employment practice laws that prohibit employers from making employment decisions on account of an employee's disability, sex, age, national origin, and other protected classifications. These laws have a "reasonable accommodation" requirement similar to the ADA's.

I cannot tell from your letter precisely why your former employer ended the employment relationship. If you were unable to perform the essential functions of your job, with or without a reasonable accommodation, your former employer had no obligation to continue the employment relationship. However, if your former employer terminated your employment because you requested and took an FMLA leave or on account of your disability, such employment termination would be in violation of these laws. If you are unclear as to why your employment ended, you might consider speaking with the human resources director or personnel manager. The administration of the FMLA and ADA are complicated because of their various and often conflicting requirements and impact on other employment laws.

As you can see from the preceding example, the ADA's "disabilities" and FMLA's "serious health condition" are different concepts. The FMLA entitles eligible employees to 12 weeks of leave in any 12-month period, whereas the ADA allows an indeterminate amount of leave, barring undue hardship, as a reasonable accommodation. In addition, the FMLA requires employers to maintain employees' health benefits during FMLA leave, whereas the ADA does not require maintenance of health insurance unless other employees receive health insurance during leave under the same circumstances.

Following are additional examples of how the ADA and FMLA compare:

1. A reasonable accommodation under the ADA might be accomplished by providing a qualified individual with a disability with a part-time job and no health benefits. In contrast, the FMLA would permit an employee to work a

reduced leave schedule until the equivalent of 12 workweeks of leave was used, with group health benefits maintained during this period.

2. A qualified individual with a disability who is also an "eligible employee" entitled to FMLA leave requests 10 weeks of medical leave as a reasonable accommodation, which the employer grants because it is not an undue hardship. The employer advises the employee that the 10 weeks of leave is also being designated as FMLA and will count toward the employee's FMLA leave entitlement. As such, the employer must continue, if applicable, the employee's health insurance coverage. This designation does not prevent the parties from also treating the leave as a reasonable accommodation and reinstating the employee into the same job, as required by the ADA, rather than as an equivalent position under the FMLA.

3. An employer may not require an employee to transfer to a different job as a reasonable accommodation in lieu of taking FMLA leave entitlement, but the ADA may require the employer to offer the employee an opportunity to take such a position. An employer may not change the essential functions of the job in order to deny FMLA leave.

4. An employer is permitted by the FMLA to require certifications of an employee's fitness for duty to return to work. However, the employer must also comply with the ADA requirement that a fitness-for-duty physical be job-related and consistent with business necessities.

Workers' Compensation

A workers' compensation absence and FMLA leave may run concurrently. If the employee's or employer's health care provider certifies that the employee may return to work in a "light duty" position and the employee's absence is also an FMLA leave, the employee may, but is not required to, accept the "light duty" position. The FMLA provides that employees are entitled to FMLA leave until they are able to return to the same or equivalent job or until the 12-week FMLA leave is exhausted. The FMLA regulations state that "the determinative factor in deciding whether or not the employee is entitled to FMLA leave under this particular set of facts is whether the employee is unable to perform any one or more of the essential functions of the employee's position."

If employees decide to take FMLA leave and decline a "light duty" position, they may no longer be qualified for workers' compensation benefits. In addition, if employees returning from workers' compensation absence are also "qualified individual[s] with a disability," they will have rights under the ADA. Therefore, employers must consider all three laws when evaluating a situation.

Because the workers' compensation absence is not unpaid leave, the provision for substitution of employees' accrued paid leave is not applicable. However, if employees elect not to perform a "light duty" job and therefore lose workers' compensation coverage, or as of the date workers' compensation benefits cease, the substitution provision becomes applicable and the employer may require employees to use accrued paid leave.

COBRA

The FMLA regulations provide guidance on how the Consolidated Omnibus Budget Reconciliation Act (COBRA) applies in relationship to the FMLA requirements. The FMLA regulations state that with respect to employees other than "key" employees,

[A]n employer's obligations to maintain health benefits during leave (and to restore the employee to the same or equivalent employment) under the FMLA ceases if and when:

1. The employment relationship would have terminated if the employee had not taken FMLA leave (e.g. if the employee's position is eliminated as part of a nondiscriminatory reduction in force and the employee would not have been transferred to another position);
2. An employee informs the employer of his or her intent not to return from leave (including before starting the leave if the employer is so informed before the leave starts); or
3. The employee fails to return from leave or continues on leave after exhausting his or her FMLA leave entitlement in the 12-month period.

If a "key" employee does not return from leave when notified by the employer that substantial or grievous economic injury will result from his or her reinstatement, the employee's entitlement to group health plan benefits continues unless and until the employee advises the employer that the employee does not desire restoration to employment at the end of the leave period, or FMLA leave entitlement is exhausted, or reinstatement is actually denied.

An employer's COBRA obligation commences when the employer's obligation to maintain health benefits ceases.

State Disability Laws

Many states have laws that provide employees financial assistance if they are unable to work due to a non-job-related disability. Numerous employers and employees erroneously believe that these state disability laws provide employees time off from work with job security and benefits in addition to the FMLA. However, as with every law, you must consider the law's purpose. The objectives of the FMLA and state disability laws are different. The FMLA protections are job security and continuation of health benefits. The right provided under most state disability laws is financial assistance. Merely because the state disability law may designate how long an employee may be eligible to collect benefits (e.g., for birth of a child), generally it has absolutely no impact upon an employee's FMLA 12-week entitlement. The state disability law does not shorten or lengthen the FMLA leave. The FMLA and state disability law are separate and distinct laws and must be viewed accordingly.

—————■ nine ■—————

Employment Separation

Employment terminations are an inevitable part of the employment relationship. As discussed in Chapter 5, absent an agreement to the contrary, employment is based on mutual consent, and either the employer or employee can end the employment relationship at any time, with or without cause or notice. However, regardless of which party is ending the relationship, certain steps must first be considered.

Employment terminations are emotional for both the messenger and the recipient. Both parties must embrace this fact to avoid creating a battleground from which no one can retreat. Employment terminations are emotional because they entail a severing of a relationship and therefore a piece of oneself. People cannot be involved in a relationship without giving something of themselves. Accordingly, they desire to infuse that missing component with something from another relationship.

The emotional aspect exists regardless of which party precipitated the ending of the relationship. Most employment terminations occur by either the employer firing the employee or the employee quitting, but these obvious scenarios have numerous variations that impact upon the future of the organization and the individual. For example, the employer may fire the employee during a probationary period, after twenty-five years of service for poor performance or gross misconduct, or as a result of a layoff or organizational restructuring. The employee may quit by providing proper advance notice, walking off the job, never reporting to work, or resigning for a better opportunity or out of disgust for the organization. How the relationship is severed affects unemployment compensation benefits, future employment opportunities, reemployment with the same organization, employee morale within the organization, and the individual's self-esteem. Therefore, before ending any employment relationship, it is imperative to consider the long-range objectives before acting upon the short-term gains.

Concluding the employment relationship amicably and voluntarily, whenever possible, serves both parties' best interest. It is human nature to desire to look good. Therefore, most disputes can be avoided by maintaining open and honest communications throughout the employment relationship. From the employer's perspective, it is immensely important to provide employees feedback on how they are performing, counseling when necessary, and documenting any problem areas. This communication, education, and documentation prevent any surprise should the relationship need to end. The interaction also gives employees the opportunity to decide to improve or to seek another employment opportunity. Employees who choose not to follow the employer's guidelines, for whatever reason, should actively look for another job, then voluntarily resign when they find other employment. The benefits of this approach are several. First, employees end their dissatisfaction as soon as possible before other problems are created. Second, it is easier to find a job while still employed. Third, being in control of your own destiny is more empowering and rewarding. Fourth, resigning is more sociably acceptable and personally comfortable.

New Job May Be the Best Option

Q. I believe I was unjustly and unfairly suspended from my job without pay due to a series of ridiculous misunderstandings. In one breath, I was given three warnings and a suspension, with my side of the story falling on deaf ears. Even if all of the allegations were true, which they were not, the punishment does not fit the crime.

The department has lost 20 employees in the past six months due to unbearable working conditions and mismanagement. I was due to transfer to another department within one week when I was abruptly suspended. My suspension was upheld, my transfer blocked, and I was told I would be required to stay in my current department for one year if I wished to remain an employee.

By now, I could not tolerate another day, let alone a year, so I resigned. This could have been what they were hoping to accomplish, given the past record of negative remarks by my former manager. My former manager and I had a tense and hostile relationship.

My question to you is, can they do this to me? Can they block my approved transfer? Can they not pay me for vacation time accrued? Do I have any legal recourse? There is no union at this company.

Anonymous

A.   Although it is never comfortable or acceptable to be accused wrongfully, you made the decision not to allow this organization's employees to disrespect you. Keep in mind that not every job is the right fit, and often it is best to end one employment relationship in order to find a better opportunity elsewhere.

From what you describe, it may be possible that the warnings and suspension you received were the result of the tense and hostile relationship you and your manager had or, as you state, "misunderstandings."

In response to your specific questions, many organizations have established policies, which are permissible, that before employees may transfer to a different department or position, they must have worked in their current position for a specified period of time and must have no current disciplinary action. If your former employer had a similar practice or policy, possibly that is why your transfer was later revoked.

In determining whether you have any legal recourse, you need to ascertain more details surrounding your transfer denial and the organization's past practices. It is also important to determine if the warnings and suspension you received were in accordance with the organization's established practice or policy and if you were treated in the same or similar manner as similarly situated employees.

Although I don't know what you mean by the statement that you and your former manager had a "tense and hostile relationship," a work environment that is hostile based upon the employee's sex, race, age, religion, national origin, disability, veteran status, or similar classification may be unlawful.

I do not have sufficient information concerning your former employer's vacation policy to answer your question on that topic. In general, an employer is not required to provide any vacation benefits. Therefore, an employer may establish any policy it desires concerning the payment of vacation time, so long as the policy is applied on a nondiscriminatory basis. Possibly, your former employer has a policy or practice of not paying any unused vacation time upon employment separation for any reason or when employees do not give proper notice of resignation.

As you did in making your decision to resign, decide what is in your best interest in living a rewarding, fulfilling, and happy life for yourself and those around you. Then take definitive action.

Unfortunately, most individuals are not proactive in taking the necessary steps to protect themselves. Even after employees have been repeatedly warned about their unacceptable employment performance, they often will remain in denial that anything is wrong or that they need to improve. Whether because of such denial, disbelief that the employer would take any adverse action, or refusal to accept personal responsibility, most employees will simply force the employer to fire them. Unfortunately, failure to act or be personally accountable does have some benefits for employees. First, they can play the victim and blame their circumstances on the employer. Second, in most circumstances, unless there is some sort of gross misconduct, they may be eligible for unemployment compensation benefits.

Because every employment termination is a potential lawsuit, the employer must view the totality of circumstances before ending the relationship. For example, has the employer treated similarly situated employees in the same or similar manner? If not, and the employee is a member of a protected group, such firing may be the basis of an employment discrimination claim. In the case of an organizational restructuring or layoff, consider whether the employment separation has an adverse impact upon persons within a protected classification. Even this unintended result may cost the organization hundreds of thousands of dollars if the employer does not devote the time to prepare properly for the employment separation. Therefore, if the employer is the party who must end the relationship, again the factors of communication, education and documentation are essential in order to establish the employer's business reason for making the employment decision should an employment-related claim be filed.

Worker Suspects Racial Prejudice

Q. I was recently let go from my job I had held for about a year and a half. I came to work one day and my boss asked me to report upstairs. He put out his hand and said he had to let me go. I asked why and he replied that I don't work hard enough and I have a bad attitude.

   However, a week prior to this, he had given me a raise of 75 cents an hour. He told me he was going to hire somebody more qualified than me.

   My boss knew that I had financial problems because my parents had died back-to-back a few months earlier. I had to pay off two funerals because neither one had any life insurance. So I really need a job in the worst way, and I am also preparing to get married.

   The person he decided to hire is a former employee who was let go for stealing and doing drugs on the job. This upset me very much because I was never late on the job and I always did my job responsibly. I was never written up for any type of wrongdoing on the job. I could not believe that he would let an honest, hard-working family man who also goes to college in the evening go for this drug addict and thief. I felt I was discriminated against because I am black and the ex-employee hired to replace me is white.

I feel that was my boss's excuse because he did not like seeing me around anymore because I was the only black person on the job. If anything, I feel he unjustly and unlawfully fired me. Do I have any rights?

M. B.

A. My heartfelt condolences to you and your family on the death of your parents.

As for your employment termination, your employer's stated reason was based upon qualifications required for the position, not upon race. The only evidence you present in your letter is your statement of your race. That alone is not sufficient to prove unlawful racial discrimination. In a case of employment discrimination based on race or other protected classifications, the complainant bears the ultimate burden of proof.

To prove unlawful employment termination, first you must prove you are part of a protected classification, you were performing the job at the level of the employer's expectation, you experienced an adverse employment action, and you were replaced by someone outside your protected class. If you meet that test, then the employer has the burden to show that it had a legitimate business interest for terminating your employment. The employer's decision will be protected so long as the decision was not motivated by a discriminatory purpose. This decision will be upheld by the courts unless you can show the reason offered is a pretext for the real motive of race discrimination.

If you believe the decision was based upon race and not your competency, then you may file a charge with the federal Equal Employment Opportunity Commission, the state Civil Rights Agency, or the state Superior Court. Often people become embroiled in litigation to the point that it consumes their lives. Do not let yourself fall into this trap.

You state in your letter that you badly need a job. Of course, you should actively seek other employment opportunities as a means of supporting yourself financially, but note also that if you pursue a claim against your former employer, you have the legal obligation to mitigate your damages by looking for other employment.

Deciding to End the Relationship

Ending the relationship can either bring closure or create costly undesired results. Therefore, before parting ways, you must review the objectives to be achieved by ending the relationship and the means by which they will be accomplished before taking any action. To assist you in deciding how, when, and under what circumstances to end the employment relationship, I outline in this section important guidelines to consider and provide you with a variety of examples.

1. First, review the employee personnel file to ascertain whether there is sufficient documentation concerning the unacceptable performance. Should an employment-related claim be filed, in most cases the employee has the burden of proving that the employer's actions were unlawful. However, most juries and administrative agencies work on the unspoken presumption that if the employer did not document the employee's poor performance or counsel the individual on the need to improve, then the employee's conduct that the employer proclaims is the reason for ending the relationship did not occur. Therefore, proper documentation is key in safeguarding the organization as well as the individual manager or supervisor.

The employee's personnel file usually contains little or no substantiation for the employment termination. In fact, the documentation often is limited to the employee's annual performance appraisal that shows a satisfactory or above-average employee. This type of file can be devastating to the organization should a claim be filed and the employee was not fired for some urgent reason, such as hitting a supervisor or stealing. Although as a general rule an employer has the right to fire an employee for any reason or no reason, with or without notice, the best defense is a good offense, especially in the employment arena where it is so easy to file a lawsuit.

Union Official Questions His Firing

Q. I read your column all the time. I am now unemployed because of my union activities. Here is my story. I organized a union and was the union representative. My boss was moved but then was transferred back again, so he is here with the union. He did not work well with the union because he had to play by the rules of the collective bargaining agreement. My boss told the people in charge to get rid of this union so he can be dictator again.

I was called in the office, and my boss told me I was not going to be hired by the new contractor because of my production. I have never been disciplined verbally or in writing about my production. My employer just wanted to get rid of me and the union. The union's labor lawyer told me to file a National Labor Relations Board charge, which was filed.

Are there any laws I can use to bring a civil suit for my loss of income and the pain and suffering this action has cost me and my family? The reason this occurred was only because I was the union steward. To me that is discrimination. I would appreciate a reply. Thank you.

T. H.

A. Your recourse is based upon the National Labor Relations Act (NLRA), which grants employees the right to join a union for the purpose of bargaining with regard to the employees' wages, hours, and other terms and conditions of employment. If employees elect to be represented by a labor union, the employer must work with the union as the employees' exclusive bargaining representative.

The NLRA refers to prohibited conduct as "unfair labor practice charges." The law has separate lists of unfair labor practice charges for employers and unions. Unfair labor practices by employers include the following:

- Interfering with, restraining or coercing employees in the exercise of their right to bargain collectively;
- Dominating or interfering with the formation or administration of any labor organization or contributing financial or other support to a labor organization;
- Discriminating in regard to hiring, tenure of employment or any term or condition of employment in order to encourage or discourage union membership;
- Discharging or otherwise discriminating against an employee because the employee has filed charges or given testimony pursuant to the NLRA; and
- Refusing to bargain collectively in good faith with the employees' representative.

Even if the employees choose to be represented by a union as their exclusive bargaining representative, the employer still retains the right to hire, discipline, and terminate employees for legitimate business reasons. An employer has the right to expect certain conduct from its employees regardless of the existence of a collective bargaining agreement.

If you believe you have been unlawfully discriminated against because of your union membership and activities, your recourse under the NLRA is to file an unfair labor practice charge with the National Labor Relations Board (NLRB) within six months of the alleged wrongful act. You have the burden of proving that you were a union member, that you were qualified for the position you held or desired, that the adverse employment action was taken because of your union activity, and that you have been damaged. If your employer then shows that it had a legitimate business reason for the action it took, you must establish that the employer's reason is not the true reason but rather is a pretext.

The NLRB will investigate the charge and may conduct a hearing. Should the NLRB find in your favor, possible remedies include reinstatement, with or without back pay, restoration of lost benefits, and an order that the employer cease and desist with regard to certain activities.

2. Examine for full compliance all employment contracts, labor agreements, employee handbooks, representations or promises, past practices, conciliation agreements, affirmative action commitments, or court orders. If any such documents or representations exist, they must be reviewed and a determination made regarding any rights or obligations by either or both parties.

Most employment contracts and collective bargaining agreements outline the reason(s), notice, and procedure that must be followed *before* and in order to end the relationship. Failure to adhere to these requirements may result in a breach of contract as well as be disruptive to the organization's operations and expensive.

Most courts have no desire to enter the employment relationship. Courts will not interfere with the employer and employee's relationship, unless in the face of a lawsuit the complained-of conduct is contrary to a specific obligation or law. The courts prefer to leave the details of the relationship to the employer and employee. Accordingly, courts generally will not direct employers in how to operate their businesses, tell them how to relate to their employees, or dictate the types of employment policies that must be in place. Thus, employers are free to develop and end their own employment relationships with their employees.

In certain circumstances, however, courts will assess the intrinsic fairness of the employer's actions. In those circumstances, the courts will evaluate the allegedly unfair behavior from the perspective of what the employer has communicated to its employees and whether the employer has honored its commitment.

As noted in the previous chapters, the employment relationship has many facets that make it operational. Some components are larger than others; however, they all contribute to whether the relationship is fully functional, working at partial capacity, or gasping for life. It is important to address even those smaller but important attributes that oil the machinery or clog its smooth operation.

Unions at Company May Obtain Different Worker Benefits

Q. I worked as a warehouseman for a company for 37 years, and last year, the company decided to close the department down. They would not talk to the union I was a member of. I was 59 years old then.

   At the same time, the company offered buyouts to other employees, who were 57 years old, in another union in the company. The company gave me 10 weeks' severance pay. I now have to scuffle and work just to pay for medical coverage, which they also took away. Did I get treated fair and square? Thanks.

   L. S.

A. I am sorry to hear about your employment separation and difficulty you have experienced. Absent an agreement or past practice, an employer has no obligation to provide employees severance pay regardless of the circumstances, including when there is a department closing, plant closing, or other reason. Similarly, an employer has no obligation to provide its employees medical insurance benefits. Rather, such an employment benefit is provided to employees as part of their compensation for services being rendered to the employer.

   However, if an employer does provide medical insurance coverage during the employment relationship and is covered by the federal Consolidated Omnibus Budget Reconciliation Act (COBRA) or similar state law, it must offer, at the employee's expense, continuation of medical coverage upon the employment separation.

   Without knowing more, I would say the fact that your employer provided you 10 weeks' severance pay appears to be a positive in light of the fact that the company may not have had an obligation to pay any severance at all.

   The part of your inquiry about whether the employer had an obligation to discuss the severance pay with your union falls under the National Labor Relations Act, which governs the relationship between employers and labor organizations. The NLRA provides that employers and unions have the obligation to meet and bargain over the union employees' wages, hours, and other terms and conditions of employment. As a general matter, this bargaining obligation would include severance pay.

In regard to your particular situation, it is possible that your employer and union previously discussed this matter and agreed that the employer would not pay any severance or would provide the severance you received. Such an agreement would most likely be found in the collective bargaining agreement.

With respect to what transpired with the other union, each union represents a specified class of employees and accordingly may bargain to receive different benefits. More information is needed to know why those union members received a buyout package.

To determine whether you were treated fairly, you would need to have more information from the union and your former employer as to how other similarly situated employees were treated. The focus of your inquiry would be if there were differences and whether they occurred for legitimate business reasons and not because of age, sex, race, disability, or other protected classification.

While you ascertain the answers to your additional questions, remember to keep focused on what you do currently possess—the ability to work to pay for your medical insurance coverage.

In my practice, I regularly counsel employers on the ever-expanding area of employee separations and severance packages. Several issues that all employers need to keep in mind are the age of the person who is affected, the reason for the separation, the class of people being separated, the age of the people in the class, and if applicable, the age of the person who replaced the separated person.

These few factors alone may involve the Age Discrimination in Employment Act, which was amended by the Older Workers Benefit Protection Act, if the employer requires the employee to sign a general release in return for severance benefits. Many traps exist for the unwary business owner, who should consult an employment attorney to avoid any unwarranted litigation in this changing and troublesome area of the law.

3. Treatment of similarly situated employees and the consequences of their actions must be consistent in order to maintain employee loyalty and avoid discrimination claims. As discussed earlier, it is relatively easy and inexpensive to file a claim of unlawful employment discrimination. Because of the multiple protected classifications, most individuals can find their way into at least one, if not several, protected groups. Accordingly, the employer must determine the reason for the employment termination and ascertain how other employees who acted in a similar manner were treated. If the result was not employ-

ment termination, it is best not to progress to that stage at the current time. The key word here is "time." Given enough time, a problem employee will usually give the employer enough opportunity to document and support the ending of the relationship. Thus, patience is a virtue, and timing is everything. These attributes are powerful employment termination considerations.

Although it is frustrating not to be able to terminate a poorly performing, disrespectful employee immediately, nothing is more devastating then being required to pay that same individual a lot of money or later reinstating the person. Rather, let nature take its course, which in most circumstances means it will be only a matter of time before the individual does something to fully support the employment termination decision. Respect and fairness are mandated at every stage of the employment relationship, right up to the end and even thereafter.

Worker Feels Coerced

Q. I have worked for a doctor for four years. The office has only two employees. I worked 35 to 38 hours a week for several years, but six months ago, my hours were cut to 28 to 32 hours a week.

The doctor's wife, who came in once a week to pay us, cut my hours, saying they had money problems. She said I could work more hours if I got paid under the table for half of my hours like the other employee.

When I refused to get paid under the table, she accepted this, but since then the doctor and other employee have been very rude and nasty to me. I filed an unemployment claim for the difference in hours, but the hours I was cut are just short of any compensation. In addition, the other employee said they are trying to get me to quit because they don't want to pay any unemployment claims.

Recently my hours were cut again, and the doctor's wife said that I needed to rest more since I was getting older. I am 53, and the other employee is 29. The doctor's wife said that she doesn't expect me to be as fast as a young person. I found this ridiculous, since I worked there for four years and never had any problem with the work. In fact, I am much faster and more proficient then my younger coworker.

As a single parent with two college students, I cannot just leave without another position. I have not found another job as yet, but feel the situation here is very hostile and I am being treated differently from my coworker. This is causing me considerable stress and anxiety.

E. S.

A.   Although you may feel ready to explode, your employer is the one with the explosive situation on his hands. Employers from time to time do incur financial difficulties, but to attempt to remedy their economic condition by engaging in unlawful conduct is reprehensible.

Your employer's attempt to entice you to receive half of your salary on the books and the other half off the books is explicitly prohibited by the federal Fair Labor Standards Act and the state Wage Payment Law. Employees who are paid off the books are prevented from accruing credits for Social Security and other governmental benefits. In addition, honest employers paying employment taxes are put at a competitive disadvantage, since the dishonest employer does not absorb this cost.

The comment made to you by the doctor's wife that you needed more rest since you were getting older is a potentially damaging statement. It indicates discriminatory thinking on behalf of the employer. It is unlawful to discriminate against an employee based upon the person's age. The federal Age Discrimination in Employment Act provides a protected classification for individuals over 40 years old. The state antidiscrimination law also prohibits employment-related decisions based upon age.

There are four elements an employee must prove to show age discrimination. You must be a member of the protected class, your work level must meet the employer's legitimate expectations, you must have been fired or otherwise adversely affected, and your employer must have hired a replacement who is substantially younger.

From the skeletal facts provided in your letter, it appears that you meet the age criteria, you work faster and more efficiently than your younger coworker, your coworker admits the doctor is harassing you into leaving, and presumably your job responsibilities would be assumed by the younger coworker or an entry-level person.

In addition, you may have a potential whistleblower claim. The state whistleblower law prohibits an employer from discharging or otherwise discriminating against an employee because the employee

- Discloses or threatens to disclose to a supervisor or to a public body an activity, policy or practice of the employer or another employer with whom there is a business relationship that the employee reasonably believes is in violation of a law;

- Provides information to or testifies before any public body conducting an investigation, hearing or inquiry into any violation of law, or a rule or

regulation promulgated by the employer or another employer with
whom there is a business relationship;

- Objects to or refuses to participate in any activity, policy or practice
  which the employee reasonably believes:

    1. is in violation of a law;
    2. is fraudulent or criminal; or
    3. is incompatible with a clear mandate of public policy concerning
        the public health, safety or welfare or protection of the environ-
        ment.

If you exercise your right to confront your employer to correct the practice of paying you and your coworker under the table, or if the discrimination continues against you for refusing to participate in this impermissible
form of payment, the whistleblower law provides you protection. Although
neither scenario is pleasant, knowing your rights will instill confidence in
your stance against participation in an illegal act.

Ending the Employment Relationship

After all the necessary documentation (e.g., the employee's personnel file) and
other pertinent information (applicable representations or past practices) have
been reviewed, the employer will have decided whether to end the employment relationship. If everything appears to be in order, the next step in executing the decision is just as important as the first step. This phrase of the
process is even more delicate because it involves delivering the message in an
empathic and firm manner, among other proactive mandates. As with step
one, failure to expend the necessary time to map out the best course of action
can have devastating and expensive results. In evaluating how best to proceed,
the employer must keep in the forefront the reason(s) for or the type of employment separation. For example, is the employment termination the result
of a large-scale layoff or corporate reorganization, or is it limited to a single
employee? Each type of employment ending has special concerns and therefore must be given individual consideration.

Accordingly, once the decision has been made to end the employment relationship, it is crucial to consider the following items:

1. *Reason for the employment termination.* As discussed in Chapter 1, honesty is
always the best and only policy. Often employers will not tell the employee

whose employment is being severed the reason for the termination or will give what they believe to be a more "palatable" reason. Both courses of conduct have negative results. In the first situation, the employee is left wondering what happened, which creates an inability to put closure on the relationship. Most employers mistakenly believe the less said the better. With some exceptions, an employer has no obligation to report to the employee the reason for the termination, but the employee often will file some type of employment-related claim that requires the employer to state the reason. Again, the long-term benefits of being respectful and properly closing the relationship produce better results. As discussed earlier, place yourself in the shoes of the employee whose employment is being ended. What would be important to you?

Unfair Decision Is Not Illegal

Q. I was working for a temporary agency at a site where a former employer frequently appeared to retrieve paperwork. Each time she came, she would look for me as well as other employees who worked for her and disturb us. We would totally ignore her, but she made her presence known.

One day, after my duties were done, my supervisor approached me and told me not to return to work until I talked to my agency. Two days later, I contacted the agency and was told that I was threatening my ex-employer, and that the company didn't want me there anymore. The agency wanted me to come and work at their main branch.

I was never asked my side of the situation, nor did I receive any write-ups. My performance at this job was always friendly and cordial. I feel as though my agency took her word over mine and that's unfair. Do I have grounds for any legal action?

Anonymous

A. It is always frustrating to have others tell lies about you. Right now you are absorbed with the perceived unfair treatment from both your ex-employer and the temporary employer. As with most decisions in life, you must evaluate how you can best profit from your most precious commodity, time.

You state this unfortunate situation occurred at your temporary assignment employer. It appears from your description that the ex-employer would frequent the establishment of the temporary employer to conduct business.

Obviously, if the temporary employer receives information that would jeopardize any of his or her business relationships, a prudent business owner would take certain steps to correct the offending conduct. In this case, the temporary employer decided to take immediate action by terminating your assignment with the business, a decision that was well within its rights to make. The decision to eliminate your temporary position is neither a bad nor a good decision. Rather, it is a business decision.

On the positive side, there is no mention in your letter of conflict at the main branch where you were reassigned. It is always better to work in an environment free from the stress you were experiencing at the temporary assignment where your ex-employer disturbed you on several occasions.

2. *Timing of the employment separation.* The adage "timing is everything" holds true in ending the employment relationship. For example, you know the employee needs to be told as soon as possible that his employment is being terminated. You also know that tomorrow he is leaving for a preapproved two-week vacation. Is it wise to tell the employee today that he is no longer an employee of the organization, or is it better to inform the individual after he has rested for two weeks in the Caribbean? Obviously, the latter option is in everyone's best interest. However, I find it amazing how little thought employers give to such an important and often emotionally devastating message.

Although you may have no legal obligation to delay the message until the employee returns from vacation, treating others as you desire to be treated will get you better results every time. Remember, we are discussing relationships, only part of which are regulated. Not regulated is the largest aspect of the employment relationship— respect and common courtesy. These characteristics must always be in the forefront of every employment decision. Time and again, employees file lawsuits because management made some error in judgment, or they believe their employer treated them unfairly. Often the employer has technically complied with the law, but there is also what Thomas Jefferson called "the spirit of the law." Many jurors side with employees out of empathy, and almost certainly most jurors will be workers, just like the person suing. This human side of the legal equation must remain in focus. Most lawsuits are filed out of anger. Thus, consider the options and consequences of your decision before proceeding. In making these determinations, check your pride and ego at the front door. "Pride goeth before destruction, and an haughty spirit before a fall." Proverbs 16:18.

3. *Delivery of the employment termination message.* Who should deliver the message and whether there should be more than one management representative present during the meeting are important questions to ask *before* ending the employment relationship. In making this decision, you must ask who is best able to

be sensitive to the employee's needs yet firm, and who has the most firsthand knowledge regarding the basis for the employment separation. Generally the "terminator" (for lack of a better word) is the employee's immediate supervisor or department head and/or the personnel manager or human resources director. These persons are the chosen communicators because of their knowledge of the individual whose employment is being ended, the reason for the termination, and the organization's position in how it has treated other similar situations.

I recommend having at least two management representatives present during an employment termination meeting. First, communicating the termination message to an individual is always a daunting task, and having another person present provides some support. Second, documentation of the employment termination meeting is important. To avoid a two-on-one situation, one person should do all the speaking and the other should serve in the supportive and documenting role. Third, a second pair of eyes and ears may be important to guard against one person's word against another's as to what transpired during the employment separation meeting. However, I do not recommend having more than two management representatives attend, because it creates the impression that management is ganging up on the employee. Again, unfairness is the last impression you want to create.

4. *Location and hour of the termination meeting.* The meeting time and location are critical components in respecting the interests of the employee being terminated and the health and welfare of the other employees. No one wants the employment separation to be the news flash of the day with unnecessary disrespect and attention directed at the employee (although in certain circumstances, the organization's best interest might dictate that security help the employee clean out his or her desk and escort the individual to the front door). Thus, consider all of the pertinent details and ask relevant questions: What is most respectful and necessary based upon the objective evidence? How often have you heard about inhuman-type firings? How did they make you feel? Most of us have heard or experienced inhuman treatment and have felt anger, fear, and betrayal even when the employer may have been justified. In throwing a person overboard without a life preserver, you must never lose sight of the remaining survivors whose well-being and loyalty are necessary in safely navigating the course.

5. *Meeting preparation.* Preparation is everything. Outline the discussion and review what to say and what not to say during the meeting. How a message is communicated is often more important than its content. Anticipate what

questions will be raised and be prepared to provide an answer. Plan and re-
hearse all aspects of the meeting to anticipate the unexpected and combat
nervousness. Ending the employment relationship is one of the least desirable
and most stressful job responsibilities. Unfortunately, this difficulty results in re
tention of many employees who should have been fired long ago. This fear is
a roadblock and can be removed by preparation, preparation, preparation.

For example, what is or is not said may result in unwanted future interactions. When an organization terminates an employee, the first reaction is
shock, hurt, and vulnerability, which the employer must address. Nevertheless,
in most severance or termination situations, not one word is either said or
written to thank these individuals for their service and the contributions they
made over the years. When the termination event occurs without any warning, softening, or showing of appreciation, the employer can expect litigation,
even if it is frivolous. If time is taken to prepare properly for the employment
separation, regardless of the reason for it, most lawsuits will be prevented. Underlying most lawsuits is not just monetary greed but the desire to inflict pain
on the other party in a greater degree than the individual experienced. If this
retributive expression is eliminated, both employers and employees will gain
from the experience. Employees will move on with their lives, and employers
will not encounter frivolous litigation. Thus, recognizing the worth and contributions of separated employees has priceless results.

6. *Employee meeting.* Get to the point quickly and tell the employee on what
grounds the decision was made. Be empathetic to the individual and his or her
personal concerns, but be sure you clearly state the person's employment is
terminated. Allow the employee to vent anger and express feelings of betrayal, mismanagement, and anxiety. It is best not to engage in a debate and
defend the organization's decision for a number of reasons. First, at this stage
in the relationship, it serves absolutely no purpose. Second, it may incite the
individual. Third, it is draining with absolutely no reward. Fourth, you want the
individual to release some of his or her anger because if the employee is
forced to repress the hurt feelings with no outlet, they generally appear later in
the form of a claim of unlawful employment termination or an act of violence.
Again, employees want to be heard. If this forum is not available, they will create one later.

Allow time for and encourage the individual to ask questions. If possible,
answer all questions, and if you do not know the answer, inform the employee you will get it and will be in touch soon. Then, without fail, follow up
on your representation, obtain the necessary information, and respond to the

individual within a reasonable period of time. If you cannot immediately discover the answer, telephone the individual and explain the situation. At all times be fair, reasonable, and honest in your communications with the person.

7. Benefits, if any, to be paid. Find out before the meeting what moneys are due to the employee for actual time worked and unused sick, vacation, or personal time. If you do not have an exact amount, at least know the employer's policies concerning these items. Know whether the employee participates in the employer's health insurance plan, pension plan, or other employer-sponsored programs and how the employee's participation in those programs is affected by the employment termination.

The key to the successful employment termination is in remembering and demonstrating through your actions that although this employee will no longer be employed tomorrow, the person still has basic needs and obligations that must be addressed. The very reasons that persuaded the employee to accept the employment opportunity are often the very items the employee does not now want to lose. Most jurors in hearing and deciding employment-related claims place themselves in the shoes of the discharged employee. Step into those same shoes before the employment termination. This perspective will guide you accordingly and in much the same manner as it does jurors. Are you and the organization being understanding, fair, reasonable? How will other employees respond when they learn of the employment termination? Is this how you desire to be treated? Is this how you desire your best friend, mother, father, spouse, son, daughter, or significant other to be treated? If you read about this action in the newspaper, how would it read? Only after you have honestly and objectively answered these questions can you proceed with confidence that you are doing the right thing.

8. General release and waiver. Often an employer desires to assist the employee during the transitional period from being unemployed to re-employed or has a real concern that the employee will file an employment-related claim. In those and other circumstances, the employer will offer the employee a severance package or other financial assistance. However, before providing any assistance that is not otherwise mandated by law or contract, the employer should first obtain the individual's written agreement not to sue the organization for any reason, known or unknown, up to the date of the executed agreement and general release. Unfortunately, many employers have provided employees severance benefits they were under no obligation to furnish, only to have the now former employee turn around and sue the employer. Merely because the employer has acted appropriately does not necessarily mean that terminated employees will conduct themselves in the same manner. Similarly, most jurors do not give an employer who has provided only average severance arrangements much benefit of the doubt in balancing the scale of justice. Money has no purchasing power for the most important life qualities, and jurors continually teach us this important lesson of life.

Even if the employer requires former employees to sign a general release in return for the benefit, the employer must ensure the agreement is properly prepared. Frequently, employers have granted benefits pursuant to a signed agreement and general release only to find later that the document is unenforceable.

Thus, the Older Workers Benefit Protection Act, an amendment to the Age Discrimination in Employment Act, provides a good guideline on how to prepare a proper general release. That statute states that a waiver of any right or claim must be "knowing and voluntary." To meet this standard, it must, at a minimum, meet the following requirements:

A. the waiver is part of an agreement between the individual and the employer that is written in a manner calculated to be understood by such individual, or by the average individual eligible to participate;

B. the waiver specifically refers to rights or claims arising under this chapter being waived or given up;

C. the individual does not waive rights or claims that may arise after the date the waiver is executed;

D. the individual waives rights or claims only in exchange for consideration in addition to anything of value to which the individual is not already entitled;

E. the individual is advised in writing to consult with an attorney prior to executing the agreement;

F.   (i) the individual is given a period of at least 21 days within which to consider the agreement; or

(ii) if the waiver is requested in connection with an exit incentive or other employment termination program offered to a group or class of employees, the individual is given a period of at least 45 days within which to consider the agreement;

G. the agreement provides that for a period of at least 7 days following the execution of such agreement, the individual may revoke the agreement, and the agreement shall not become effective or enforceable until the revocation period has expired;

H. if the waiver is requested in connection with an exit incentive or other employment termination program offered to a group or class of employees, the employer (at the commencement of the period specified in subparagraph [F]) informs the individual in writing in a manner calculated to be understood by the average individual eligible to participate, as to—

(i) any class, unit or group of individuals covered by such program, any eligibility factors for such program, and any time limits applicable to such program; and

(ii) the job titles and ages of all individuals eligible or selected for such program, and the ages of all individuals in the same job classification or organizational unit who are not eligible or selected for the program.

Because of some current judicial decisions, it is also advisable to include in the agreement that the employer is not responsible for paying the individual's attorneys' fees or any other fees or expenses. Or if attorneys' fees or other specified expenses are to be paid, then expressly state in the agreement the purpose of the payment. Similarly, because the purpose of the settlement agreement is to avoid any and all current and/or future litigation and amicably resolve the parties' differences, a statement needs to be included in the agreement that the employee is not a prevailing party in any action or lawsuit. Failure to specify such provisions has resulted in employers paying more than originally anticipated.

9. *Exit interview.* Exit interviews with employees who quit or are discharged are beneficial to both the employer and employee for a number of reasons. First, it brings closure to the relationship. The importance of this closure is usually underestimated. Most persons have difficulty moving forward without having resolved open issues. No one is served well by having lingering disturbances persist. If not addressed as completely as possible, they will reappear in current or prospective employees and customers as well as the employee's future employers. Second, the exit interview is an opportunity to have all property belonging to the organization returned, such as keys, computers, employee handbooks, telephone lists, prescription cards, and identification badges or, if the individual has lost any property, to ensure its replacement or payment for its replacement. Third, use this time to furnish information regarding the individual's final paycheck and benefits. Fourth, the interview is an opportunity to discuss the former employee's experiences with the organization and make any suggestions for improvements. This may possibly be the most honest and valuable communication of the entire relationship. Thus, invest the time to

learn and avoid future mistakes. You need not agree with what is being said, but there may be a grain of truth in the comments. Fifth, the exit interview is a time for both parties to move forward together and discuss future plans.

10. *Written confirmation of the employment separation.* Document through and up to the end of the employment relationship. Close out an employee's personnel file with a memorandum or letter reciting the reason for the employment separation and the last day of work. Like a good book, the employment relationship has a beginning and an ending. Similarly, the personnel file has a commencement date and an ending date. Make your records complete. You might not have the opportunity to speak with the individual personally to communicate the employment ending because the employee walked off the job or simply failed to report to work; nevertheless, document the facts and confirm the same in writing to the employee. Following is an example of this type of letter sent to the employee by regular and certified mail, return receipt requested:

> This letter is to confirm that you have voluntarily resigned your employment with the organization, effective [insert last day worked]. The organization's established policy and practice are that any employee who does not report or call in to work for more than three consecutive days will be deemed to have resigned voluntarily. You last worked on [insert date]. You did not report or call in to work on [insert date], [insert date], [insert date], and [insert date]. Therefore, you have chosen to no longer be employed by the organization as of [insert last day worked]. We wish you well in your future endeavors.

This type of documentation will also serve the employer well in disputing the employee's eligibility for unemployment compensation benefits should a claim be filed.

Retaliation

For anyone deciding to end an employment relationship, it is important to remember that employers provide employment opportunities. The basis of the opportunity is usually dependent on the employer's needs and the employee's performance, skills, experiences, and abilities. Absent the fulfillment of these factors, the reason for the relationship disappears. The law does not require an employer to change its business operations, policies, rules, or procedures because some employees refuse to abide by them. When an employer has informed such employees about their performance deficiencies and the employees still refuse to recognize their problem, the employer at that point may exercise its legitimate business interest in ending the relationship. Although all individuals are subject to the imperfections of being human, they have the ability to address their mistakes and thus to better themselves. Unfortunately, some employees refuse to rectify their mistakes when given repeated opportunity. Consequently, these employees choose a course of indifference.

If employees continually reject the constructive directives of their superiors, only one decision is left for management: What is in the best interest of the organization, its customers or clients, and the other employees? A healthy organization has no place for individuals who will not give their best. Many employment terminations are elected solely by employees based upon their chosen conduct. Many employees fail to see their responsibility in the employment relationship and believe that the employer owes them more than their paycheck. Unfortunately, this thought process prevents such employees from seeing how their actions impact upon the work environment.

Unlawful employment retaliation claims are on the rise. Webster's defines "retaliation" as "to return like for like, to get revenge." Federal and state employment laws prohibit employers from retaliating against employees and provide that an employer may not discharge or otherwise discriminate against an individual for having (1) filed a claim or causing to be instituted an action against the employer under one of the employment laws; (2) given or about to give any information in connection with any inquiry or proceeding relating to any employment rights; or (3) testified or about to testify in any inquiry or proceeding relating to any employment rights. Following is an example of an employee's claim that she was fired because she filed a complaint of age discrimination against her employer. Although the employer will probably argue that it fired the employee because it confirmed its initial suspicions that she stole company computers, the timing of the alleged retaliatory act—the employment termination—is also an important fact that will need to be addressed.

Unequal Treatment and Retaliation

Q. I worked for a large and respectable company but the managers shafted me. They came up to me and told me I stole $20,000 worth of computers. I did not do any such thing. They suspended me without pay for six weeks. On the second week I went to the state Civil Rights Agency. People there determined that based on the facts, there was an age discrimination case, so I signed a complaint. As soon as the company was served with the papers, I was immediately fired with no explanation. I could not collect unemployment benefits because my employer had me on the books still.

I had planned on retiring from this company I used to respect. My employer made me look like a criminal to my peers and feel humiliated and played with the unemployment laws so I could not collect sooner. Does the fact that I stood up and fought back give the company the right to put me through this? What rights does a person have? How long will it take for truth to prevail, for them to apologize, and how can corporations be stopped from hurting innocent people, imposing blatant discrimination, and taking belligerent actions against people?

J. K.

A.   As it appears you have learned, the state Civil Rights Office is the administrative agency authorized to enforce the state antidiscrimination law. The state legislature in enacting the law expressly declared "that practices of discrimination against any of its inhabitants, because of race, creed, color, national origin, ancestry, age, sex, affectional or sexual orientation, marital status, familial status, liability for service in the Armed Forces of the United States, or nationality are matters of concern to the government of the State, and that such discrimination threatens not only the rights and proper privileges of the inhabitants of the State but menaces the institutions and foundation of a free democratic State."

The law prohibits unlawful discrimination based on one of the protected categories listed and provides a remedy if such actions are found to have occurred. In addition, the statute makes it unlawful for any person or entity to take any reprisals or retaliatory action against individuals because they have opposed any practices forbidden under the law or because they have filed a complaint, testified, or assisted in any proceeding under this law.

If you believe you were fired because you filed a claim with the Civil Rights Agency, you may amend the complaint you already filed with the state agency to include retaliatory discharge. The agency will investigate your allegations as well as the company's defenses and make a determination as to whether there is sufficient recorded evidence to support a finding of probable cause of unlawful employment discrimination. In addition, you may also file or request the agency to have the matter dually filed with the federal Equal Employment Opportunity Commission (EEOC) under the Age Discrimination in Employment Act.

Because of the large number of complaints, there is currently a three- to four-year investigation period at the state level. The backlog at the federal level is also quite extensive. However, the EEOC is charged with completing its investigation within 180 days, or the individual may request a "right to sue" letter authorizing the individual to file a lawsuit in federal court. You will probably never receive an apology, and I suggest you abandon that objective. With respect to your question about getting corporations to stop unlawfully discriminating, the purpose of the various employment laws is to prevent and deter others from treating persons differently based upon their membership in a protected classification.

Your concerns regarding unemployment compensation benefits should have been addressed with the state Department of Labor, Division of Unemployment and Disability Insurance, at the time you filed your claim or received notice of your eligibility and date of eligibility or ineligibility to receive benefits. Depending on how long it has been since the department rendered its determination, you may still seek to have the matter addressed.

Good luck in seeking to have the truth heard. Keep in mind that during this process you have the legal obligation as well as the responsibility to yourself to mitigate your damages by looking for other employment.

When people believe their rights have been violated or they have not been treated fairly and with respect, human nature is to get even. Although one avenue for employees is to file a retaliation claim with a federal or state court or administrative agency, following is another option employees pursue.

Most Workers on Job During Lunch Must Be Paid

Q. My former employer violated the wage laws. I know this for a fact because I called Wage and Hour (the state Office of Wage and Hour Compliance) and they confirmed the violation. The violation was that my company insisted that all supervisors take a half hour lunch if they work more than six hours in one day and then they had to sign out and could not leave the premises. In other words, supervisors are forced to take an unpaid lunch and be on-call in case they are needed, and many a time, they are.

When you stand on your feet all day dealing with customers, one-half hour of reprieve can really clear your head and make for a better employee. My suggestion is either give all employees the responsibilities to be able to run the store in the supervisor's absence, or pay them for their lunch time.

I do not plan to file a claim regarding this issue. This was a major reason I left the company. I just wanted people to be aware that according to Wage and Hour, if the company insists that you stay on the premises and does not pay you for lunch, it is violating the law. Here is my question: Why are so many employers getting away with forcing their supervisors to stay on the premises during their lunch without pay?

K. H.

A.   The state Wage and Hour Law establishes, among other items, minimum wage and overtime pay. The Wage and Hour Regulations, which interpret the statute, state that employees shall be paid for all hours worked. The regulations further provide that for purposes of computing all hours worked, all time that employees are required to be at their place of work or on duty shall be counted as hours worked.

However, an employer is not required to pay employees for hours they are not required to be at their place of work because of holidays, vacation, lunch hours, illness, and similar reasons. As you pointed out, when employees are required to remain on the employer's premises and are not free to engage in their own pursuits, that time may be computed as hours worked because it is subject to restrictions on the employees' freedom to engage in personal activities.

Computing the number of hours employees work is necessary for determining not only the regular rate of pay but also overtime pay. Overtime compensation is required to be paid to those employees who work more than 40 hours in any week and are not exempted from the overtime-pay provisions. Exempt employees are not entitled to any additional compensation for working extra hours beyond a 40-hour workweek. These employees are paid on a salary or fee basis, not hourly.

Although each case is reviewed on its particular facts, generally those employees who work in a managerial or supervisory capacity are exempted from the overtime provisions. Absent an agreement to the contrary between the employer and the employee, these employees are not entitled to additional compensation for working during lunchtime. The basis for this rule is that exempt employees are paid a salary from which, with limited exceptions, no deductions may be made for time not worked. This form of compensation is also balanced by the greater freedom managers and supervisors experience in the workplace because they have more responsibility and accountability and are not paid on an hourly basis.

As you can see from the preceding discussion, many considerations must be reviewed, analyzed, and discussed *before* an employer lays off or terminates employees' employment or employees leave their employment. The more thought, time, and documentation expended in the preparation of the employment separation, the more successful the transition will be for both the employer and employee. From the employer's perspective, there will be continuation of smooth operations, maintenance of employee morale, and avoidance of potential litigation. For the employee, there will be continuation of pride and dignity, maintenance of self-esteem and good relations, and avoidance of future pitfalls.

Time and again employees file lawsuits due to some error in judgment by management or they believe they were treated unfairly by their employer. I have heard tragic stories of thirty-year workers who were properly dismissed in accordance with the technical aspect of the law but not within the spirit of the law. When employees receive their final paycheck with a COBRA notice and vacation pay, the employer may have complied with all the proper notices except one: appreciation. A common question executives ask when first learning of a lawsuit is, "What will it take (money) to settle the case?" The better question is, "What problem do we have that needs to be corrected?" As touched upon earlier, money will not solve the human problems. Rather, properly instructed personnel will prevent the situation from arising in the first instance. Approximately ninety percent of the time, if management personnel had only fulfilled their responsibility, the explosive situation would never had arisen, thus averting human loss and costly litigation. In considering any employment separation, the human factors need to be evaluated as well.

Employee Considerations in
Ending the Employment Relationship

On the other side of the equation is the fact that many employment terminations are elected by employees—from landing a more satisfying job to forcing a termination as a result of consistently disrespectful behavior, such as failing to report to work on time for two months.

In most circumstances, retaliation serves no one. Therefore, employees also must consider and review their options as to how and when to end their employment relationship and what course of action will best support their future plans. Like anyone, employers talk among one another and share information about employee conduct.

The guidelines that follow will assist employees in charting a proper employment closure, which will help ensure a professional and positive termination:

Respecting the employer
   Provide two to four weeks' advance notice of employment resignation.
   Complete and/or organize all projects to allow for a smooth transition.
   Educate and/or train employee assigned to take over employment duties.

Furnish contact number should former employer have any future inquiries concerning job responsibilities.

Return all property and equipment in as good condition as when it was received and/or replace any lost or damaged property or equipment.

Respecting yourself

Burn no bridges, as you may need to cross them again.

Obtain a job while still employed.

Request a letter of recommendation.

Never speak poorly of or ridicule your former employer or any coworker.

Clarify what happens to unused employment benefits and the continuation of any health insurance or similar employee programs.

As discussed in earlier chapters, the employment relationship is a dual equation. Again, I have shown how similar are the interests of both the employer and employee in having and using good communication. The objective in severing employment is to bring full and proper closure to the employment relationship.

—————■ ten ■—————

Planning for Life After Employment Termination

Like death and taxes, employment termination is a certainty of life. In today's society in which people are more mobile and marketable, employment termination is increasing in our economy. For most employees, concluding an employment relationship is difficult and often personally devastating, even when employees voluntarily choose to terminate the relationship. Like any other closure in life, termination is a natural process that must be experienced—denial, anger, bargaining, and acceptance. However, from my seventeen years of practicing labor and employment law and my life's experiences, I have found that 99 percent of the time, ending of the employment relationship is mutually beneficial to the employee and employer.

In general, each employment opportunity is like every life relationship—a stepping stone to acquiring new information or abilities that are infused into the next relationship or phase of life. Again, regardless of the underlying factors for employment separation, employees must examine the part they played in bringing it about. After this self-analysis, they will be able to extract the essential positive components from their prior employment and use that powerful knowledge for the next employment relationship. Employees who fail or refuse to see their role in ending the relationship usually will be doomed to repeat the same behavior in their next employment relationship. Any problematic traits will persist until they are reviewed and corrected.

People don't want to look into life's mirror for fear of seeing their true image, but not looking means never discovering the truth. The reflection in the mirror will reveal the frailties and faults we all possess. Taking the time to build upon our strengths and face our shortcomings will let us see any undesirable underpinnings that can then be replaced by more admirable characteristics.

"Proud men end in shame, but the meek become wise." Proverbs 11:2. We all bear responsibility for the relationships we enter and therefore must be honest with ourselves about both our strengths and weaknesses.

Shedding false images will enable individuals to improve upon those areas that need attention, and surprisingly, most people discover their positive attributes are suddenly more pronounced to others. Like Snow White and the Seven Dwarfs, employers and employees must ask themselves the following rhyme:

> *Mirror, mirror, on the wall*
> *Who knows the fairest assessment of them all?*
> *For it is I who have looked and lo and behold*
> *It is I and only I who can reveal what I have been told.*

In assessing our characteristics or in deciding to make an important decision that will have lasting effects on our well-being, it is always helpful to speak with a respected colleague, mentor, or trusted friend. Obtaining another person's perspective on a situation can have only positive rewards. Choosing to act alone can lead to negative consequences, as demonstrated in the next example.

Job Seeker Is Not Protected

Q. Recently I was fired from my job. I was fired for asking for a letter of reference for a future job. On a Friday I asked my department manager to write the letter, and he ignored me.

Later in the day I went to the store manager and asked him to write the letter. He sighed and said he would have to ask one of his superiors. Assuming everything was all right, I finished my shift and went home.

When I returned to work on Monday, nothing was said about the letter. But around 1 p.m. the store manager approached me and said that I should have kept the job I was applying for to myself and that he had to let me go, on orders from his superior. I was fired for asking for a letter.

I would appreciate it if you could give me your opinion on this matter and if taking further action is necessary. Thank you for your time.

M. H.

A. The general rule of law is that without an employment agreement, representation, or collective bargaining agreement, or in the absence of unlawful conduct, the employment relationship is at-will. Under the employment-at-will doctrine, the employer or employee may end the employment relationship at any time, for any reason or no reason, with or without advance written notice.

There is no protection for employees who ask their current employer for a reference letter for a future job. Your former employer's negative reaction to the request was not unusual. When employees are actively seeking another job while currently employed, most will ask the prospective employer to keep the application confidential until an employment offer has been made, so as not to jeopardize the current relationship.

The employment offer may be conditioned upon receiving a favorable reference from the current employer. Most people understand the sensitive nature of changing allegiance to a new employer.

In this explosive arena of employment litigation, most employers will not even provide reference letters. Most organizations have a firm policy that the only information they will provide to a prospective employer is the employee's date of hire, title, and salary.

The courts have consistently ruled that trust and loyalty are the two primary components of the employment relationship. When these characteristics are absent, so is the relationship. Apparently this is how your former employer felt.

When employees make it clear that their interests or loyalties are divided, employers often will end the relationship immediately out of concern for the organization and its assets. History has shown that divided loyalties result in disloyalty. Employers must take action to protect their assets. Consequently, your asking for the reference letter may have precipitated your employment firing; however, it most likely was not the reason for your termination.

Like employees, employers owe a responsibility to their organization, their employees, and their clientele to review the ending of each employment relationship. In order to strengthen current morale and all future relationships, employers must determine what they could have done differently in the employment relationship. As I discussed in Chapter 3, each employee hiring is expensive in terms of resources and financial commitment and therefore is an investment in the organization. Therefore, when the relationship ends, the reason for the ending must be similarly reviewed. "Taking stock" is an important tool in every facet of life.

To conduct this review, accurate and complete information is necessary. These details enable both parties to assess fairly where they have been and what is in their best interests in moving forward. False or scarce information can create frustration and unnecessary problems. These difficulties are expensive emotionally, physically, mentally, and financially.

Worker Gets Mixed Messages from Her Former Employer

Q. I worked for a company for over two years. In that time, I moved up to the position of assistant manager. My manager never told me that I was doing anything but an excellent job.

While she was on vacation, one of the employees who had already given notice that she was quitting cursed at me and was insubordinate. I gave her the choice of changing her attitude or forgetting her notice and leaving that day. She chose to leave.

When my manager returned from vacation, I was told to take a week off with pay. I was called in for a meeting at the end of that week and was fired. I was told at the termination that I had not done anything but an excellent job, but that my job was being eliminated.

I was also told that perhaps I did not have enough experience. Meanwhile, I had already managed two small establishments that were much busier than the position I was being terminated from. I found out that two weeks later, another employee who had less than half of the experience I had was promoted and given my position.

What recourse, if any, do I have?

C. M.

A. From what you report, it appears that your former employer was not entirely forthright with you. Although an employer generally has the right, absent a contract to the contrary, to fire you at any time for any reason, or even for no reason, so long as the firing is not in violation of the law, most employers do not fire employees who are doing an "excellent job."

The confusing aspect of your employer's explanation at the termination meeting is that your job was being eliminated but that perhaps you did not have enough experience. If your job was being eliminated, how much experience you had is irrelevant. That statement alone shows inconsistency on the part of the employer.

In trying to discern the true reason for an employee's termination, the courts often look at what took place close in time to the employee's firing. In your situation, you may have ruffled some feathers by giving your subordinate the choice of changing her attitude or leaving.

However, from your perspective, the most important factors are whether your position was eliminated, and if not, whether you were replaced by someone of a different sex, race, age, religion, national origin, or similar characteristic over which you have no control and who possesses fewer qualifications than you.

If you believe your employment was terminated because of how you treated your subordinate, you may or may not have any legal recourse depending on how other similar situations were handled, any applicable employment policies, or other pertinent facts. If you believe your employment was terminated because of your membership in a protected group, you may file a complaint with the state Civil Rights Agency, the state court, or the federal Equal Employment Opportunity Commission.

Should you elect to file a complaint, you still have the obligation to mitigate your damages by actively seeking other employment opportunities. It is never easy to decide whether to institute a lawsuit. Therefore, it is wise, as you are doing, to gather as much information as possible.

With the ending of each employment relationship, employers need to reflect upon a number of questions: Should this person have been hired? Should this person have been fired sooner? Was the documentation sufficient? If not, what needed to be done differently? Who was responsible for creating the documentation? What were the initial warning signs that there was a problem? Were these warning signs ignored, and if so, why? How did this employee affect the workplace and other employees? Is repair work necessary? Are there more problems that need to be addressed? Most important, how will things be done differently going forward?

Employer and Employee Habits

The employment relationship is based on the universal laws of human nature. When habits are formed early and correctly in life, they serve the person well for a lifetime. Both the employer and employee need to practice good employment relationship habits in order to create a harmonious workplace. Unfortunately, many individuals do not regularly demonstrate a strong work ethic or other quality characteristics. Similarly, many employers need to be better servants to their primary resources—their employees. Following is an unfortunate example that gives life to the universal laws of human nature and the importance of forming good habits early in life:

Manager Doesn't Follow Rules

My 16-year-old daughter has been having problems with one of her managers regarding her breaks and lunches. This manager has shown up at work out of uniform, which is against the employee handbook, and he does not work as a team player, which is also a rule in the handbook. The handbook also clearly states that the employer works with students knowing that grades are important. My daughter went from all Bs to Cs and Ds since she started working. I told my daughter she is only to work three evenings a week and one day on the weekend. The manager told her he is cutting her pay if this happens. He is constantly picking on her for every little thing she does.

If my daughter did not love her job so much, I would tell her to quit. This is her first job, and she has never had a nice comment from the manager. I have met the owner of the establishment who seems to adore my daughter and is a very happy, upbeat person. The owner was told of the manager's attitude. What can I do as a parent to stop this guy from sending my daughter home feeling like a piece of dirt?

C. P.

A. You may contact the federal or state Department of Labor's Office of Wage and Hour Compliance to request that a copy of the child labor laws and regulations be sent to you. These laws are very specific regarding such matters as breaks, meals, how many hours a minor may work, and what hours they may work on school days. Request also from the agency a copy of the notice that employers are to post in a conspicuous place in the workplace. You may obtain these telephone numbers in the blue pages of the telephone book.

I read conflicting scenarios in your description of how the manager is treating your daughter versus your statement that your daughter loves her job. The fact that this is your daughter's first job may be why she loves it. It is natural for a person, especially a child, to desire to succeed at her first job. However, from what you describe, there is plenty of objective evidence that this particular work environment is not a good learning opportunity or safe and healthy. As with any first experience, it is invaluable to have a mentor from whom admirable qualities can be mimicked and acquired.

A loyal and dedicated hard worker is to be respected, not demeaned. Regardless of whether the owner of the establishment is a happy, upbeat person, apparently he does not work with the manager all day. If the owner knows how his manager is treating the employees, he has a legal and moral obligation to take immediate corrective action. His failure to do so sends a clear message as to what he thinks of his employees.

Possibly your daughter's grades have fallen not because of the number of hours she is working but rather as a result of how she is being berated and threatened by her manager. From her perspective, he is someone in a position of authority who possesses more experience and is in charge of the very environment where she naturally wants to do well.

Like most people, your daughter will probably have several jobs during her lifetime. Her school grades and self-esteem are more important than working, especially with this manager, because success in these basic fundamentals will enable her to obtain better employment opportunities. Trying to get the manager to change is nearly impossible, and fighting the bad work environment while your daughter remains employed may be more destructive.

Most employers who become embroiled in employment litigation have been lax in enforcing appropriate standards that unfortunately metamorphose into bad habits. The resultant deplorable corporate culture then permeates managers, supervisors, and employees, sending the whole organization into disarray. All parties must commit to reform their collective past traits to form the basis of the proper employer-employee relationship.

Bad habits must be confronted and substituted with positive attributes. Reinforcement of these affirmative tools is the key that will transform the undesirable habits. Repetition. Repetition. Repetition. It is often said that "imitation is the sincerest form of flattery." When employees begin to imitate management's commitment to positive habits, the signs of having won the battle will be self-evident. "The character of even a child can be known by the way he acts—whether what he does is pure and right." Proverbs 20:11.

As in the preceding example, sometimes it is the employer who has set the stage for the demeaning, unacceptable habits that permeate the entire workforce. In those situations, employees may have few choices, but one alternative they always have, and that is the most important, is the decision to take care of themselves. The law may provide some limited remedies, but seeking an amicable resolution is usually the preferred option.

Boss Who Uses Foul Language Is Abusive

Q. I am an avid reader of your column, and I have always found your advice and views to be enlightening and helpful in today's working environment.

I have been having a serious problem at my workplace. I am working at a small-size organization. I have a very short-tempered boss (who is a partner of the company also) who tends to use foul language every now and then. He always uses abusive language when talking to his employees. For each sentence he speaks, he throws out three or so four-letter words and much more.

I cannot take it anymore. It is affecting my work ability and personal life. It is also adversely affecting my mental and physical health, as I am tense all the time. I don't complain against him because of fear of losing my job. The same is happening with all other staff, but people aren't going to complain against him from fear of losing their jobs. Even if anybody complains, others might not support it for fear of losing their jobs.

What kind of legal recourse can I take in this matter? Kindly advise me as to whom I should contact for this. Your help in this matter will be highly appreciated.

B. P.

A. Your workplace seems to be very unpleasant. Even more important is that you and your coworkers are being disrespected. No law expressly prohibits the conduct you and your coworkers are experiencing. However, if your boss is using harassing language against you or other employees who are members of a protected group and the language is based on protected characteristics, such as race, sex, disability, or some other minority classification, then you may have a discrimination claim against the employer. The law does not provide a remedy for every action, even if the behavior is seemingly unfair.

You don't mention wanting to quit your job, but if you decide the situation is intolerable, you may be eligible to receive unemployment compensation benefits. Generally, unemployment compensation benefits are provided to individuals who become unemployed through no fault of their own, such as a layoff. However, when employees have good cause to end the employment relationship, they may receive benefits. Your state Unemployment Compensation Board has ruled that an employer's persistent use of foul language and abusive conduct are good cause for an employee to terminate the employment relationship and has awarded unemployment benefits in those cases.

However, before pursuing that option, you might consider talking with your boss and making him aware of your discomfort with his foul and abusive language. During that conversation, which should focus solely on how you feel in that situation without any judgment of his behavior, make him aware that you are not the only employee who is being adversely affected. Start the meeting by setting forth the reasons you enjoy working with him and his organization; then explain how the language distracts from the workplace and employee productivity. Because no one has complained to your boss regarding his poor choice of descriptive words, he may not even be aware of how he is negatively affecting the workplace.

I understand you would rather not speak with your boss about this problem. Confrontation is always difficult, but what are your alternatives? You can say nothing and be miserable when he may not know there is a problem; you can say nothing and quit; or you can communicate the problem in such a way that he can hear your concerns so that you possibly get the result you desire.

Another option is for you and a coworker to educate your boss about the situation so that your boss understands that it is not just your limited perception of the work environment. You might also consider talking with another company partner and ask for advice on how to proceed.

Another possibility is to outline your skills, work experience, and career objectives and start pursuing other employment opportunities. Keep in mind that it is best to find a job while still employed. Although your situation is frustrating, you do have options.

In the meantime, while you are deciding in what direction to proceed, remember that his language is a reflection of him and what is going on in his world; it has nothing to do with you. With that in mind, you can at least be grateful that you stand in your own shoes and not his, since he does not appear to be happy. Although it is unfortunate that he is making others miserable as well, you need not travel that path with him.

As with every applicant interview and employee hiring, every employee termination is a potential lawsuit. Usually after the initial shock or wave of reality that the employment relationship is over, employees will ask, if they can sue their employer. Gone are the days of introspective reflection on what they have learned and how they have grown from their life experience and what goals they desire to pursue with this enrichment. Rather, the focus is on what monetary or emotional gain they can reap from a lawsuit against their former employer.

Many employees still fail to recognize what they did receive during the employment relationship. I am amazed to see their incredulous look when you remind these employees that in return for providing a service to the employer, they were paid a salary or wages and furnished numerous benefits. For them, the basic tenet underlying the employment relationship suddenly has become a foreign concept. They understood compensation from the outset of the relationship as the basis for accepting the employment opportunity. Why then do employees now think that agreement was insufficient and they are entitled to more?

Although getting even or believing you are entitled to more may feel good, at least momentarily, it usually does not win the day. Even though it may be easy to file a lawsuit to set your now former employer straight or receive monetary benefits, you must have a basis for bringing the action. In the employment setting, employees generally have the burden of proving their case. If they file a groundless claim, they may be liable for filing a frivolous action.

Discrimination Claim Must Be Backed by Evidence

Q. I worked for an employer for two years. I was hired as a manager. Recently three employees were accused of causing an economic loss to the employer's business. The next day upper management fired all 18 employees in the company.

I felt this was a wrongful discharge and discrimination against me for things other employees did to the company. I feel I was not an at-will employee.

I would like to know if I have grounds to file a lawsuit against the company and management for wrongful discharge and discrimination against me.

E. F.

A. What you experienced must have felt terrible. In a similar vein, what the employer experienced was also tragic. Unfortunately, it takes only a few people to make life miserable for many.

If you have facts to support your feeling that you were not an at-will employee, that information would make a difference as to whether you have a basis for filing a lawsuit against your former employer.

The general rule governing at-will employment is that absent an employment agreement, collective bargaining agreement, or representation, employees may quit their job or an employer may fire employees at any time for any reason or no reason, with or without advance notice. The courts have created exceptions to this general rule based primarily on the rule of law that the employment termination may not be contrary to law or public policy.

As for a discrimination lawsuit, you must have a legal basis for the filing of such an action. Employees who assert that they were unlawfully discriminated against must show that they are a member of a protected group, that they were performing at the level expected, that they suffered an adverse employment action, and that they were treated differently from employees outside their protected group. Protected classifications include sex, race, color, religion, creed, national origin, age, disability, marital status, and veteran status.

From what you describe, the employer may have had a concern about employee trust and loyalty. Without these two essential elements, no relationship can exist. It is not possible to know the employer's thought process for the mass firing without having more information.

Regardless of what action you choose to take, it is important to pursue your personal and legal obligations in finding other employment. In all employee firings, even if unlawful, employees have the obligation to mitigate their damages by actively looking for other, similar employment.

Employment terminations are an important marking in navigating future conduct. They clearly demonstrate the value of information and how the failure to communicate and empathize fully and honestly can have devastating consequences. In deciding how best to move forward after an employment separation, employees must seek as many details as possible about their employment circumstances. This information will guide their course in deciding whether to file an employment-related claim against the employer or take no action. Therefore, as discussed in the previous chapter, the value of informing employees truthfully why their employment is being ended is immeasurable. If the information furnished employees does not withstand logic and reason or is later contradicted, the employer's perceived betrayal often creates a direct path to the attorney's office.

Frequently life does not give us what we desire or anticipate. Of utmost importance is how we respond to those situations based on what is in our control. The first step in deciding how to proceed when a situation goes contrary to plan is to gather as much information regarding the circumstances as possible, then act accordingly. The next example illustrates the value of taking the time to ascertain alternatives before acting.

Employee Wonders What to Do About Firing

Q. My employer recently laid me off from my position as production manager. The reason given for my dismissal was "We are going to liquidate the division." Thereafter, I found out that my former employer bowed to pressure and will continue the business for at least another season. Do I have any legal recourse?

K. M.

A.   Without a representation or contract to the contrary, an employer has the right to fire a worker for any legitimate business reason. You apparently do not dispute the reason your employer provided for laying you off, and at the time of your employment separation, the reason provided was truthful. Without an enforceable agreement entitling you to employment, there does not appear to be any legal recourse against your former employer.

However, the absence of a legal remedy does not preclude you from pursuing other options. For example, you might consider telephoning your former employer to schedule a meeting to discuss the possibility of your resuming your job responsibilities. However, even if you do return to work there, it is uncertain how long the company will continue its operations. Because you are most likely receiving unemployment compensation benefits as a result of having been laid off, you might consider using this time to secure a more stable job.

The decision of whether to file a lawsuit entails evaluating the realities of what litigation involves and the likelihood of success. In making this important life decision, many individuals do not consider how this step will impact upon their life and the lives of their other relationships, personal and work. Litigation is an ordeal, and you must enter it with eyes wide open.

The Litigation Process

The purpose of the following discussion is to explain the litigation process for employees who are contemplating whether to file a lawsuit against their employer or former or prospective employer. This information is equally important for managers and supervisors who are either named in a lawsuit or asked to assist in the defense of the action filed against the employer.

The initial step employees will take in seeking a remedy from the employer for a perceived wrong is to contact a plaintiff's attorney—an individual who represents employees. Increasingly, the plaintiff attorney profile for an employment case is an attorney who has previously been practicing in personal injury cases, such as automobile accidents, slip-and-falls, and medical malpractice. These individuals are keenly aware of the financial rewards of employment litigation. Equally important is that the plaintiff's attorney in presenting the case has cleared a huge hurdle—jury identification is usually with the employee rather than the employer. Translation: Plaintiffs' attorneys are reaping huge settlements with less outlay of time compared with personal injury lawsuits. In addition, society has communicated that it is acceptable to sue your employer or prospective or former employer.

Plaintiffs' attorneys are generally aggressive in representing their clients' interests. The reason, in part, is that these attorneys have a financial interest in the outcome of the case because in most cases they receive money only if the action is settled or decided in the employee's favor. This arrangement is usually called a contingency fee.

Aggression alone, however, does not win lawsuits. Knowledge is powerful, and an attorney's understanding of the employment laws may win or lose the case. Therefore, as in any decision, careful selection and professionalism are essential criteria that must be considered in deciding how best to proceed. Because of the emotional aspects of employment cases, it is also important to retain an attorney who will be supportive, available, and attentive. Your future and personal reputation are on the line. You must place yourself in the best possible posture to confront this situation.

After the employee selects an attorney and provides legal counsel all pertinent details and documents concerning the employer's alleged wrong, the first volley in the legal process is the filing of the complaint. This document sets forth the alleged facts and law on the disputed matter from the employee's viewpoint.

As a general rule, everyone who participated in the adverse employment decision may be a named party to the action. The impact of filing a complaint, as it is a public record, and of being named a defendant in the lawsuit is stressful, distracting, and worrisome. There is no turning back; the allegations are visible for all to examine. Regardless of the role people have in the litigation, it almost always brings their actions or judgments into public view or question. How many people want a jury to become Monday morning quarterbacks analyzing each facet of their conduct or decision?

Employers are amazed that a seemingly trivial employee discussion is now the centerpiece of the plaintiff's complaint. Because any action or word may be scrutinized later in the context of litigation, make sure you do not do or say anything you will later regret. If management personnel always had in the back of their minds that a particular decision has the potential to be examined by an objective outside third party, how many of their decisions would be reversed? If none, then fear of a jury is unwarranted, but if the answer is qualified or different, they should begin to count the zeros in the jury's damage award.

The defendant(s) must file an answer to the complaint, or all the facts will be presumed to be admitted, whereupon judgment may be entered in the employee's favor. The defense counsel who represents the employer will respond on behalf of the organization and/or named individuals. The average time period to answer a complaint is within 35 days of the complaint being served. This period is often enlarged, with the parties' consent, in order for defense counsel to meet with those persons who have knowledge of the alleged facts and to review pertinent documents.

Management's role at this critical juncture cannot be underestimated, for now is the time that the players and their roles come to life. Questions must be answered and the truth revealed. Allegations commonly asserted are that the supervisor knew of the alleged unlawful act, did nothing to stop the complained-of conduct, participated in the unlawful behavior, or assured the complaining employee the matter would be resolved in a positive manner. What a vivid reminder to always make the right decision for the right reasons every minute of every day.

The litigation impact upon everyone's daily life is now just starting to settle in. The time commitment and intensity will only continue to heighten over the duration of the litigation. Once the litigation door is opened, the dust begins to stir. Valuable time must be spent on answering the allegations in the complaint and marshaling facts to support the defense. Failure at this stage not to establish the underpinnings of the litigation plan can be even more costly later.

After the initial pleadings (the complaint and answer) have been filed, the next stage of litigation is the discovery period. The initial discovery phase includes interrogatories and document requests. Interrogatories are written questions sent to a party to be answered under oath and can range in number from 25 to 250. Determining what questions to ask depends on knowing what information is needed. Therefore, time, the most crucial and valuable element, must be expended in reviewing and preparing the case.

No pilot leaves the airport without filing a flight plan. No litigation can accurately be pursued or defended without a similar determination being made as to the direction of the litigants' strategy. Interrogatories are one part of that strategy. Once the list of questions is finalized, it is served upon the opposing party who must, by law, answer each question truthfully. Depending on the length of the interrogatories and the complexity of the case, the investment of time in answering the interrogatories could range from one to ten or more days.

Document production is a request for a vast array of written materials to assist in establishing the plaintiff's case or defending against the alleged wrongdoing. As with the other discovery devices, the search for all information and requested documentation will take away from performance of your job duties and other responsibilities.

Generally, after the parties exchange written discovery, depositions are taken. Depositions are questions asked orally by the plaintiff's or defendant's attorney and answered under oath, with everything transcribed by a court stenographer. Depositions have the full effect of law as if they were conducted in a court of law. They can range from a few hours to several days, depending on the attorney and the complexity of the case, and this does not include the time required to prepare for the depositions. The preparation time includes reviewing the complaint, answer, interrogatory answers, and documents produced and received and meeting with the plaintiff or defense counsel and other key players. Again, preparation cannot be overemphasized, because the deposition transcript may be used in support or defense of a motion filed with the court requesting certain relief, in settlement discussions, or possibly introduced at trial. Most important, all information given at the deposition must be truthful.

Unfortunately, preparing for the deposition may need to be repeated once, twice, even three or four times, since depositions are typically rescheduled for a variety of reasons. Because of the importance of the deposition and the time lag not only between their scheduling but also since the alleged unlawful act, all pertinent materials must be reviewed to refresh one's memory of important facts and dates. The deposition itself is even more stressful, because it can often be demeaning and filled with tricky or brutalizing tactics used by attorneys. Few people would volunteer to participate in the deposition process or would delight in repeating the opportunity.

All of these steps are in preparing the case for trial. When the trial date has been scheduled, each potential trial witness will need to prepare for providing testimony to the court, and where applicable, the jury. This preparation is even more time-consuming than the deposition preparation.

In addition to reviewing the same materials pertinent in preparing for a deposition (the complaint, answer, etc.), and meeting with the plaintiff or defense counsel and other key players, witnesses must review their deposition transcript and learn about the trial procedure and their role in the trial. Like the deposition, the trial will usually not be held on the first date scheduled but rather will be rescheduled a number of times for a variety of reasons. Nevertheless, everyone must be fully prepared to proceed to trial on every date scheduled, and this can mean preparing for trial (e.g., reviewing key information, documents) multiple times. This is a laborious, stressful process, filled with uncertainty, that permeates every aspect of life and takes valuable, irreplaceable time from your personal and business affairs.

Even if individuals elect or are required to file their complaint with an administrative agency instead of the court, much of the process I have discussed will still occur, except it will be less formal, usually not as time-consuming, and possibly not as stressful. However, the loss in time and energy will never be recouped.

The trial finally arrives. The length of the trial depends on whether it is a jury trial, the number of witnesses, including experts, and other matters. The trial can range from one day to three weeks or more. The same negative factors are even more present in the trial—stress, tension, anxiety, uncertainty, and lost time. There is good reason most lawsuits are settled before they are decided by the administrative agency, judge, or jury.

The result of all your painstaking work is the verdict. At the end you will be either the winner or the loser. Even if you are the winner, have you really won? Be honest. Look at the difficult path you have just traversed. Can you recoup that expenditure of energy, loss of interest in matters other than the upcoming trial, unsettled feelings, worry, financial loss, damage to relationships and reputation, and the list goes on? Years may pass with anniversaries and wedding celebrations identified by the marking of a particular case name. Which would you prefer?

Even if you were not a primary participant in the litigation process—or even if you were the winner—you still paid for this employment litigation. How, you ask? Quite simply by virtue of your status as a consumer and taxpayer. What happened to the productivity of the plant manager, the front-line supervisor or department head, and disgruntled employees who were required to spend time away from performing their job responsibilities to prepare the case for trial or be in attendance at trial? What happened to the distraught former employee, coworkers, and managers who are distressed by the overwhelming unwieldy legal process? Are they more or less productive at work? Did they even go to work today, yesterday, or the day before that? Has their diverted focus affected other employees in the workplace? As I have discussed, no one involved in an employment relationship lives in a vacuum. Employment litigation affects everyone. Juries these days are awarding higher and higher dollar amounts in their decisions. And who ultimately pays for each award? Yes, each one of us as a taxpayer and consumer.

If a case reaches the verdict stage, the court enters a final order in the action, after which both parties have the right to appeal from the decision. Although the appeal process primarily entails the review of the trial transcript and preparation of an appellate brief and other supporting papers, the uncertainty of the litigation process remains, and the parties may still have to participate. On appeal, the case may be affirmed, reversed, or remanded for additional evidence or further consideration based upon specified reasons. Like the discovery stage, pretrial period, and trial, the appellate procedure requires dedication, commitment, and time.

Before embarking on the litigation path, you must fully assess all available options, the consequences of your decisions, and your ability to achieve the desired result. In making these assessments, you must start at the end. Failure to evaluate your situation fairly and honestly without a navigation chart or without consulting wise, disinterested advisors often invites more destruction.

Giving Your Life Positive Meaning and Remembrance

As you can see from the preceding discussion, the preferred route is to apply the tools I have discussed throughout this book and practice their implementation daily to prevent the litigation of tomorrow. If you adhere to these time-tested methods, they will serve both you and your colleagues as well as society. You will demonstrate your life's greater purpose by being a leader in human relations. He who loves wisdom loves his own best interest and will be a success. Proverbs 19:8. By taking prudent steps, you will not be a victim and will have prevented frivolous litigation. In this manner, you will enable your employment opportunity to survive and head off the long, agonizing process of litigation.

In understanding the importance of this message, you must bear in mind at what point in time employment lawsuits commence. The answer is not when applicants, employees, or former employees files their complaint with the appropriate legal authority, but when the disrespect, unfair treatment, unlawful conduct, or other similar action occurred. It is this injury that caused the relationship to fall ill. As in medicine, the damage must be repaired, or it will continue to fester and cause further harm. Failure to address the problem will affect every living organism associated with the entity and will have far-reaching effects.

If you encounter an unhealthy employment relationship, you have an obligation to assist in remedying the situation by making the relationship healthy again. If the matter is not handled properly, unnecessary litigation may begin. And who wins at litigation? *No one!* What have you done to create a workplace environment free of tension between management and employees? Each employee regardless of whether you are a management or a nonmanagement employee has a clear duty to take strong and aggressive measures in creating and maintaining strong and healthy employment relationships and to correct and remedy promptly any ill conduct when it occurs. Knowing and using the workplace tools discussed in this book will decide to a large extent your workplace future.

After an employment separation, employees have the obligation to mitigate their damages by seeking other employment, regardless of whether the employee's termination was justified or unjustified. This obligation to mitigate has been defined as to seek comparable work and pay. Employees' damages may be reduced by actual earnings or by what employees reasonably could have earned. Employees may not lower their sights by accepting a lower-paying job until they have sought comparable employment for a reasonable period of time and been unsuccessful.

As I have discussed numerous times, honesty and living by your employment commitment to serve your employer and its employees and customers to the best of your ability everyday may prevent future losses. The courts take these employee responsibilities seriously. In 1995 the United States Supreme Court, in *McKenon v. Nashville Banner Publ. Co.*, 513 U.S. 352 (1995), ruled that the amount of an employee's damages may be limited when the employer would have terminated the employment relationship if the employer had known of the employee's wrongdoing at the time of the discharge. The Court stated that the after-acquired evidence "must be taken into account, we conclude, lest the employer's legitimate concerns be ignored." Therefore, the importance of the employee's conduct is "to take due account of the lawful prerogatives of the employer in the usual course of its business and the corresponding equities that it has arising from the employee's wrongdoing."

Again we are reminded of our basic human duties. The individual and the family unit were present in the forefront of my mind while I was writing this book. My hope is that readers will avoid employment pitfalls that can inflict years of havoc upon themselves and their families. No one wins in litigation. The time spent in litigation can never be returned to the participants. We all have a "lease on life" that has an expiration date filled in on life's contract. I hope the book provides those employees currently experiencing an unrewarding employment experience the opportunity to cancel that status and start afresh with a new lease on life.

Instead of sitting on the sidelines of life, make a commitment to create a work environment where everyone can learn, everyone is welcome, and everyone will succeed. Take the challenge to explore yourself in charting a new direction in expanding and transforming your workplace and reaping the rewards. The goal is to eliminate disappointment and discrimination in the workplace and yield a rejuvenated and energized work experience for all. The accomplishment is realizing the common desire of both employers and employees—a mutually rewarding relationship with our fellow human beings. *Let the employer-employee relationship revolution begin!*

Index